DATE DUE

			Printed in USA

Psychology

Reference Sources in the Social Sciences Series

Lubomyr R. Wynar, Series Editor

No. 1 *Sociology: A Guide to Reference and Information Sources*. By Stephen H. Aby.

No. 2 *Education: A Guide to Reference and Information Sources*. By Lois J. Buttlar.

No. 3 *Public Relations in Business, Government, and Society: A Bibliographic Guide*. By Anne B. Passarelli.

No. 4 *Political Science: A Guide to Reference and Information Sources*. By Henry E. York.

No. 5 *Cultural Anthropology: A Guide to Reference and Information Sources*. By Josephine Z. Kibbee.

No. 6 *Psychology: A Guide to Reference and Information Sources*. By Pam M. Baxter.

Psychology

A Guide to Reference and Information Sources

PAM M. BAXTER

1993

LIBRARIES UNLIMITED, INC.
Englewood, Colorado

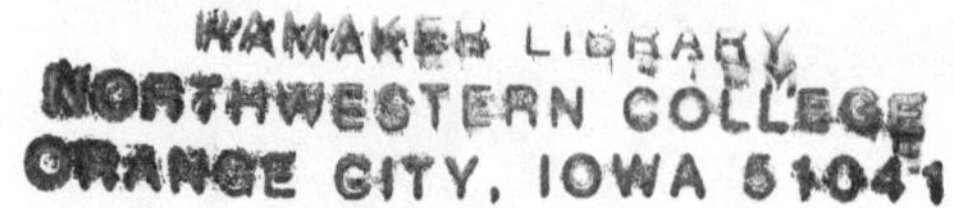

LIBRARIES UNLIMITED, INC.
P.O. Box 6633
Englewood, Colorado 80155-6633

Library of Congress Cataloging-in-Publication

Baxter, Pam M., 1955-
Psychology : a guide to reference and information sources / Pam M. Baxter.
xxi, 219 p. 17x25 cm. -- (Reference sources in the social sciences series ;)
Includes bibliographical references and index.
ISBN 0-87287-708-6
1. Reference books--Psychology--Bibliography. 2. Psychology--Bibliography. I. Title. II. Series.
Z7201.B39 1993
[BF121]
016.15--dc20

93-13182
CIP

For Gordon

CONTENTS

Part I
General Social Science Reference Sources

Part II
Social Science Disciplines

Part IV
Special Topics in Psychology

FOREWORD

This series, Reference Sources in the Social Sciences, is intended to introduce librarians, researchers, and students to major sources within the social sciences disciplines. The series covers the following disciplines: sociology, history, economics and business, political science, anthropology, education, psychology, and general social science reference sources.

The organization and content of each volume are shaped by bibliographic forms and subject structures of the individual disciplines. Since many subject areas within the social sciences are interrelated, some reference sections in the various volumes will have certain features in common (e.g., a section on general social science sources). Each volume in the series constitutes a unique reference tool, stressing the informational subject structure of the discipline, major reference publications, databases, and other relevant sources including serials, major professional organizations, and research centers.

It is hoped that *Psychology: A Guide to Reference and Information Sources* will fill an important gap in professional social sciences literature and provide a useful tool for research in psychology. The volume is divided into four parts and covers all major reference sources on psychological disciplines, including over 600 selected sources. The emphasis is placed on reference titles published from 1970 through late 1991. A few imprints published in 1992 are included, and reference sources published before 1970 are covered only in case they represent "classic works" or are unique in their coverage. Ms. Pam M. Baxter, psychological and social sciences librarian of Purdue University, published several articles and bibliographies related to psychology and reference librarianship and is very active in various professional organizations.

This guide is for reference librarians, researchers, and students. Practitioners in applied psychology and clinical practice may find this publication very useful in their research and professional work.

Lubomyr R. Wynar
Series Editor

FOREWORD

ACKNOWLEDGMENTS

My quest for printed materials, both common and obscure, made reliance on the collections of the following libraries a necessity.

Cornell University
Indiana University
Indiana University—Purdue University at Indianapolis
Purdue University
State University of New York at Albany
University of Michigan
University of Rochester
Any errors or omissions are entirely my own.

The interlibrary loan staff of Purdue University addressed my needs with their customary diligence. My staff at the Psychological Sciences Library displayed their usual good humor as I accumulated towers of volumes and paper on my desk.

I am pleased to recognize the editorial staff of Libraries Unlimited, who surely have the collective patience of Job. Editors certainly have a way of transforming pedestrian text.

And finally, megathanks to my husband, to whom this work is dedicated.

INTRODUCTION

In the nineteenth century, psychology emerged as a discipline distinct from those which it derived its roots: philosophy, medicine, and biology. The American Psychological Association (APA), the first such professional organization in the United States, was formed in 1892. The academic credentials of its early officers reflected the intellectual traditions from which psychology emerged: William James, whose writings were influential in both philosophy and psychology and who completed medical studies; George Trumbull Ladd, possessor of a degree in divinity; John Dewey, known by most as a philosopher; and G. Stanley Hall, recipient of the first doctoral degree in psychology awarded in the United States. Indeed, those individuals we readily recognize as influential to the development of psychology were products of a wide variety of backgrounds. Alfred Binet received training in science and the law; Sigmund Freud, Carl Jung, Alfred Adler, and Ivan Pavlov were physicians; and Alfred Kinsey received his doctorate in zoology and began his career lecturing in that area.

Therefore, it is not surprising that psychology's research literature originally appeared in publications that now would not be considered psychological. Perusing the first issues of *Psychological Index*, one is immediately struck by three elements that distinguish it from its successor, *Psychological Abstracts*: the sizable representation of foreign-language publications, primarily German, French, and Italian; the prevalence of book literature, as opposed to that from journals; and the representation of literature from other disciplines. Contributions that would now be placed squarely in the realm of psychological research appeared in anatomy, zoology, ethnology, and pedagogy publications, among others.

G. Stanley Hall initiated *American Journal of Psychology*, the first American psychology journal, in 1887. By 1927, the first volume of *Psychological Abstracts* began to reflect psychology's body of literature. This reference tool still indexed publications from related disciplines and also included subject-relevant articles from general-interest magazines, such as *American Mercury*, *New Republic*, and *Scientific American*. However, it now covered the body of literature that appeared in numerous new psychology journals founded after the turn of the century.

As a discipline, psychology is now not only a child but a parent, with impact on areas of research that some might regard as far flung. The interdisciplinary area known as psychohistory emerged from the work of Freud and Erik Erikson. Human factors—the effect of work and home environment and design on human comfort, motivation, and productivity—combines a number of distinct areas: psychology, urban planning, industrial engineering, and so forth. Applications of psychological research on problem solving and decision making include management information systems, business management, and marketing and retailing. An even more up-to-date example: The study of mind and consciousness is being applied to the development of artificial machine intelligence. The list of examples seems endless.

As are psychology and the interests of psychologists (whether teacher, researcher, or practitioner), psychology information sources are diffuse, not simply in a handful of printed sources with the word "psychology" in their titles. A good example is the broad topic of substance abuse. Such literature can, of course, be found in numerous psychology sources. Depending on the specific information need, it can also be found in the literatures of sociology (e.g., as a social or family problem), anthropology (e.g., cross-cultural differences in counseling), criminology (e.g., criminal behavior), biomedicine (e.g., its effects on physiological responses), and education or social work (e.g., children as victims of dysfunctional families, as abusers themselves).

Compounding the intellectual sprawl of the literature is the variety of search strategies and information formats that researchers and students must consider. Citation searching—the ability to locate current references citing an important, seminal body of literature—gained quick acceptance among the social sciences. Computerized literature searching now involves not only bibliographic files but also textual and statistical databases. CD-ROM technology and user-friendly retrieval software make this research option even more accessible. In psychology, to a greater extent than in the other social sciences, the journal has supplanted the book as the primary method of scholarly communication. At present, the refereed electronic journal, accessible via telephone lines and international computer networks, is in its infancy but developing quickly. That said, some traditional research shortcomings remain; information on and access to limited circulation technical reports, unpublished conference papers, and other fugitive literature remain elusive.

Scope and Purpose

This volume brings together information on over 500 selected sources in psychology, the social sciences, and related non-social science disciplines. The primary audience consists of undergraduate and graduate students. Researchers and librarians will also find it a helpful resource when seeking information outside their areas of subject specialization. Additionally, practitioners in applied psychology areas and clinical practice may find many sources of interest, although these individuals are a secondary audience.

Most of the information sources in this guide are print reference tools published from 1970 through late 1991 with a few 1992 imprints. Works published before 1970 are included if they offer unique coverage of a topic or body of research or if they represent a classic work in the reference literature. Although emphasis is on English-language material, a large number of guides, bibliographies, and indexing tools cover research published in other languages or are otherwise international in scope. With few exceptions, descriptions and evaluations of sources represented in this volume are based on examination by the author.

A few definitions are in order. Reference literature in psychology is, of late, replete with publications containing the terms *guide*, *handbook*, and *annual review* in their titles. Actually, many of these works do not serve the purposes that these terms traditionally convey. Therefore, I have employed a few distinct definitions when selecting titles for inclusion, using the *ALA Glossary of Library and Information Science* (1983 edition) for guidance.

A *handbook* is a volume or series of volumes intended to discuss major theories, research strategies, and special topics within a given subject. Ideally, a handbook is a collection of essays by researchers who can convey and evaluate this body of knowledge, cite seminal and current literature reflecting research trends, and help the user consider future directions of the field. Two outstanding examples in this bibliography are the two-volume *Handbook of Social Psychology* and the four-volume *Handbook of Child Psychology*. Too many recent handbooks contain chapters on very narrow areas of interest and thus do not allow the student or researcher an appreciation of the topic. Handbooks of this nature have been excluded.

There has also been an increase in annual publications calling themselves "Annual Review of . . ." or "Progress in. . . ." In fact, many are annual publications that contain chapters reflecting empirical, methodological, or theoretical contributions. Others consist of articles reprinted from journals or other sources. To quote from the *ALA Glossary*, an annual review is "a bibliographic survey of the major publications in a subject field. . . . Such surveys provide a state-of-the-art summary when they emphasize the significance and implications, rather than the specific content, of the publications" (p. 9). The best example of an annual review that meets this definition is the *Annual Review of Psychology*, although others are cited in this guide.

How is a *guide* different from a *bibliography*? The *ALA Glossary* definition of a bibliography is straightforward: "A list of works, documents, and/or bibliographic items, usually with some relationship between them" (p. 22). They can be published or unpublished. With few exceptions, I have included bibliographies containing citations produced over a span of a decade or more. Conversely, a *guide* can be a bibliography. However, it considers information sources in other formats (e.g., organizations, machine-readable files, the names of individuals). A guide may also be a work whose intent is to introduce basic titles in the literature and, in addition, to convey an appreciation of a discipline's bibliographic "geography."

Finally, some publications are derived from other, larger works and are reworked, repackaged, and remarketed to meet the needs of a specific audience. For example, the American Psychological Association produces a series of subject-specific *PsycSCAN* periodicals, consisting of citations and abstracts extracted from the PsycINFO database. These cover discrete areas of interest (e.g., psychoanalysis, applied psychology) and are intended as current awareness sources for practitioners and researchers. The APA has also produced several bibliographies derived from the PsycINFO database that cover topics of current research interest, such as AIDS and learning disabilities. Most works whose contents are almost totally derived from another source have been excluded. Those that are cited note the relationship with a parent volume in the annotation and are included because they have been substantially revised or updated, because they meet the needs of a specific audience, or because there are few (if any) similar works.

Format

Most entries for printed sources begin with the bibliographic citation: author(s) or editor(s), title, place of publication, publisher, date of publication, pagination or number of volumes, and presence of indexes. As appropriate to each source, bibliographic information also includes a series statement, a Library of Congress (LC) card number, and an International Standard Book Number (ISBN). If available, a series report number and a Superintendent of Documents (SuDocs) classification number are included for federal government publications. Prices for in-print books reflect 1991 prices as found in *Books in Print* or current publishers' catalogs. Each item is followed by an annotation of approximately 100 words that describes and evaluates the work. The annotation also compares a publication to similar or related titles if they exist, whether or not they are cited elsewhere in the guide.

Journal and other serial publications include the volumes and publication dates, place of publication, publisher, and the International Standard Serial Number (ISSN). Journal subscription prices were obtained from the most recent issue available, from publishers' catalogs, or from *Ulrich's International Periodicals Directory*, and they reflect the cost of an institutional subscription (if different from an individual rate). Annotations for journals are also descriptive and evaluative but are briefer than for serials such as index and annual review publications. Titles under which a serial was previously published are noted.

Several sections of the guide contain nonprint information sources. Some provide directory information for professional associations and publishers. For these, data include name and address of the organization or publisher and a brief description. Online databases constitute yet another nonprint format. Their entries consist of the name of the file, the location and name of the producer, and the earliest date for which that file is available. For each database, information on the database vendors systems making the file available includes the name of the file on that system, the frequency of updates, and the price per connect hour. In the case of files available through BRS Information Technologies, the rate given is for "open access," meaning that subscribers to the service have not contracted for a minimum number of usage hours.

Organization and Content

This guide is organized into four sections. "General Social Science Reference Sources" includes information on reference tools of interest to the broad range of social science disciplines. Each item cited has applicability to psychology, which is noted in the annotation. References are categorized according to reference format: guides, indexes and abstracts, dictionaries and encyclopedias, sources of statistical information, directories, and biographical sources.

Part 2, "Social Science Disciplines," contains sections for each of seven disciplines or fields of study whose literatures are important to psychology students and researchers: education, economics and business, sociology, social work, anthropology, history, and political science and criminal justice. Under each, sources are listed by publication format: guides, bibliographies, indexes and abstracts, handbooks, and dictionaries and encyclopedias. Not all publication formats are represented under each discipline. Although the titles included are selective, some unbalanced coverage among the disciplines is inevitable due to the relative unevenness of reference publishing among the social science disciplines. For example, education is served by an abundance of current, comprehensive, and high-quality dictionaries and encyclopedias; anthropology as a discipline is not. The areas of economics and business are supported by several guides to information sources, each reasonably current and useful for applied psychology research. History, however, does not have a large number of resource guides, and few are useful in psychological research.

Broad-based information sources of interest to psychology are categorized in part 3: guides to the literature, bibliographies, indexes and abstracts, online databases, handbooks and yearbooks, dictionaries and encyclopedias, biographical sources, journal titles, professional and scholarly organizations, publishers, and biographical and institutional directories.

The largest section, part 4, consists of information sources grouped according to categories that represent subdisciplines of psychology. These categories are loosely based on the content classifications used in *Psychological Abstracts*. As in part 2, this organization is adapted to accommodate publication patterns. Relatively narrow subfields in psychology, such as political psychology and health psychology, have a definite presence in the journal literature, including one or more unique journal titles. However, they are not well represented by reference tools whose contributions differ substantially from those already available. Rather than include a topical category under which is listed one work, I have opted instead to include those citations under a larger classification. They may be easily located through the subject index.

Due to the inherently interdisciplinary nature of many of psychology's subfields, a number of nonpsychology reference sources are cited. For example, those seeking literature in the areas of health psychology, psychiatry, or physiological psychology should utilize *Index Medicus*, which complements coverage of *Psychological Abstracts*. Conversely, those who need literature in the area of ergonomics are already well served by *Ergonomics Abstracts* and need not resort to the exhaustive *Engineering Index*.

Part I

GENERAL SOCIAL SCIENCE REFERENCE SOURCES

GUIDES

1. Freides, Thelma. **Literature and Bibliography of the Social Sciences**. Los Angeles, Melville, 1973. 284p. index. (Information Sciences Series). price not reported. LC 73-10111. ISBN 0-471-27790-8.

Aimed at undergraduate and graduate students, this work is not so much a research guide as an attempt to convey the structure and purpose of bibliography in the social sciences as part of a scholarly communication network. The age of the volume means that the sources discussed may no longer be the best available. However, the book retains value as a discussion of research communication and the integration of printed information research tools in the disciplines of anthropology, geography, history, political science, psychology, sociology, and education.

The first series of chapters surveys the development, evolution, and structure of scientific research and its literature. Part 2, "Structure and Components of the Social Science Literature," discusses the roles of various types of communication mechanisms: scholarly journals, books and research reports, review publications, handbooks, and survey works. Part 3 covers methods of retrieval and presents an annotated list of such reference tools as library catalogs, bibliographies, and literature guides. There are subject and author/title indexes.

2. Li, Tze-chung. **Social Science Reference Sources: A Practical Guide**. 2d ed. Westport, Conn., Greenwood Press, 1990. 590p. index. (Contributions in Librarianship and Information Science, no.68). $75.00. LC 90-2733. ISBN 0-313-25539-3.

Originally compiled as a library science text for the social sciences, this title introduces approximately 2,200 basic reference tools in a variety of formats; most are American and were produced before 1978. Part 1 considers the needs of social science students and researchers and the nature of information sources. A discussion of social science sources follows, including guides, bibliographies, indexes, directories, encyclopedias, statistical sources, periodicals, government publications, and data archives and online services.

Part 2 consists of discipline-specific chapters: cultural anthropology, economics and business, education, history, law, political science, psychology, sociology, and geography. Each chapter provides an introduction to the field and its sources of information. Only the most basic tools in psychology are listed. Although not as comprehensive as *The Social Sciences* (see entry 8) or *Sources of Information in the Social Sciences* (see entry 10), the contribution of this title remains the presentation of the literature's structure and the information needs of researchers.

3. Lu, Joseph K. **U.S. Government Publications Relating to the Social Sciences: A Selected Annotated Guide**. Beverly Hills, Calif., Sage, 1975. 260p. index. o.p. LC 74-77288. ISBN 0-8039-0402-9.

Lu cites over 700 government-produced books and serials published through mid-1973 that will be of interest to social science researchers, students, and teachers. The table of contents, with its hierarchical subject outline, provides subject access under 12 broad categories and myriad subcategories. In addition to basic bibliographic information, citations include Superintendent of Documents Classification numbers and brief, descriptive annotations. There are also name and title indexes. Appendixes list other guides to government publications, general information on ordering documents, and depository libraries.

Predictably, American history, business and economics, legislative and political policy, area studies, law, and labor and manpower are emphasized. There is also extensive coverage of research produced and access tools in education and special education, criminal justice, minority groups, substance abuse, services to the elderly, demographics, and social welfare, all of interest to the social science disciplines. Although it is in need of updating, this remains a valuable guide to government publications in a broad spectrum of social science disciplines.

4. McInnis, Raymond G., and James W. Scott. **Social Science Research Handbook**. New York, Garland, 1984. 436p. index. $40.00. LC 83-49158. ISBN 0-8240-6368-6.

This edition reprints the original 1975 (Barnes & Noble) publication, discussing approximately 1,500 reference works in the social science disciplines of anthropology, demography, economics, geography, history, political science, and sociology. The volume's first section consists of eight chapters, one for each discipline and another for general social science reference works. Each chapter is further subdivided by type of reference tool (e.g., atlases, handbooks and yearbooks, bibliographies). McInnis opts for a bibliographic essay format, with each source coded to correspond to an extensive bibliography in the back of the volume.

A second section consists of nine essays that outline an area studies approach to each discipline. Throughout, the essays compare works similar in format and content, making this an important evaluative source. Despite this book's age, many works presented within retain their usefulness or can be easily traced to more recent editions.

5. **Political and Social Science Journals: A Handbook for Writers and Reviewers**. Santa Barbara, Calif., ABC-Clio, 1983. 236p. index. (Clio Guides to Publishing Opportunities, no.2). o.p. LC 82-18455. ISBN 0-87436-026-9; 0-87436-037-4pa.

The introduction states that the volume "provides prospective authors with specific and current information on the editorial policies and procedures of journals accepting and publishing articles and reviews in political science, social science, and related disciplines." Accordingly, it has advice on manuscript preparation, journal selection, copyright, and book reviewing.

The remainder of the work is a title listing of over 440 English-language journals. The primary focus is on political science, with coverage of related topics such as international and area studies, law, public administration, and urban studies. Other areas with some coverage are sociology, labor and economics, history, and minority and women's studies. The selection of titles listed in the subject index under "Behavioral Science" and related headings is severely limited.

Three types of information are given for each title. First is a description of its purpose and readership, frequency and circulation, cost, editor's name, editorial address, and where it is indexed. Next, manuscript submission and preparation requirements cover editorial style, referee process employed, languages of publication, and percentage of manuscripts accepted for publication. Finally, information on book reviews is provided for potential reviewers.

6. Sheehy, Eugene P., ed. **Guide to Reference Books**. 10th ed. Chicago, American Library Association, 1986. 1560p. index. $65.00. LC 85-11208. ISBN 0-8389-0390-8.

7. **Guide to Reference Books. Supplement to the Tenth Edition**. Robert Balay, ed. Chicago, American Library Association, 1992. 613p. index. $85.00. LC 92-6463. ISBN 0-8389-0588-9.

Sheehy divides the universe of reference literature into five sections: general works, the humanities, the social and behavioral sciences, history and area studies, and science and medicine. These broad categories are generally subdivided into about 10 subject disciplines with their own subject subdivisions. For example, the section on linguistics is divided by languages and language groups, while economics has categories for accounting, business management, advertising, and the like. The section covering psychology and psychiatry contains 153 titles, including literature guides, bibliographies, periodicals, indexes and abstracts, handbooks, dictionaries and encyclopedias, directories, and directories of tests. Use of the combined author, title, and subject index is essential as a supplement to the hierarchical arrangement. Balay's *Supplement* includes over 4,000 items (about 60 titles in psychology and psychiatry) published from 1985 through 1990; it uses the same organizational structure and indexing features.

Because their intent is to guide librarians, researchers, and students to reference books, the volumes' emphasis is on items of a research nature, although works of interest to those in general settings are well represented. Although the most current tools are given preference, important retrospective titles are included if warranted. (Retrospective access is amply provided by the many editions since the first in 1902.) Citations are to books of all types and reference periodicals, with brief and descriptive annotations. Tools are listed regardless of country of publication or language if deemed important to a discipline's reference literature.

Sheehy and Balay do not substitute for *Sources of Information in the Social Sciences* (see entry 10) nor *Research Guide for Psychology* (see entry 120). Instead, when used with *Walford's Guide to Reference Material* (see entry 9), they provide excellent, comprehensive, and systematic coverage of an expansive literature.

8. **The Social Sciences: A Cross-Disciplinary Guide to Selected Sources**. Nancy L. Herron, general ed. Englewood, Colo., Libraries Unlimited, 1989. 287p. index. (Library Science Text Series). $35.00; $23.50pa. LC 89-12802. ISBN 0-87287-725-6; 0-87287-777-9pa.

This is a comprehensive guide to the most important reference books and serials in the social sciences. Although considerably more selective than *Sources of Information in the Social Sciences* (see entry 10), it is more current and offers descriptive, critical, and comparative annotations, some approaching the format of short review articles. Each of 12 chapters is preceded by a concise, informative essay defining the discipline, its major areas of research and professional involvement, and the structure of its literature. Although some chapters (e.g., law) employ what is essentially an essay format interspersed with annotated citations, most categorize citations by reference format (e.g., guides, bibliographies, directories).

Part 1 consists of a chapter on social science reference tools. Chapters covering political science, economics and business, history, law, anthropology and sociology comprise part 2. Education, psychology, and communication are categorized as "emerging disciplines" in part 3, with geography, demographics, and statistics covered in part 4. The format of each chapter varies with the literature important to the discipline, such as maps in geography, government publications in political science, and tests and measurements in psychology. Nonprint sources such as databases and CD-ROMs are also included. There are author, title, and subject indexes.

9. **Walford's Guide to Reference Material. Volume 2: Social and Historical Sciences, Philosophy and Religion**. 5th ed. Alan Day and Joan M. Harvey, eds. London, Library Association; dist., Lanham, Md., UNIPUB, 1991, 1992. 942p. index. $180.00. ISBN 0-85365-539-1.

Walford's is intended as an entry to the published book and serial reference literature for librarians and researchers. Although its emphasis is on English-language publications with a distinct British flavor, it affords better international coverage than, for example, *Guide to Reference Books* and its supplement (see entries 6 and 7). Recent titles are preferred over older ones, although a significant number of references are to retrospective, core reference works. This volume groups all disciplines covered under the headings "Philosophy & Psychology"; "Religion"; "Social Sciences"; and "Geography, Biography, History." (Companion volumes cover science and technology and languages, literatures, and the arts.) Each area is broken down by discipline. An estimated 5,000 citations are provided, with additional sources discussed in the annotations.

For psychology, citations to reference books and serials cover general works, experimental psychology, child psychology, personality, intelligence, creativity, psychoanalysis, psychiatry, and mental tests. Because fewer than 100 sources are listed in this section, *Walford's* serves as only a brief introduction to any single discipline's literature. There are an author/title and a subject index.

10. Webb, William H., ed. **Sources of Information in the Social Sciences: A Guide to the Literature**. 3d ed. Chicago, American Library Association, 1986. 777p. index. $75.00. LC 84-20494. ISBN 0-8389-0405-X.

This is the single most comprehensive view of social science sources available. Webb has compiled a massive list of information sources spanning the breadth of social science literature. Most works cited are current through the mid-1980s, although the importance and continuing contributions of classic works are recognized. There is a section for general social science literature, but most entries are grouped under history, geography, economics and business, sociology, anthropology, psychology, education, or political science. Each discipline-specific chapter is preceded by a discussion of the literature and its structure. Citations to seminal and survey books follow under subdisciplines; for example, psychology includes sections for learning, motivation and emotion, personality, and clinical. Some works are individually annotated, others are discussed together. A second section in each chapter cites reference and information sources by format: current and retrospective bibliographies, directories, dictionaries and encyclopedias, literature guides, databases, organizations, and journals. The index to authors, titles, and subjects is essential to locate information on interdisciplinary areas such as social psychology and political behavior.

INDEXES AND ABSTRACTS

11. **Bibliographic Index**. Vol. 1- . Bronx, N.Y., H. W. Wilson, 1937- . semiannual, with annual cumulations. service basis. LC 46-41034. ISSN 0006-1255.

This title is an excellent source for locating literature reviews. It serves as a subject index to book-length bibliographies, those appearing in books and pamphlets, or those appended to articles selected from over 2,600 source periodicals. Although most are published in English, there is some coverage of European languages. The primary selection criteria is that the bibliographies cited contain at least 50 references. Subject coverage includes almost every discipline and interdisciplinary area in the humanities, social sciences, sciences, and technology.

12. **Book Review Index**. Vol. 1- , No. 1- . Detroit, Gale, 1965- . bimonthly, with quarterly and annual cumulations. $195.00/yr. ISSN 0524-0581.

This index cites reviews from over 500 popular, academic, and professional periodicals and from selected daily and weekly newspapers. It is not limited to popular and scholarly works; reference and children's book and periodical title reviews are also included. Citations are listed under author's or editor's last name and thereunder by title, followed by a list of citations to published reviews. There is also a title index.

Although *Book Review Digest* (H. W. Wilson, 1905-) provides better retrospective coverage and brief excerpts from reviews, its policies for inclusion of book titles limits its usefulness to popular and heavily reviewed books. *Book Review Index* is a better choice for review citations in scholarly and professional works, in addition to its popular book coverage.

13. **Book Review Index to Social Science Periodicals**. Arnold M. Rzepecki, ed. Ann Arbor, Mich., Pierian Press, 1978. 4v. $275.00/set. LC 78-51070. ISBN 0-87650-026-2(v.1); 0-87650-110-2(v.2); 0-87650-049-1(v.3); 0-87650-114-5(v.4).

Each volume of this set indexes reviews from approximately 300 journal titles in economics and management, education, history, anthropology, area and ethnic studies, political science, and sociology. Volumes are arranged according to years covered. One deals with 1964-1970, 1971 and 1972 each have a single volume, and the final volume spans from 1973 to March 1974. Despite the limited years of coverage, this set compensates for lack of access to scholarly reviews before they were indexed consistently in *Social Sciences Index* (see entry 26). This set also supplements general book review indexes, such as *Book Review Digest* (H. W. Wilson, 1905-) and *Book Review Index* (see entry 12).

Within each volume, reviews are listed by book author and title. The scope of the books reviewed, of course, is determined by the reviews in the list of source journals. There is some coverage of journal titles in the behavioral sciences, primarily in the areas of social organization and problems, public opinion, and group behavior.

14. **Bulletin of the Public Affairs Information Service.** By Public Affairs Information Service. Vol. 1- , No. 1- . New York, Public Affairs Information Service, 1915- . monthly, with quarterly and annual cumulations. $395.00/yr. ISSN 0898-2201.

This bulletin is a hodgepodge of publication formats and subject focuses. It indexes selected government documents and books, reports from research centers, and articles from scholarly and special interest periodicals, all encompassing the broad area of public policy. For this reason, it is especially strong in its coverage of issues surrounding mental health services, educational policy, political and group behavior and attitudes, and survey research.

Citations are arranged by subject, with many subheadings and abundant cross-references. Titles that do not adequately indicate content are often accompanied by brief descriptive annotations. The annual bound cumulations contain author indexes. Although headings are selected from the 2d edition of *PAIS Subject Headings* (Public Affairs Information Service, 1990), they are not necessary for successful use of the index.

15. **Combined Retrospective Index to Book Reviews in Scholarly Journals, 1886-1974.** Evan Ira Farber, ed. Woodbridge, Conn., Research Publications, 1982. 15v. index. $1,650.00. LC 79-89137. ISBN 0-8408-0167-X.

This is a massive index to over one million reviews appearing in 459 scholarly journals selected from the disciplines of history, political science, and sociology. Volumes 1 through 12 list review citations by primary author and book title, with cross-references from secondary authors. Volumes 13 to 15 consist of a title index. This should be a useful supplement to *Book Review Index* (see entry 12) and *Book Review Index to Social Science Periodicals* (see entry 13).

16. **Comprehensive Dissertation Index, 1861-1972.** Ann Arbor, Mich., University Microfilms International, 1973. 37v. $180.00/v.; $6,660.00/set. LC 73-89046. ISBN 0-8357- 0080-1.

17. **Comprehensive Dissertation Index. Supplement.** Ann Arbor, Mich., University Microfilms International, 1973- . annual. $745.00pa.; $605.00 (microfiche) (institutions). LC 76-642006. ISSN 0361-6657.

The original retrospective set cites more than 417,000 dissertations accepted as requisites of doctoral degrees in the United States, with selected coverage of foreign dissertations. The first 32 volumes are organized by broad subject areas, such as psychology, education, communication and the arts, and business and economics. Each of these volumes or sets of volumes consists of a keyword index made up of significant words in titles. Many, but not all, of the citations contain cross-references to *Dissertation Abstracts Annual* (*DAI*) (see entry 20), which provides lengthy abstracts. Volumes 33 through 37 consist of an author index to the entire set.

The annual *Comprehensive Dissertation Index* is a five-volume supplement to *DAI* that contains a keyword subject index. Volumes 1 and 2 cover the sciences (e.g., agriculture, health sciences, engineering), and volumes 3 and 4 deal with the humanities and social sciences, including psychology. Volume 5 contains the author index. Within each grouping, the keyword indexes are arranged under disciplines. Topics in interdisciplinary areas necessitate searching under more than one discipline and often through more than one volume. In addition to authors, dissertation titles, and year completed, there is a citation to the corresponding citation and abstract in *DAI*.

18. **Current Contents: Social & Behavioral Sciences.** Vol. 1- , No. 1- . Philadelphia, Institute for Scientific Information, 1969- . weekly. $340.00/yr. ISSN 0092-6361.

In the course of a year, *Current Contents* reproduces tables of contents from over 1,300 journal titles. Each issue organizes that week's journals under broad subject areas such as psychology, psychiatry, social issues, and rehabilitation. In addition, the contents of several edited books are included in each issue. A subscription may be received in paper or in floppy disk format for use with personal computers.

Issues contain a title keyword index, an author index and address directory to aid in requesting reprints, and a journal publishers' address directory. Some of these indexes cumulate on a regular basis: the journal index cumulates triannually, and a comprehensive list of journal titles and books covered is produced biannually. But despite the cumulated indexes and book coverage, the primary value of this serial lies in its current awareness function and its rapid, comprehensive access to the journal literature in the social sciences.

19. **Directory of Published Proceedings: Series SSH-Social Sciences/Humanities.** Vol. 1- , No. 1- . Harrison, N.Y., InterDok, 1968- . quarterly. $325.00. ISSN 0012-3307.

This directory provides international coverage of professional and research conferences, symposia, and meetings. It cites preprints of proceeding papers as well as those published in books and journals and as limited distribution research papers. Primary arrangement is by year and month of the conference, and individual paper listings include where each was published and purchasing information (aided by a publisher and distributor directory). Indexes are provided by editor, meeting location, and subject and sponsor; all cumulate in the fourth issue of the year. In the past, entries and indexes have been republished in four-year cumulations. Because it is not as comprehensive as the *Index to Social Sciences and Humanities Proceedings* (see entry 23), this title should be considered as a supplementary source of such information.

20. **Dissertation Abstracts International.** Vol. 30- . Ann Arbor, Mich., University Microfilms International, 1969- . monthly. $595.00pa./yr.; $395.00/yr. (microfiche) (pts. A and B). ISSN 0419-4209(pt.A); 0419-4217(pt.B).

21. **Dissertation Abstracts International. Part C: Worldwide.** Vol. 50- . Ann Arbor, Mich., University Microfilms International, 1989- . quarterly. $750.00/yr. ISSN 1042-7279.

Dissertation Abstracts International (*DAI*) began publication in 1938 under various titles, such as *Dissertation Abstracts* and *Microfilm Abstracts*. It is published in three parts. Part A is "The Humanities and Social Sciences," part B is "The Sciences and Engineering," and part C is "Worldwide." In the cases of parts A and B, copies of most dissertations accepted in fulfillment of doctoral degrees in the United States (and selected Canadian and British institutions) are submitted to UMI for announcement in this source. Each entry is accompanied by a lengthy abstract provided by the dissertation's author. Order numbers are included with bibliographic information such as author and institutional affiliation, title, date, pages, and dissertation director. Part C contains similar information (with translated titles and abstracts) for foreign dissertations and began publication in 1976 under the title *European Abstracts*.

Within parts A and B, citations and abstracts are arranged under broad subject areas and subareas. Most fields of psychology are covered in part B, with numerous subheadings, including clinical, personality, and psychometrics. However, part A includes languages and linguistics, education (including testing and counseling), sociology, and gerontology. Only author indexes, which cumulate annually, are provided with *DAI*. More detailed subject access can be found in the annual supplement *Comprehensive Dissertation Index* (see entry 17), which has a keyword index constructed from titles. As a set, the three parts provide comprehensive, exhaustive access to the original research inherent in dissertations.

22. **Government Reports Announcements and Index.** Vol. 1- . Springfield, Va., U.S. Department of Commerce, National Technical Information Service, 1946- . semimonthly. $450.00/yr. ISSN 0097-9007.

Government Reports Announcements and Index (*GRAI*) is usually associated with technical reports in the sciences and engineering. It indexes unclassified research reports, often of limited circulation, generated as a result of research sponsored and funded by the federal government; it also covers some foreign research reports. As such, it is a source of fugitive research literature not published in other formats. Documents may be ordered from the National Technical Information Service (NTIS) in paper or microfiche; some libraries and information centers subscribe to all or part of NTIS documents in microfiche.

Reports are organized under 38 subject categories and numerous subcategories, with indexes by keyword, personal author, corporate author, contract/grant number, and NTIS number. Included in a citation are the author, report title, contract information (including sponsoring agency), language of publication, ordering information, and a lengthy nonevaluative abstract. Indexes cumulate annually as the multivolume *Government Reports Annual Index*.

This service and the NTIS documents it indexes provide very good coverage of reports in human factors, ergonomics, personnel administration and general management, and social services practice and delivery. The "Behavior and Society" category includes employment and career development, social issues, and selected areas of experimental psychology.

23. **Index to Social Sciences and Humanities Proceedings.** Philadelphia, Institute for Scientific Information, 1979- . quarterly. $775.00/yr. ISSN 0191-0574.

Papers presented at professional conferences, conventions, and symposia in practically any discipline are difficult to locate, either bibliographically or in their entirety. This work indexes papers from these sources that are eventually published in books, journals, or reports or as preprints. Coverage is international and multilingual, with a subject scope that covers the breadth of the humanities and social sciences as well as many interdisciplinary areas. Among these are psychology, psychiatry, education, criminology, communications, sociology, management, political science, and anthropology.

Primary arrangement is by conference accession number. Entries provide basic information on the papers, where they were published, and the locations and dates of the conferences. The many indexes provide access by broad subject categories, subject keywords, meeting or conference sponsor, author or editor, meeting location, and corporate affiliation of first authors. All issues, including the indexes, cumulate annually.

24. **Monthly Catalog of United States Government Publications.** Washington, D.C., Government Printing Office, 1895- . monthly. $167.00/yr. ISSN 0362-6830.

The *Monthly Catalog*, also available as a bibliographic database, is the single most important entry to the vast body of federal government publications. Its broad spectrum incorporates legislative hearings, research reports, educational and informational materials, and studies in every discipline. Many documents included are acquired by libraries to afford availability to patrons according to a depository program.

Practically every area of research and public service is included, and the work is a particularly rich source of statistical and demographic data. Citations to reports are arranged according to the publishing agency within monthly issues. Issues also contain seven indexes, the most useful of which are author, title, subject, series or report, and title keyword. Some indexes cumulate semiannually and annually. An annual *Periodicals Supplement* lists publications produced three or more times a year.

25. **Social Sciences Citation Index**. Vol. 1- , No. 1- . Philadelphia, Institute for Scientific Information, 1969- . triannual, with annual cumulations. $3,950.00. ISSN 0091-3707.

As an index to approximately 1,500 social science journals, *SSCI* incorporates many of the features found in other indexes. Its "permuterm" subject index allows access by significant words or word combinations in the titles of articles indexed. Listing by first author is the primary arrangement in the source index to articles indexed in that issue or year, accompanied by an author affiliation and address, basic bibliographic information, and a list of references cited by the authors. There is also a corporate index, allowing searching by the primary author's corporate or academic affiliation.

What sets *SSCI* apart is that it gives one the ability to search published literature by tracking the citations used by authors in their reference lists. Citation searching is based on the practice that authors cite seminal and other work related to their own and on which their research is predicated. Therefore, by using the citation index, one may find who has cited previously published research for a given year, then find the complete citation in the source index. Although a complex indexing tool to use, this title provides a unique and unequaled entry into a vast body of research literature.

This title comprehensively covers every social science discipline. Source journals in other disciplines, such as history, philosophy, medicine, and the physical sciences, are included selectively, having been derived from the ISI companion publications *Sciences Citation Index* and *Arts and Humanities Citation Index*. Multiyear cumulations extend *SSCI* coverage back to 1966, with a retrospective set covering 1956-1965. It has excellent interdisciplinary coverage of such topics as area studies, demography, international relations, minority studies, and geography.

26. **Social Sciences Index**. Vol. 1- , No. 1- . Bronx, N.Y., H. W. Wilson, 1974- . quarterly, with annual cumulations. service basis. ISSN 0094-4926.

Indexing over 300 journals in the social sciences and interdisciplinary areas, *Social Sciences Index* (*SSI*) provides an abundance of cross-references, subject headings based on a natural language-controlled vocabulary, and hierarchical subheadings within the subject heading scheme for ease of retrieval. The body of the index contains entries for subjects and authors (including cross-references for joint authors), with a separate book review section organized by book author in the back. Aside from the core journal literature in psychology and its subareas, *SSI* indexes interdisciplinary titles in aging and gerontology, social psychology, marriage and family studies, and cross-cultural psychology and ethnopsychology. This title supersedes, in part, *Social Sciences and Humanities Index* (volumes 19-27, 1965-1974) and *International Index to Periodicals* (volumes 1-18, 1907-1965).

HANDBOOKS AND YEARBOOKS

27. **Books in Print**. New Providence, N.J., R. R. Bowker, 1948- . annual. $349.95/set. LC 4-12648. ISSN 0068-0214.

28. **Subject Guide to Books in Print**. New Providence, N.J., R. R. Bowker, 1957- . annual. $239.95/set. LC 4-12648. ISSN 0000-0159.

Books in Print (*BIP*) is a comprehensive listing of books currently available for purchase in the United States. Over 30,000 publishers are represented, including trade presses, university and scholarly presses, research centers, and advocacy groups. Titles published abroad often are included if they are available through U.S. distributors. The number of volumes in the set varies, although at present the first three volumes are a listing of books by author, with the title listing comprising volumes 3 through 6. Bibliographic information always includes author, title, and publisher and often supplies ISBNs, prices, formats available, number of pages, and series. Because information on the approximately 850,000 titles is supplied by publishers, the completeness of entries and the accuracy of bibliographic information can vary. A directory volume contains information on publishers and distributors, and there is a volume for titles out-of-print and out-of-stock indefinitely.

The *Subject Guide* rearranges *BIP* titles (except most fiction and juvenile titles) under subject headings. Currently four volumes in size, it is supplemented by *Volume 5: Thesaurus*, a guide to over 100,000 subject headings used. Because titles are listed under Library of Congress subject headings, they can be cited more than once.

R. R. Bowker produces several related publications that are helpful but not essential for most users of *BIP*. A midyear supplement includes new titles and those recently out-of-print. The monthly *Forthcoming Books* provides an author, title, and subject listing to newly published books and advance listings of titles. The semiannual *Paperbound Books in Print* and several annual subject-oriented volumes are also available, as is Books in Print Plus, a CD-ROM version of *BIP* and its related publications.

DICTIONARIES AND ENCYCLOPEDIAS

29. Seligman, Edwin R. A., ed.-in-chief. **Encyclopaedia of the Social Sciences**. New York, Macmillan, 1930-1935. 15v. n.p. LC 30-3962.

This classic set was produced under the joint sponsorship of 10 preeminent American professional associations representing anthropology, social work, economics, history, political science, psychology, sociology, statistics, law, and education. A series of introductory essays in volume 1 defines and surveys development of the social science disciplines from ancient times to the postwar period. A second set of essays concentrates on the disciplines' evolution in 11 countries and geographic areas (all European except the United States, Latin America, and Japan).

Topical articles range from 3 to 10 pages in length. Biographies of deceased individuals whose contributions were significant to activity and research in the social sciences are shorter than the norm. Conceptually broad articles, such as those on children, education, and trade unionism, consist of multipart, multiauthor contributions. Reference lists are lengthy and now, of course, serve historical purposes. Each volume is preceded by a list of articles contained in that volume, and there are abundant cross-references. However, a cumulated classification listing categorizes articles under 55 broad areas. A traditional subject index follows.

Obviously, the encyclopedia serves a historical function now, and one with a predictably Eurocentric point of view. That said, it provides a unique and important service in the reference literature, reflecting research activity and emphases during a particularly important time of development in the social sciences. For this reason, it is only partially superseded by the later *International Encyclopedia of the Social Sciences* (see entry 30).

30. **International Encyclopedia of the Social Sciences**. David L. Sills, ed. New York, Free Press/Macmillan, c1968, 1977. LC 68-10023. 8v. $310.00/set. ISBN 0-02-895700-8.

31. **Biographical Supplement**. David L. Sills, ed. New York, Free Press/Macmillan, 1979. 820p. $85.00. LC 68-10023. ISBN 0-02-895510-2.

32. **Social Science Quotations**. David L. Sills and Robert K. Merton, eds. New York, Macmillan, 1991. 437p. index. $95.00. LC 68-10023. ISBN 0-02-928751-0.

Intended as a successor to *Encyclopaedia of the Social Sciences* (see entry 29), this work's subject scope, format, and in-depth coverage mirrors that of its predecessor. It focuses on the theories, research methods, and concepts associated with anthropology, economics, geography, history, law, political science, psychiatry and psychology, sociology, and statistics. The basic set contains biographies of approximately 600 influential individuals; the supplement has biographies of 215 additional people.

Organization in this set is similar to the *Encyclopaedia*, with an extensive index in volume 17, abundant cross-references linking related articles, lengthy essays, and a few statistical charts and tables. Conceptually broad articles, such on those on attitudes and psychoanalysis, are divided into shorter, focused essays. Again similar to the original *Encyclopaedia*, articles in the newer set focus on theory and concepts rather than applied areas of the disciplines.

Published as volume 19, *Social Science Quotations* provides lengthy quotations ("memorable ideas memorably expressed") from the works of writers who have had a significant impact on social science thought and development. Individuals quoted range from historians Thucydides and Ibn Khaldun to psychologists Carl Rogers and Edward Thorndike.

33. Kuper, Adam, and Jessica Kuper, eds. **The Social Science Encyclopedia.** New York, Routledge, Chapman & Hall, 1985. 916p. $75.00; $35.00pa. LC 84-27736. ISBN 0-7102-0008-0; 0-415-040821-7pa.

This is an excellent, authoritative, one-volume encyclopedia to the diverse social sciences. Over 700 entries cover theories, methods, issues, and individuals important to the history, development, and research of the social science disciplines. The preface claims over 500 contributing authors. Along with the core disciplines of anthropology, economics, political science, psychology, and sociology, there is excellent coverage of demography, linguistics, psychiatry, and applied areas (e.g., management and personnel, counseling and therapy, social work and criminology).

Averaging two to three pages in length, essays cover the scope, philosophical and theoretical underpinnings, and evolution of a concept, citing both seminal and current secondary literature. A list of further readings is usually appended. There are numerous cross-references and a guide that lists articles under disciplines or cross-disciplinary areas.

STATISTICS

34. **Statistical Abstract of the United States.** Washington, D.C., Bureau of the Census; distr., Washington, D.C., Government Printing Office, 1878- . annual. $25.00. ISSN 0081-4741.

This one-volume statistical compendium is chock-full of statistical tables on U.S. demographics, mortality, housing, employment, industrial and agricultural production, and finance. It is hard to imagine any aspect of life not represented by data compiled and presented in this source. Tables often provide statistics for a range of years, which, combined with this work's longevity, make it an excellent retrospective source. Because the tables are often highly condensed versions of government statistical reports, figures also include a full citation to the original source of information.

35. **Statistics Sources: A Subject Guide to Business, Social, Educational, Financial, and Other Topics for the United States and Internationally.** Jacqueline Wasserman O'Brien and Steven R. Wasserman, eds. Detroit, Gale, 1962- . 2v. annual. $305.00/set. LC 84-82356. ISBN 0-8103-4699-0.

This is a comprehensive directory to approximately 2,000 published and unpublished sources of statistical information. Among the published sources are trade and industry journals; documents of the United Nations and federal, state, and other governmental bodies; publications from professional and research associations and institutes; and serial and research reports from a wide variety of sources. In addition, clearinghouses and agencies are cited as sources of unpublished statistical information.

Features of recent editions include a list of federal offices and regional contacts for specific statistical information, including the name of a contact person. Citations are arranged under subject headings, with additional subject geographic subheadings as appropriate. Psychologists will find this title of interest because of the broad range of statistics indexed, especially those dealing with employment, retailing, education, and demographics.

DIRECTORIES

36. **Directories in Print**. Detroit, Gale, 1980- . 2v. $250.00/set. ISBN 0-8103-2948-4. ISSN 0275-5580.

Until 1988, previous editions of this annual were published under the title *Directory of Directories*. It contains approximately 10,000 entries representing a variety of directory sources: professional, trade, and avocational organizations; book and periodical publications; and machine-readable files. Among the directories listed are educational and business establishments, clearinghouses, membership rosters, and practically any other directory of name and address information. In addition to professional and association directories of individuals, the title cites directories of psychological software, treatment and research programs in mental health care and delivery, library collections, and periodical publications.

Each entry contains the name and source of the directory, its scope and format, a description of its contents, and its availability and cost. Entries are arranged under 16 broad subject areas, although more efficient access is provided through the subject and title/keyword indexes. Gale publishes *Directories in Print Supplement* as an updating source between editions.

37. **Research Centers Directory**. Detroit, Gale, 1960- . biennial. $390.00. LC 60-14807. ISSN 0080-1518.

Listed in this directory are 12,000-plus research centers and institutes affiliated with universities and other nonprofit organizations that represent all disciplines, from the humanities and arts to the sciences and social sciences. This publication is limited to continuing research programs in the United States and Canada. A supplemental publication, *New Research Centers*, updates contents between editions.

Entries are grouped under five broad subject areas—life sciences, physical sciences and engineering, public policy, multidisciplinary areas, and social and cultural studies—and thereunder by 17 additional categories. Psychology in general is covered under behavioral and social sciences; psychiatry is included under the section for medicine. Each entry provides the name and address of the research program, a brief description and history of the organization and the scope of its research, staffing and special facilities, director, and publications and special services offered. Access points include indexes by subject and a master index in which centers are listed alphabetically and under their university affiliation.

38. **Ulrich's International Periodicals Directory.** New Providence, N.J., R. R. Bowker, 1965- . 3v. annual. index. $339.95/set. LC 32-16320. ISSN 0000-0175.

The first two volumes of this set consist of entries for over 116,000 serials published at both regular and irregular intervals. Titles are arranged according to a subject classification scheme, a guide to which precedes the entries. Each entry consists of the serial title, publisher information, ISSN, frequency and price, editor, availability of the text in alternate formats, and indexing and abstracting sources in which it is included.

Volume 3 consists of supplemental lists of serials: those in machine-readable format, a selective list of refereed serials, recently ceased titles, an index to titles published by international organizations, and ISSN and title indexes. The annual editions are supplemented by Bowker's quarterly *Ulrich's Update*. Although information on periodicals is in constant flux, this is an indispensable source of information on journals and other serials.

39. **World Directory of Social Science Institutions**. 5th ed. Paris, Unesco; distr., Lanham, Md., UNIPUB, 1990. 1211p. index. $43.00. ISBN 92-3-002552-6.

Revised at approximately five-year intervals, this edition contains descriptions of over 2,000 research organizations worldwide. The body of the work organizes the research centers under country of location, with those of an international nature listed in a separate section for international and regional centers. Each entry consists of address, information on publications issued, types of research it supports and in what geographic area, and size and composition of staff. There are indexes to names and acronyms, directors or executives of the research centers, and subjects and areas of geographic research interest.

40. **World List of Social Science Periodicals**. 8th ed. Paris, Unesco; distr., Lanham, Md., UNIPUB, 1991. 1264p. index. (World Social Science Information Directories). $40.00. ISBN 92-3-002734-0.

Prepared by the Unesco Social Science Documentation Centre, this work lists 4,459 periodical titles that publish the results of research of interest to social scientists. Secondary periodicals, including bibliographic indexing services and review serials, are included, although statistical and news publications are not. Entries are arranged by country of publication and alphabetically thereunder by title, and each contains a brief annotation that describes coverage, the average number of articles and pages in each issue, editorial responsibility and publisher information, languages of publication, variant titles, and the like.

A title index precedes the entries, and a subject index lists titles according to broad categories. A simliar subject index is provided for bibliographic indexes. The disciplines covered are wide, including economics, statistics, political science, anthropology and sociology, social welfare, geography, management science, and philosophies of the disciplines covered. Psychology as a discipline is not covered (presumably it is considered a science), although many areas of human behavior are, including social psychology, human geography, and personnel and labor relations.

41. **World of Learning**. London, Europa; distr., Detroit, Gale, 1947- . annual. $290.00. ISSN 0084-2117.

This is a unique worldwide directory to institutions of cultural and scholarly endeavor: universities, learned societies, libraries, research centers, and so forth. Its primary arrangement is by country and then by type of organization or institution; international organizations precede the national ones. Location information is provided for each entry, as well as size and composition or organization (e.g., schools, administrative units, departments).

This is one of the few sources in which one can locate information on scholars and staff affiliated with foreign institutions. Listings for many entries include faculty members, affiliated scholars, and others; at the very least, they name heads of departments. There is an index by institution name.

BIOGRAPHIES

42. **American Men and Women of Science: Social and Behavioral Sciences**. 13th ed. New York, R. R. Bowker, 1978. 1545p. index. $69.95. ISBN 0-8352-1018-9.

Originally produced as a companion to *American Men and Women of Science* (R. R. Bowker, 1975-), this is unfortunately the last such volume to cover individuals in the social and behavioral sciences. It is one of the few titles providing biographical sketches of American academics and other researchers across the spectrum of the social sciences. Its continued usefulness despite its age attests to its unique content and to the difficulty of locating similar information in other sources.

Individuals are alphabetically listed. Each entry provides some personal information, institutions attended and degrees held, employment history, important publications, areas of current research interest, and a mailing address. There are indexes by field of research and by geographic location (state and city).

43. **Biography Index.** Vol. 1- . Bronx, N.Y., H. W. Wilson, 1946- quarterly, with annual cumulations. $100.00/yr. ISSN 0006-3053.

This is a handy tool for locating English-language biographies and autobiographies of living and deceased individuals from all walks of life. Book-length biographies, information contained in collections of biographical essays, and magazines and journals are all covered. A supplemental index by occupation of the biographees is most useful for locating information on important, but not always prominent, individuals from a variety of disciplines.

Part II

SOCIAL SCIENCES DISCIPLINES

EDUCATION

Guides

44. Berry, Dorothea M. **A Bibliographic Guide to Educational Research**. 3d ed. Metuchen, N.J., Scarecrow, 1990. 500p. index. $49.50. LC 90-48184. ISBN 0-8108-2343-8.

This work is an annotated list of 1,050 English-language printed sources on education. Reference materials are categorized by format: access to books (e.g., card catalogs and their subject classification schemes, bibliographies); periodical directories and indexes; ERIC and other sources of unpublished documents; dissertations; government documents; reference tools for children's literature; textbooks; and media, tests, and general reference materials. Also included are guides to research methods, style manuals for writers in education, and reference and research guides in other social science disciplines. There are indexes by author/editor, title, and subject.

Because Berry concentrates on printed sources, the book is less comprehensive than Woodbury's *Guide to Sources of Educational Information* (see entry 46). However, this volume does cover national, state, and international publications more thoroughly, and material is more comprehensibly organized for the beginning user.

45. Freed, Melvyn N., Robert K. Hess, and Joseph M. Ryan. **The Educator's Desk Reference: A Sourcebook of Educational Information and Research**. New York, Macmillan, 1989. 536p. index. (American Council on Education/Macmillan Publishing Company Series in Higher Education). $49.95. LC 88-9249. ISBN 0-02-910740-7.

Education practitioners, researchers, and students will find this an excellent one-volume reference resource. The first section consists of an annotated list of 134 printed reference sources by format and an "information locator" of common questions asked during the information search process, followed by suggested sources for answers. The second section lists and describes over 100 professional journals, over 60 book publishers, and approximately 60 software producers of interest to potential authors.

Other sections list and describe microcomputer software for professionals, about 100 standardized testing instruments commonly used in educational settings, and designs and models used in educational research.There is also a directory with detailed descriptions of national and regional professional and research organizations. Finally, there is a combined index to organizations, titles, and subjects.

46. Woodbury, Marda. **A Guide to Sources of Educational Information**. 2d ed. Arlington, Va., Information Resources Press, 1982. 430p. index. $39.95. LC 82-80549. ISBN 0-87815-041-2.

Woodbury takes a format-of-information approach to education sources, with sources divided between print and nonprint formats. Printed sources are organized by type of reference tool: directories, encyclopedias, guides to the use of statistics, bibliographies and review sources, and current-awareness tools. Nonprint sources include organizations and clearinghouses, databases, research centers, and state library services and resources for educators. A section of more specialized sources lists tools in special education, educational finance, instructional materials, and tests. Each section is preceded by a brief description of the types of sources available and their value in the information search process. All citations, regardless of format, have descriptive and evaluative annotations.

An introductory chapter discusses the production and dissemination of educational information, the types and diversity of source materials, and an outline of the research process. A final chapter lists printed guides to assist in composing written reports, proposals, and other documents. There is a combined subject, title, and author index.

Bibliographies

47. Cabell, David W. E., ed. **Cabell's Directory of Publishing Opportunities in Education.** 2d ed. Beaumont, Tex., Cabell Publishing, 1989. 2v. index. $59.95. LC 89-162981. ISBN 0-911753-03-6.

Cabell's primary audience is researchers and practitioners in all areas of education who seek a medium of publication. Over 400 English-language journals are represented in education at all levels, settings, and disciplines; special education; and counseling and student services. In addition, core journals are selected from the disciplines of psychology, communications, library science, anthropology, sociology, and the creative arts. Journals are listed alphabetically, and there is a subject index in volume 2.

For each title, extensive information is provided on the review process, circulation data, subject areas considered appropriate for publication, brief information on publication guidelines, and addresses for manuscript submission. In most cases, information on submission procedures and manuscript guidelines and preparation is reproduced from the journals themselves or from information available from the publisher or editor. Although listing fewer titles than *Education Journals and Serials* (see entry 48), it covers only journals and, of those, the titles of most interest to potential authors. It also includes information on manuscript acceptance rates, percentage of invited articles, and other data difficult to locate elsewhere.

48. Collins, Mary Ellen, comp. **Education Journals and Serials: An Analytical Guide.** Westport, Conn., Greenwood Press, 1988. 355p. index. (Annotated Bibliographies of Serials: A Subject Approach Series, no.12). $49.95. LC 87-31442. ISBN 0-313-24514-2.

Collins lists almost 800 journals, newsletters, and other serial publications. The discipline is interpreted broadly, with coverage of relevant titles in child development, developmental and educational psychology, sociology, and a wide variety of interrelated disciplines.

Entries are arranged under four broad concept areas: education in general, educational levels, curricular areas and professional issues, and other topics. These chapters are further subdivided to provide subject access under approximately 50 categories, supplemented by a subject index. There are also indexes by publisher, geographic origin, and current title.

In addition to standard information such as publisher, price, and editorship, each entry contains a wealth of bibliographic and publishing data: title changes and mergers; policies on manuscript selection, special issues, advertising and illustrations, and book reviews; reprint and microfilm availability; and print and online indexes in which the title is included. Most entries contain descriptive and evaluative annotations, which vary greatly in length.

Indexes and Abstracts

49. **Current Index to Journals in Education**. Vol. 1- , No. 1- . Phoenix, Ariz., Oryx Press, 1969- . monthly, with semiannual cumulations. $207.00/yr. ISSN 0011-3565.

CIJE is the journal indexing component of the ERIC (Educational Resources Information Center) system of the U.S. Department of Education. As such, it indexes articles from nearly 800 education and education-related journals. "Education" is interpreted broadly as being any factor or process affecting the learning process, including public policies, teacher preparation, environmental and social factors, and psychological effects. All levels, from preschool education through post-graduate to independent learning, are included.

The main entry section organizes citations and their brief annotations under one of the 16 subject clearinghouses responsible for its indexing. The primary access is through the subject index, which uses the *Thesaurus of ERIC Descriptors* (see entry 53) as its controlled vocabulary. Terminology in the subject index is not restricted to thesaurus terms, as uncontrolled terminology, called identifiers, provides access by proper names and other terms not represented in the controlled vocabulary. There are also indexes by author and by journal title and issue. The main entry section and all indexes cumulate semiannually. ERIC also issued a *CIJE* cumulative author index covering 1969-1984.

50. **Education Index.** Vol. 1- , No. 1- . Bronx, N.Y., H. W. Wilson, 1929- . monthly, except July and August, with annual cumulations. service basis. ISSN 0013-1385.

Education Index cites articles from over 300 journals and annual publications of interest to students, researchers, and professionals. Citations are listed by author and subject, with abundant cross-references for secondary authors and alternate subject headings. A separate section of book review citations was added with volume 26, 1975. Monthly issues are cumulated quarterly, then annually in the bound volume.

In addition to coverage of educational and instructional psychology, many key serials in counseling, developmental psychology (especially children and adolescents), and education of exceptional individuals are indexed. Although there is substantial overlap with *Current Index to Journals in Education* (see entry 49), some of the source journals are unique to this index. The "natural language" subject approach and use of subheadings within subjects make it easier to use.

51. **Exceptional Child Education Resources.** Vol. 9, No. 1- . Reston, Va., Council for Exceptional Children, 1977- . quarterly. $75.00/yr. ISSN 0160-4309.

ECER lists about 3,000 entries per year, representing citations from more than 200 journals in addition to books, research reports, government publications, and dissertations. (The work was previously published as *Exceptional Child Education Abstracts* from 1969 to 1977.) It is intended for practitioners in education and psychology; researchers; and students interested in the education and welfare of the physically and mentally impaired, the learning disabled, and the gifted. The literatures of medicine, the psychology of learning and education, education and special education, and rehabilitation and therapy are well represented. Although the primary focus is on children and the educational process, the scope also includes prenatal influences and handicapping conditions, the learning styles and rehabilitation of handicapped adults, and the education and learning of all exceptional learners regardless of context or setting.

Because the Council is one of the ERIC clearinghouses, there is some duplication between *ECER* and the other ERIC indexes. The format of entries is similar, with bibliographic information accompanied by nonevaluative abstracts and the list of subject descriptors assigned. Entries are listed in two sections: books and journal articles, and dissertations (the latter section without abstracts). There are author and title indexes and a subject index that uses *Thesaurus of ERIC Descriptors* (see entry 53) terminology. All indexes cumulated annually. There is an identically named database equivalent of this index.

52. **Resources in Education.** Vol. 10- , No. 1- . Washington, D.C., U.S. Department of Education, National Institute of Education, 1975- . monthly, with annual cumulations. $66.00/yr. ISSN 0098-0897.

RIE indexes "fugitive," nonserial documents, such as conference papers and proceedings, research reports, position papers, curriculum guides, and lesson plans. The vast majority are unpublished and difficult to locate through other means. Material is submitted to one of 16 subject clearinghouses by professional associations, institutions of higher education, local school districts, individuals, and a variety of other sources. These clearinghouses abstract, index, and disseminate information about these documents, coordinated by ERIC (Educational Resources Information

Center), which produces *RIE* and provides document delivery services in microfiche or paper for approximately 95% of the items listed. Libraries and other institutions may also subscribe to a monthly microfiche service, by which these documents are received automatically in conjunction with the *RIE* issue. Doctoral dissertations and published books are cited but are not available through the document delivery service or in microfiche.

Each *RIE* issue lists about 1,000 documents. Every "document resume" lists title and publication information, availability (from ERIC or other sources), sponsoring agency, a physical description, an ERIC price code, publication type, subject descriptors and identifiers assigned to the document, and a lengthy abstract. The subject index uses terminology from the *Thesaurus of ERIC Descriptors* (see entry 53), supplemented by an uncontrolled vocabulary represented by identifiers (usually geographic or proper names or terminology too new to be a part of the thesaurus). There are an institutional index by the name of the sponsoring or producing agency, an index by publication type, and an author index. These indexes cumulate semiannually (published by ERIC) and annually (published by Oryx Press). Volumes 1-10 (1966-1974) were published under the title *Research in Education.*

Psychologists will be particularly interested in the coverage of educational psychology, testing, counseling, and child development. In addition, papers presented at professional psychology conferences, especially at state and regional levels, occasionally find their way here, and the ERIC Document Reproduction Service makes them easy to obtain.

Handbooks and Yearbooks

53. **Thesaurus of ERIC Descriptors**. 12th ed. Phoenix, Ariz., Oryx Press, 1990. 627p. $69.50. LC 87-647380. ISBN 0-89774-561-2.

This volume constitutes the controlled vocabulary for *Current Index to Journals in Education* (*CIJE*) (see entry 49), *Resources in Education* (*RIE*) (see entry 52), and ERIC online products. Primary vocabulary arrangement is alphabetical, with over 5,200 postable terms used as subject headings and another 4,100 cross-references to postable terms. For postable terms, the date first used as a descriptor, the number of postings in *CIJE* and *RIE* publications, and "used for" terms are listed, as well as related, broader, and narrower terms. Brief scope notes clarify terms with ambiguous or dual meanings or otherwise delineate their use as a subject heading.

The *Thesaurus* also includes a rotated descriptor section, under which all descriptors and cross-reference terms are listed by each significant word. Another section lists terms according to a hierarchical arrangement of descriptor concept families. There is a listing of all descriptors under 41 "Descriptor Groups," providing rudimentary table-of-contents access to the main alphabetical list.

New editions of the *Thesaurus* are frequent, generally every five to seven years. Changes to the terminology or additions between editions are included in the back of monthly issues of *CIJE* and *RIE.*

Dictionaries and Encyclopedias

54. **Encyclopedia of Education**. Lee C. Deighton, ed.-in-chief. New York, Macmillan, 1971. 10v. index. $199.00/set. LC 79-133143. ISBN 0-02-895300-2.

There are more current encyclopedias for the discipline of education. Yet this set remains a classic, comprehensive, and substantial source of information. More than 1,000 articles encompass the breadth of education at all levels, from preschool to professional, from home-based to correctional facilities, from administration to individualized instruction, and from urbanization to agricultural education. Coverage is international in scope, with emphasis on the effects of political, social, economic, and cultural trends on educational institutions, processes, and theories.

Essays are conceptually broad, and contributors place particular emphasis on the historical context and evolutionary developments of institutions. Extensiveness of the bibliographies varies but generally encompasses the core literature. Articles range in length from under a page to over 50 pages, with longer articles usually divided into smaller segments. Although most concern concepts or techniques, a few are biographical, cover associations, or discuss specific geographic regions of the world.

Cross-references and *see* references are sparse, although the index in volume 10 is detailed and extensive. This volume also contains a "Guide to Articles," which acts as a broad outline to articles and their *see* and cross-references. As the scope of education has been interpreted so broadly, interest in this title goes well beyond educational psychology to encompass developmental, social, and counseling psychology areas, among others.

55. **Encyclopedia of Educational Research**. 6th ed. Marvin C. Alkin, ed.-in-chief. New York, Macmillan, 1992. 4v. index. $315.00/set. LC 91-38682. ISBN 0-02-900431-4.

Sponsored by the American Educational Research Association, this work has over 300 conceptually broad essays that discuss issues in and approaches to educational research. Volume 1 provides a hierarchical listing of articles arranged under 16 broad areas. Because of the conceptually wide topics of articles, use of the index in volume 4 is essential for access to proper names and topics of narrower interest, supplemented by cross-references in the articles themselves. An appendix in volume 4, "Doing Library Research in Education," guides novice researchers through the types of reference materials available.

Articles discuss areas or concepts in historical, social, and intellectual contexts, and contributors cite liberally from both the seminal, historical literature and from recent publications through the 1980s. Several categories of articles are relevant to psychology, especially those concerning handicapped and gifted education, research in personality and perception, specific areas in social and developmental psychology (e.g., aging, attitudes, racism), and testing and measurement techniques and issues.

56. **Encyclopedia of Special Education**. Cecil P. Reynolds and Lester Mann, eds. New York, John Wiley, 1987. 3v. index. $250.00/set. LC 86-33975. ISBN 0-471-82858-0.

Entries from over 300 contributors cover every aspect of the education of the handicapped and gifted. Ranging in length from less than half a page to several pages, articles encompass biographies, mental measurements and tests, rehabilitation and intervention, descriptions of handicapping conditions, legal and public service issues, research issues and methods, and such miscellaneous topics as professional associations and journals. They are usually appended by brief reference lists and cross-references. An appendix reprints the groundbreaking P.L. 94-142, and there are name and subject indexes in volume 3.

Not strictly for the professional, articles are comprehensible by the educated layperson and beginning students in a variety of disciplines.

Particularly relevant to psychology is coverage of developmental disabilities, learning and language disabilities, and cognitive and communication disorders. There are also entries for individual evaluative measures of aptitude and impairment as well as extensive coverage of behavioral approaches to diagnosis and treatment.

57. **International Encyclopedia of Education**. Torsten Husen and T. Neville Postlethwaite, eds.-in-chief. Oxford, England, Pergamon Press, 1985. 10v. $2150.00/set. LC 84-20750. ISBN 0-08-028119-2. **Supplement. Volume 1**. Elmsford, N.Y., Pergamon Press, 1989. 864p. index. $195.00. LC 88-39814. ISBN 0-08-034974-9.

This encyclopedia is a major undertaking to provide both an international and multidisciplinary approach to education and its intersecting disciplines. Its scope and currentness make it an essential complement to *Encyclopedia of Education* (see entry 54).

Article length varies from a page to over 50 pages. Emphasis is on issues, policies, and approaches in education rather than individuals or organizations. Separate entries for individual countries discuss the structure and organization of their educational institutions, trends, and areas of concern. Literature cited in bibliographies includes both the current and the classic. Articles fall under one or more conceptual cluster areas: human development, policy, and economics; curriculum and teaching; evaluation and research; comparative education; and social science and humanities disciplines that concern education. Coverage of areas in educational psychology focuses on counseling and therapy, evaluation, discussion of developmental stages, and theories of educational psychology.

Volume 10 contains several supplementary access tools. A classified list of entries organizes articles hierarchically under 24 broad categories, subdivided into narrower interest areas. There are author and subject indexes and a title list of major educational journals.

58. Shafritz, Jay M., Richard P. Koeppe, and Elizabeth W. Soper. **The Facts on File Dictionary of Education**. New York, Facts on File, 1988. 503p. $40.00. LC 88-24554. ISBN 0-8160-1636-4.

The entries in this work are of two types: brief definitions of terms and longer explanations of concepts and other phenomena in education or related fields with an impact on education. The latter feature makes this title more useful than the former does by describing theories, movements, organizations, judicial and legal proceedings, standardized tests and journals, and biographical entries of both living and deceased individuals. Longer entries include one or two citations to relevant literature and discuss the development and implications of the issue at hand. This work also serves as a directory, with address information for associations and journal publications, and as a sourcebook, with its tables on competency testing and compulsory school attendance in the United States and standardized IQ classifications. Although there are no indexes, there are numerous cross-references.

ECONOMICS

Guides

59. Daniells, Lorna M. **Business Information Sources**. rev. ed. Berkeley, Calif., University of California Press, 1985. 673p. index. $40.00. LC 84-2546. ISBN 0-520-05335-4.

Intended as "a guide to the vast and varied sources of business information for the business-person, student, and librarian," this work cites a variety of print formats, including texts and handbooks, journal titles, and reference serials, to meet a wide variety of needs. Inclusion is selective, with emphasis on U.S. English-language sources published in the late 1970s to mid-1980s. A few chapters discuss the variety of business library collections, list general reference works and computer-readable files, and cover a wide range of sources for economic and industrial statistics. Others focus on sources about specific topics within business: investment and banking, accounting and taxation, computer applications and management information systems, and management and personnel. All are accompanied by descriptive annotations, and there is a combined author, title, and subject index.

Although not as wide-ranging as *Encyclopedia of Business Information Sources* (see entry 60), this work affords solid coverage of basic sources in the behavioral sciences: marketing and buyer behavior, human resources management, employment and industrial relations issues, and organizational behavior.

60. **Encyclopedia of Business Information Sources.** 7th ed. James Woy, ed. Detroit, Gale, 1988. 896p. $220.00. LC 84-643366. ISBN 0-8103-2764-3.

This is an exhaustive guide to over 20,000 print, organization, and online sources. With comprehensive coverage of management and finance, personnel, economics, and marketing, it should be of particular interest to those involved in consumer behavior, advertising, and human resource management.

Sources are topically arranged under more than 1,000 categories. An outline of contents precedes the entries, acting as a thesaurus to the subject headings, including references that range from unacceptable to usable terminology. Sources are listed under each subject category by format, with bibliographic or location information provided for each source, as appropriate. Among these are formats for reference tools (e.g., bibliographies, indexes and abstracts, almanacs and yearbooks, directories), professional sources (e.g., manuals, selected periodical titles), statistical sources, databases (text, bibliographic, and statistical), and research centers and trade associations.

61. Fletcher, John, ed. **Information Sources in Economics.** 2d ed. Boston, Butterworths, 1984. 339p. (Butterworths Guides to Information Sources). $70.00. ISBN 0-408-11471-1.

After an introductory article on the scope of the economic literature and literature search methods, a series of bibliographic essays focus on a variety of research formats: bibliographic guides, periodicals, machine-readable bibliographic and statistical sources, and public documents. These are followed by contributed essays on topics within economics and relevant information sources.

Fletcher's focus is decidedly British, yet similar U.S. sources tend to focus more on business, management, and finance rather than economic literature. Therefore, this volume earns a niche as a guide to information in economic behavior and decision making.

62. Schlessinger, Bernard S., ed. **The Basic Business Library: Core Resources.** 2d ed. Phoenix, Ariz., Oryx Press, 1989. 278p. index. $38.50. LC 88-37381. ISBN 0-89774-451-9.

Schlessinger's primary audience is business librarians. Of most interest to students is part 1, "Core List of Printed Business Reference Sources": serials, books, indexes, and so forth. Each of the 177 references includes a description and evaluation of the source. Part 2 consists of articles and books on business reference work and librarianship published from 1976 to 1987. Nine contributed essays comprise part 3 and focus on topics in business information sources and services: machine-readable sources, organization and collection development issues, investment sources, and government publications. There is a combined author, title, and subject index. Although intended as a collection development tool for small and medium-sized libraries, this work introduces library users to essential business sources and the wealth of business information to be found in general reference sources.

Indexes and Abstracts

63. **Business Periodicals Index.** Vol. 1, No. 1- . Bronx, N.Y., H. W. Wilson, 1959- . monthly, except August, with annual cumulations. service basis. ISSN 0007-6961.

Despite the abundance of economics- and management-related indexing sources in both print and machine-readable format, *BPI* retains its role as the standard general index in business-related fields. As such, it covers many areas of interest to applied psychologists: organizational behavior and decision making, behavioral aspects of marketing and advertising, employee relations, and personnel issues.

BPI indexes a variety of publications, from scholarly and academic journals to trade and industry magazines and professional publications. Its ease of use, natural-language subject headings, abundant cross-references, and familiarity as one of the family of Wilson indexes also make it a first stop for many students.

64. **Index of Economic Articles.** Vol. 8, No. 1- . Nashville, Tenn., American Economic Association, 1966- . annual. $90.00/yr.(institutions). ISSN 0536-647X.

This title was previously published as *Index of Economic Journals*, with seven multiyear volumes covering 1886 to 1965. The annual publication schedule, which often runs late, limits its usefulness. However, it provides coverage of articles in scholarly and professional journals and books in a broad spectrum of economic areas. Among these subject areas are managerial organization and decision making, decision theory, marketing and advertising, labor force training, human resource development, and consumer economics. The index is published in two parts each year. Basic arrangement is provided in the first part under a hierarchical subject arrangement requiring use of the detailed outline in the front of the issue. The second part is an author listing.

SOCIOLOGY

Guides

65. Aby, Stephen H. **Sociology: A Guide to Reference and Information Sources.** Littleton, Colo., Libraries Unlimited, 1987. 231p. index. (Reference Sources in the Social Sciences Series). $36.00. LC 86-27573. ISBN 0-87287-498-2.

This book takes an interdisciplinary approach to the literature of sociology and a multiformat approach to information sources. Part 1 consists of reference tools in the broad area of the social sciences. Part 2 contains research guides, indexes, handbooks, encyclopedias, and other tools in six social science disciplines: education, economics, psychology, social work, anthropology, and history.

Part 3 has a section of general reference sources in sociology, including guides, bibliographies, and indexes and abstracts; a list of journals, professional organizations, and research institutes; primary publishers; dictionaries and encyclopedias; handbooks and yearbooks; and online databases. Finally, the field is divided further into 23 subareas. Psychologists will be interested in the coverage of clinical sociology and social work, aging, family psychology, gender roles, women's studies, and research methods. Over 650 sources are represented, each with complete bibliographic and purchasing information (if in print) and a lengthy descriptive and critical annotation. There are author/title and subject indexes.

66. Brown, Samuel R., comp. **Finding the Source in Sociology and Anthropology: A Thesaurus-Index to the Reference Collection.** Westport, Conn., Greenwood Press, 1987. 269p. index. (Finding the Source, no.1). $45.00. LC 86-31879. ISBN 0-313-25263-7.

This is a guide to selected monographic and serial reference tools: indexing and abstracting services, bibliographies, directories, encyclopedias, dictionaries, handbooks, atlases, and compendia of statistics. The emphasis is on materials primarily (but not exclusively) published after 1970. Users will not find many highly specialized sources. Instead, Brown guides users to an easily accessible core collection of materials. The value of this work is its keyword approach to 586 reference tools in sociology and anthropology, their subareas, and interdisciplinary areas. Primary arrangement for the unannotated references is under 10 subject categories, including general, social sciences, anthropology, sociology, and several interdisciplinary topics. There are author and title/subject indexes. Subject access is primarily through the "thesaurus-index." Broad topics such as psychological anthropology, social attitudes, and mental health list entries by a hierarchical arrangement, subdivided by population, bibliographic format, and subject-oriented subheadings. Thesaurus features such as scope notes; *see* references; and referral to narrower, broader, and related terms are provided.

67. McMillan, Patricia, and James R. Kennedy, Jr. **Library Research Guide to Sociology: Illustrated Search Strategy and Sources.** Ann Arbor, Mich., Pierian Press, 1981. 70p. index. $25.00; $15.00pa. LC 80-83513. ISBN 0-876-50121-8; 0-876-50122-6pa.

Intending their work for sociology undergraduates, McMillan and Kennedy illustrate the step-by-step use of basic sources in the discipline. Preliminary chapters focus on selecting and narrowing a search topic. Others focus on using the traditional card catalog and evaluating the contents of books. Some basic indexes are covered as well: *Sociological Abstracts* (see entry 72), *Social Sciences Index* (see entry 26), and *Social Sciences Citation Index* (see entry 25), as well as some general interest indexing sources. Other chapters focus on government documents and statistical sources, dictionaries and encyclopedias, and using guides to the literature. Illustrations are plentiful, with large illustrations demonstrating the use of the source and how to find appropriate citations.

The most helpful section is appendix 2, which contains basic reference sources for a course in sociology: a classified, unannotated listing of reference books, guides, bibliographies, and indexing tools that provide a narrower focus than the sources discussed. Especially strong is coverage of ethnic studies and social problems. Because most works are pre-1978, however, its usefulness is now dated.

Bibliographies

68. Huber, Bettina J., comp. **Publishing Options: An Author's Guide to Journals.** Washington, D.C., American Sociological Association, 1982. 157p. index. (ASA Professional Information Series). $18.00pa.

69. Sussman, Marvin B., ed. **Author's Guide to Journals in Sociology & Related Fields.** New York, Haworth Press, 1978. 214p. index. (Author's Guide to Journals Series). $32.95. LC 78-1952. ISBN 0-918824-03-8.

Both of these works provide information on journals—specifically their manuscript submission and publication procedures—that will be of interest to potential authors. Included are the primary journals in sociology and its subareas, interdisciplinary areas such as demography and area studies, and selected primary titles from other social science disciplines, such as psychology, education, social work, economics, anthropology, law, and political science.

Primary arrangement of these works is alphabetical by title, with the following information consistently provided for each entry: publisher, editor, manuscript address, publication's audience, subscription price, frequency and circulation, indexing tools in which it is included, style requirements and review process, restrictions on length and content of articles, and reprint policies and charges. Completeness of entries varies, as most were procured directly from journal publishers. Huber's list is preceded by a list of titles organized under 101 broad subject areas, bringing together all journals that publish in specific content areas. It also has a cross-reference list of superseded titles. Sussman has a combined subject, title, and keyword subject index. Selected British, Canadian, and regional journals are included in Sussman, whereas Huber restricts her titles to United States and Canadian ones. The focus of both is overwhelmingly on U.S. titles, with all published primarily in English.

As with all works of this sort, some information is subject to almost constant flux. The numerous interdisciplinary titles begun in the 1980s are not represented. Sussman has better coverage of core journals in psychology, psychiatry, and areas of mental health care and counseling, many of which are not in Huber. Additionally, Sussman has more titles (350-plus), including British publications, than Huber, who lists 257 titles.

70. Wepsiec, Jan. **Sociology: An International Bibliography of Serial Literature 1880-1980.** London, Mansell, 1983. 183p. index. $57.00. LC 83-217098. ISBN 0-7291-1652-X.

This impressive catalog lists over 2,000 serial publications in sociology and related areas in philosophy, biology, psychology, and a host of interdisciplinary studies. As the title indicates, the scope is international and multilingual.

Titles are arranged alphabetically by journal name or transliterated title and accompanied by publication data such as publisher, dates published, and frequency. Brief annotations provide variant titles, languages of publication, changes of publisher over the publication span, subtitles where appropriate, and the indexing and abstracting services in which they are included. Liberal use of cross-references allows access by previous titles, and there are two supplements of titles too recent for the initial compilation. The work has a detailed subject index.

Indexes and Abstracts

71. **International Bibliography of Sociology**. Vol. 5- . New York, Routledge, Chapman & Hall, 1955- . annual. (International Bibliography of the Social Sciences). $110.00/yr. ISSN 0085-2066.

This is one of four annual bibliographies prepared by the International Committee for Social Science Information and Documentation on behalf of UNESCO. It was preceded by five issues of the publication *Current Sociology* that covered 1951-1954. Citations from over 800 serial publications are organized by a rather complex, detailed classification scheme, so that the unannotated citations are listed under approximately 200 subject categories. Good coverage is provided for group and individual social interaction, attitudes and perceptions, and marriage and the family, especially cross-cultural perspectives. There are a subject index, especially helpful for locating items about a country or geographical region, and an author index. The geographically broad coverage makes this publication truly international. One serious problem is lag time: A volume covering the publications of a given year is often published three years later.

72. **Sociological Abstracts.** Vol. 1- , No. 1- . San Diego, Calif., Sociological Abstracts, 1953- . 6 issues per year. $400.00. ISSN 0038-0202.

As the primary index for serial literature in sociology and its related disciplines, this work includes articles from 1,200 journals, annual reviews, and research paper series. Each issue contains three sections. The main body lists citations and abstracts under one of 33 broad subject areas, with some categories further subdivided, as outlined in the table of contents. Journal citations are accompanied by lengthy, descriptive abstracts, which may contain references to historically relevant citations or those previously cited in this serial. References cited in one of its companion publications, such as *Linguistics and Language Behavior Abstracts* (see entry 406), are cited here, but users are referred elsewhere for the abstract. Citations to dissertations do not include abstracts.

A second section, also known as "International Review of Publications in Sociology," provides abstracts of current books in sociology, often including extensive tables of contents, and cites book reviews appearing in journals. This section contains its own author, source, and reviewer indexes. The last section contains the *SA* author index, a source journal and issue index, and a subject index. After April 1986, subject terms were assigned from the *Thesaurus of Sociological Indexing Terms* (see entry 75). All indexes cumulate annually.

In the past, *SA* has contained a bewildering and varied array of supplements: bulletins, abstracts of papers presented at professional conferences, annotated proceedings, and various other publications from regional and international associations of sociology. The most consistent of these has been the *Bulletin* of the International Sociological Association.

Psychologists will find excellent, exhaustive coverage of social psychology areas complementing coverage afforded by *Psychological Abstracts* (see entry 129), especially the sociology of organizations and social group interaction and conflict. The cross-cultural perspective provided by the source journal list is generally better than that provided by *Psychological Abstracts*.

Handbooks and Yearbooks

73. Bart, Pauline, and Linda Frankel. **The Student Sociologist's Handbook.** 4th ed. New York, Random House, 1986. 291p. index. $10.95. LC 85-19399. ISBN 0-394-35109-6.

Intended for undergraduates, this work combines an overview of sociology as a discipline and the structure of its research literature with the qualities of a library research guide and writing manual. There is also selected coverage of research and applied methods in sociology.

The first chapter, "Perspectives in Sociology," discusses the interpretations and approaches applied to the study of human social behavior, both historical and contemporary. Chapter 2 describes the types of sociology papers typically undertaken by students, including fieldwork, library research, and analytical papers, with some hints on selecting a topic and writing styles. The next chapter covers library mechanics: the organization of libraries, interlibrary loan, book classification systems, and card catalogs. Chapter 4 discusses the importance of the journal literature and describes over 100 journal titles in sociology; related titles from economics, law, and psychology; and interdisciplinary areas. Chapter 5, "Guides to Research and Resource Materials," evaluates all types of printed references tools, including general and specialized indexes and abstracts, recurring and retrospective bibliographies, handbooks and guides, encyclopedias, and dictionaries. There is an excellent overview of sources of United States and United Nations data, the Human Relations Area File, and other information for the student researcher. The final chapters describe computer applications in sociological research (already out of date) and ethical and career issues. Appendixes include outlines of pertinent sections of Dewey Decimal and Library of Congress classification systems. There is a subject, title, and author index.

This guide is strong in its coverage of Marxist literature, women's studies, and alternative sociology. The chapter on statistical sources is particularly noteworthy and will be comprehensible to the serious student.

74. Smelser, Neil J., ed. **Handbook of Sociology.** Newbury Park, Calif., Sage, 1988. 824p. index. $89.95. LC 87-36762. ISBN 0-8039-2665-0.

Sociology has lacked a comprehensive, solid, and current handbook to the discipline until the publication of this volume. Composed of 22 chapters by 33 authors, this handbook conveys the breadth of sociological research and its implications, applications of sociological theory, and current research issues, while slighting only a few areas.

Part 1 contains chapters on methodological issues and sociological theory, with special attention on social structure, sociological data, and research methodology. Part 2, "Bases of Inequality in Society," contains four essays on causes of social conflict: economic inequality, race and ethnic relations, age, and sex roles. Part 3 examines social institutions, such as education, religion, medicine, the mass media, politics, the family, science, and work. The four chapters in the final section focus on social change: deviance and control, spatial and environmental processes, social movements, and international development and the world economy. Each chapter is appended by an extensive reference list citing both classic and current works, some as recent as 1987. There are subject and name indexes.

75. Booth, Barbara, and Michael Blair. **Thesaurus of Sociological Index Terms**. 2d ed. La Jolla, Calif., Sociological Abstracts, 1989. 320p. $65.00. LC 89-60757. ISBN 0-930710-06-1.

Beginning with the first edition (1986), the *Thesaurus* represents the controlled vocabulary to the subject indexes in *Sociological Abstracts* (SA) (see entry 72). Similar to *Thesaurus of Psychological Index Terms* (see entry 163), it consists of a basic alphabetical list, including cross-references from unacceptable terms and suggested related terms, and a "rotated" list of terms, arranging each by significant words.

Between 1953 (when the abstracts were first published) and 1986, *SA* subject headings were composed of essentially standardized keywords or phrases, and much of the *Thesaurus* is based on those subject headings. This fact and the recent development of the *Thesaurus* mean that it does not function as a list of standard terminology to the discipline to the same extent as, for example, the ERIC and *Psychological Abstracts* thesauri. However, numerous historical notes attached to terms in the *Thesaurus* are helpful for using the relatively loose controlled vocabulary in older volumes as well as finding current subject headings.

Dictionaries and Encyclopedias

76. Borgatta, Edgar F., and Marie L. Borgatta, eds. **Encyclopedia of Sociology**. New York, Macmillan, 1992. 4v. index. $340.00/set. LC 91-37827. ISBN 0-02-897051-9.

In terms of scope and authority, this set is probably the next best thing to an updated edition of *International Encyclopedia of the Social Sciences* (see entry 30). Over 350 essays, each at least several pages in length, interpret the discipline broadly to include a wide variety of topics, such as violence in the family and society, social gerontology, health behavior, aggression and criminology, sex differences and gender roles, statistical and research methodologies, demographics, and interpersonal and intergroup behaviors. There are essays on history and theory of social science research as well as topics of current research interest (e.g., white-collar crime, sexually transmitted diseases, homelessness, comparable worth). Articles avoid highly technical jargon without sacrificing quality and comprehensiveness of coverage. They are appended by references cited and lists of suggested readings. An exhaustive index supplements many cross-references.

This is an important reference for those in social psychology. Coverage of topics in organizational behavior, environmental psychology, personality, deviant behavior and psychopathology, and cross-cultural psychology expands the importance of this tool in the discipline. Overall, this set is an excellent source for students of all levels and those seeking information outside their area of expertise.

77. Mann, Michael, ed. **International Encyclopedia of Sociology**. New York, Continuum, 1984. 434p. LC 83-15340. ISBN 0-8264-0238-0.

This one-volume work provides definitions of current terms such as white-collar crime, compensatory education, and welfare economics. Originally published in Great Britain, the book has a distinct (but not overwhelming) British flavor. There are about 700 entries, a significant number being biographical or eponymous. Mann admits inconsistencies in length, with some areas covered by numerous brief articles and others by fewer, lengthier contributions. Some articles contain references to other works or are appended by a few suggested books, and there are sufficient cross-references in lieu of a subject index.

SOCIAL WORK

Guides

78. Mendelsohn, Henry Neil. **A Guide to Information Sources for Social Work and the Human Services**. Phoenix, Ariz., Oryx Press, 1987. 136p. index. $28.50. LC 87-12253. ISBN 0-89774-338-5.

Mendelsohn provides an organized, systematic approach to the library research process and the breadth of social work literature. There is standard information on and citations to reference books, journal and newspaper indexes, journals, books, and documents. Most useful are the discipline-specific discussions of public documents and legal materials, statistics, historical materials, and current awareness sources and strategies. Coverage of social work journals, statistical sources, and federal government publications is particularly strong. The table of contents affords a detailed topic approach, although there is a combined author/title/subject index.

The strength of this volume lies in its description of the literature search process, although it does list resource materials. As such, beginning clinical students and clinicians will find it useful for an introduction to the literature.

Bibliographies

79. Conrad, James H. **Reference Sources in Social Work: An Annotated Bibliography**. Metuchen, N.J., Scarecrow, 1982. 201p. index. o.p. LC 81-21219. ISBN 0-8108-1503-6.

Conrad limits his sources to those published from 1970 to early 1981, although the section on the history of social work contains earlier citations. In addition to general and historical works, chapters focus on allied disciplines such as urban affairs, sociology, political science, and psychology. Others deal with specific aspects of social work practice: work with the handicapped, family groups, substance abuse, social work as a profession, and legal and administrative topics in social service delivery. Within each category, descriptive and comparative annotated entries are listed by reference publication type (e.g., directories, indexes and abstracts, statistical sources).

Author, title, and subject indexes are provided. An appendix lists social work journals, significant social work library collections, professional and advocacy organizations, and clearinghouses.

80. Fritz, Jan M. **The Clinical Sociology Handbook**. New York, Garland, 1985. 292p. index. (Garland Bibliographies in Sociology, v.7; Garland Reference Library of Social Science, v.134). $47.00. LC 82-49133. ISBN 0-8240-9203-1.

In the introduction, Fritz defines clinical sociology as using "sociological perspectives to analyze and design intervention for change at any level of social organization," whether it be an entire social system or a small group. Therefore, there are correlates between social work and the scope of this publication, although not on the therapeutic/advisory level of intervention. After a review essay on the history of the field, over 800 annotated citations to journal literature, books, doctoral dissertations, research reports, conference papers, and other unpublished sources are listed under 13 subject categories. These include a general overview, aging, the community, counseling, criminology, education and training, sexuality and the family, health, inequality, the workplace, policy issues, group dynamics, and material that does not fall into the above categories. Some foreign materials are cited, although most are English-language references published between 1931 and 1981. Following the bibliography is a description of the Clinical Sociology Association and the interorganizational interests of its members, a section on education and training of clinical sociologists, and an author index.

81. Mendelsohn, Henry N. **An Author's Guide to Social Work Journals.** 2d ed. Silver Spring, Md., National Association of Social Workers, 1987. 153p. $10.95. LC 87-1707. ISBN 0-87101-144-1.

This is a basic reference for prospective authors in social work research. Mendelsohn provides information for 100 titles of interest to researchers and practitioners in human services: social work, social policy, clinical psychology and sociology, child and family studies, psychotherapeutics, gerontology, and interdisciplinary areas.

The information for each entry includes subject or content focus, specific manuscript format and preparation requirements, submission and review procedures, circulation data, subscription information and cost, indexing and abstracting tools in which a title is included, reprint policy, publication lag time, and manuscript acceptance rate. An appendix lists writing guides and style manuals.

Indexes and Abstracts

82. **Social Work Research and Abstracts.** Vol. 13- , No. 2- . Silver Spring, Md., National Association of Social Workers, 1977- . quarterly. $82.00/yr.(institutions). ISSN 0148-0847.

This publication serves two functions: research journal and abstracting tool. As a research journal, it contains two to four articles in each issue, with its primary focus on research strategies and methods, review articles, and theoretical issues. As an abstracting tool, it continues the publication *Abstracts for Social Workers* (1965-1977) by selectively indexing almost 200 source journals of interest to social workers, emphasizing U.S. publications. Abstracts are descriptive and usually range in length from 60 to 300 words; some are cited but not abstracted. Government reports, publications from professional or service organizations, and dissertations are also included and often annotated. The quarterly author and subject indexes cumulate annually. Citations are organized under almost 30 subject categories, including separate sections for psychiatry/medicine and psychology/social psychology.

Dictionaries and Encyclopedias

83. Barker, Robert L. **Social Work Dictionary.** Silver Spring, Md., National Association of Social Workers, 1987. 207p. $18.95. LC 87-5501. ISBN 0-87101-145-X.

In this work brief definitions are provided for over 3,000 terms associated with social work administration and practice, clinical diagnosis and treatment, human development and social organization, and public policy and legislative issues. Although definitions are as short as 5 words, the average is 50 words. Entries include not only concepts but also descriptions of organizations, governmental agencies, landmark legislation proposed or enacted, and philanthropic organizations. There are no biographical entries, and there are few citations to items for further reading. A chronology details landmark events in social work from 1750 B.C. to A.D. 1987, and the NASW Code of Ethics is reproduced.

84. **Encyclopedia of Social Work.** 18th ed. Anne Minahan, ed.-in-chief. Silver Spring, Md., National Association of Social Workers, 1987. 2v. index. $75.00/set. LC 30-30948. ISBN 0-87101-141-7.

85. **1990 Supplement.** Silver Spring, Md., National Association of Social Workers, 1990. 348p. index. $20.95. LC 30-30948. ISBN 0-87101-178-6.

86. **Face of the Nation, 1987**. Sumner M. Rosen, David Fanshel, and Mary E. Lutz, eds. Silver Spring, Md., National Association of Social Workers, 1987. 124p. price not reported. LC 86-18219. ISBN 0-87101-142-5.

Since 1960, editions of the encyclopedia have appeared every six years or so to keep its content and emphasis current in the changing field of social work. The 225 articles in the basic set of two volumes reflect increasing interest in American social work problems in the 1980s (e.g., abortion, services to the elderly, family violence, unemployment) and update coverage of clinical practice and theory. Articles average about 6 to 10 pages, are well written and clearly organized, and rely on recently published literature. Reference lists are supplemented by lists of suggested readings. The subject index to both volumes is included in each for ease of use, and there are abundant cross-references. Charts and tables are provided throughout.

A separate biographical section in volume 2 profiles 100 individuals important to the development of social work theory and practice. Although about half a page each in length, they focus on the nature of the contribution, biographical data, selected publications, and citations to other biographies. Appendixes include various NASW documents, such as the Code of Ethics, curriculum policy for degree programs, standards for clinical practice, and a guide to welfare agency information. The *Supplement* contains 20 articles and follows the format of the original set, covering such issues of recent interest as AIDS, homelessness, youth gangs, and ethnoviolence. *Face of the Nation* acts as a statistical supplement to the *Encyclopedia*; it contains over 100 tables and charts of demographic, economic, and health-related data.

ANTHROPOLOGY

Guides

87. Kibbee, Josephine Z. **Cultural Anthropology: A Guide to Reference and Information Sources**. Englewood, Colo., Libraries Unlimited, 1991. 205p. index. (Reference Sources in the Social Sciences Series, no.5). $47.50. LC 91-14042. ISBN 0-87287-739-6.

Kibbee lists and annotates 668 selected sources. Most represent printed reference works, and coverage is retrospective through 1990; a few citations refer to relevant articles within reference works, such as literature reviews appearing in annual review volumes. Works of a general nature are arranged under broad sections such as social science sources and bibliographic works (including library book catalogs and databases), and thereunder by publication format. There are separate sections for core journal titles in the field, publishers, important organizations, and libraries and archives with noteworthy holdings in anthropology.

The organization of much of the book mirrors that of the discipline. A large section on area studies organizes published material by geographic area, whereas another section includes special topics or materials, such as visual materials in anthropological research, the history of the discipline, and research methods. By far the largest section categorizes materials by anthropology's subfields: archaeology, urban anthropology, psychological anthropology, physical and medical anthropology, and the like. There are author/title and subject indexes.

88. Weeks, John M. **Introduction to Library Research in Anthropology**. Boulder, Colo., Westview Press, 1991. 281p. index. $22.95pa. LC 90-24177. ISBN 0-8133-7454-5.

Weeks states in his preface that this is not intended as an exhaustive guide but is meant for the undergraduate student preparing for a research project. The brief introductory chapters discuss the subdivisions of anthropology and its relation to other social sciences; the structure of research literature, constructing a search strategy, and formats of research materials; and library catalogs (card and online).

The remaining 18 chapters will also be of interest to advanced students and faculty seeking basic reference tools outside their areas of expertise. Each is preceded by a brief essay on the importance of a particular information format. Chapters cite and annotate published catalogs and subject and regional bibliographies; tools for locating dissertations, manuscript collections, audiovisual material, government publication, and biographical information; selected journals and online databases; reference materials, such as atlases, handbooks, encyclopedias, and indexes and abstracts; and the Human Relations Area File (HRAF). Appendixes detail sections of the Library of Congress classification scheme relevant to anthropology, important anthropology collections in the United States and Canada, and the classification schemes used to organize information in the HRAF collection. Indexes to authors, ethnic groups, and geographic area are provided.

Bibliographies

89. Driver, Edwin D., ed. **The Sociology and Anthropology of Mental Illness: A Reference Guide**. rev. ed. Amherst, Mass., University of Massachusetts Press, 1972. 487p. index. $35.00pa. LC 71-103476. ISBN 0-87023-062-X.

Because it only contains items produced between 1956 and 1968, this bibliography is suitable largely for retrospective searching. Still, the 5,910 unannotated citations represent an excellent source of research on social psychiatry, or the effect of social relationships on the formation, manifestation, and treatment of dysfunctional behavior. This entails considerable cross-cultural examination, also represented among the works cited. As might be expected, a large number of non-English (and non-Western) citations are included. Formats include journal articles, books, dissertations, and technical reports.

References are listed under nine broad categories, such as general studies, attitudes, the prevalence and demographics of mental illness, mental health care delivery, and crime and suicide. Most provide subheadings for access under more than 40 categories. There is a combined author and subject index.

90. Farazza, Armando R., and Mary Oman. **Anthropological and Cross-Cultural Themes in Mental Health: An Annotated Bibliography, 1925-1974**. Columbia, Mo., University of Missouri Press, 1977. 386p. index. (University of Missouri Studies, v.65). $30.00. LC 76-48620. ISBN 0-8262-0215-2.

Anthropological psychiatry is a broad area covering the definition, etiology, and manifestation of deviant and aberrant behavior across social and cultural organizations. The historical evolution of this interdisciplinary area is expertly explored in this work's two forewords and introduction.

The bibliography is composed of English-language journals in psychiatry, psychology, and mental health. Titles from some areas of psychology are covered more fully than others: Psychoanalysis, social psychology, and medical psychology are afforded excellent coverage, in part because of the longevity of primary journals in these areas. Anthropological journals per se are not covered. Therefore, the 3,634 items cited reflect the influence of social and cultural anthropology research on mental health research and practice.

References are listed chronologically, with brief and descriptive annotations. There is an author index, and the detailed subject index is particularly helpful for finding studies on particular cultural or ethnic groups or those located in specific geographic areas.

91. **Catalogue of the Library of the Peabody Museum of Archaeology and Ethnology. Authors (Vols. 1-26). Subjects (Vols. 1-27)**. Harvard University. Peabody Museum. New York, G. K. Hall/Macmillan, 1963. 53v. $6410.00/set. ISBN 0-8161-0647-9.

92. **First Supplement** (1970). **Authors** (6v.) **Subjects** (6v). $1775.00/set. ISBN 0-8161-0861-7.

93. **Second Supplement** (1971). **Authors** (2v.) **Subjects** (3v). $920.00/set. ISBN 0-8161-0960-5.

94. **Third Supplement** (1975). **Authors** (3v.) **Subjects** (4v.) $1060.00/set. ISBN 0-8161-1168-5.

95. **Fourth Supplement** (1979). **Authors** (3v.) **Subjects** (4v.) $1080.00/set. ISBN 0-8161-1400-5.

This is a unique source to an unusual and important collection in archaeology, ethnology, and physical anthropology. It reproduces the card catalog of the Tozzer Library's collection, beginning with the basic retrospective set and extending through 1977 (the cutoff date for the fourth supplement). Along with the collection's depth and chronological span of coverage is the variety of material represented in the catalog: maps, books and analytics for book chapters, journal articles, pamphlets, and dissertations.

The subject volumes use the library's *Index to Subject Headings*, revised edition (Boston, G. K. Hall, 1971), as its controlled vocabulary. This set is especially noteworthy for worldwide coverage of research materials and will be of particular interest to those in the areas of cross-cultural psychology and psycholinguistics. It is, for the most part, updated by the indexing source *Anthropological Literature* (see entry 98).

96. Smith, Margo L., and Yvonne M. Damien, eds. **Anthropological Bibliographies: A Selected Guide**. South Salem, N.Y., Redgrave Publishing, 1981. 307p. index. $22.50. ISBN 0-913178-63-2.

Compiled under the auspices of the Chicago-area Library-Anthropology Resource Group, this is a list of over 3,200 bibliographies and mediagraphies as published in serials, books, and research reports. Most bibliographies are listed under six geographic regions (e.g.. Africa, Asia, Oceania); each section is further subdivided by region or countries. There is a separate section for bibliographies that cover more than one region or that have no specific geographic focus.

Included are bibliographies published in anthropology journals, academic pamphlets with limited circulations, and exhaustive bibliographies produced by international organizations. Some citations are annotated, usually with just a few sentences on the scope of publications included or a physical description. There is no restriction on language of publication or geographic origin. A combined subject and author index is supplied.

Indexes and Abstracts

97. **Abstracts in Anthropology**. Vol. 1- , No. 1- . Amityville, N.Y., Baywood Publishing, 1970- . 8 issues/yr. in 2 volumes. $219.00/yr. ISSN 0001-3455.

Although its emphasis is on cultural and physical anthropology, anthropological aspects of linguistics, and archaeology, this index derives its source journal list from a broad spectrum of disciplines outside the core anthropology literature: psychology, sociology, medicine, and related health sciences areas. Until 1987, each quarterly issue covered all topic areas, with citations organized under narrower areas, such as psychological anthropology, psycholinguistics, minority studies, and social organization. The author and subject indexes did not cumulate from issue to issue. At present, two quarterly issues are published concurrently: One covers linguistics and cultural anthropology, and the other covers archaeology and physical anthropology. Each has an annual cumulated index by author and subject.

98. **Anthropological Literature: An Index to Periodical Articles and Essays.** Vol. 1- , No. 1- . Cambridge, Mass., Tozzer Library, Harvard University, 1979- . quarterly. $125.00/yr.(institutions). ISSN 0190-3373.

This index serves as a continuation of the Peabody Museum library catalog volumes. In a given year, articles are selected from approximately 1,000 journals and collections of essays owned by the Tozzer Library, Harvard's library of anthropology. Each quarterly issue includes over 2,000 items. Coverage is international, with an emphasis on English and European languages.

Full bibliographic entries are listed by author in the classified section within five subareas of anthropology: archaeology; biological/physical anthropology; cultural/social anthropology; linguistics; and methodology, theory, and general materials. Entries are also listed in a subject section according to Library of Congress subject headings to allow access by ethnic group, geographic location, site, and archaeological topics. The author index lists all authors and the location of the complete bibliographic entry as cited in the classified section.

As a research tool, this should be considered a supplement to *Abstracts in Anthropology* (see entry 97). It provides better coverage of foreign-language material and unique access to collections of essays.

Handbooks

99. Williams, John T., comp. **Anthropology Journals and Serials: An Analytical Guide.** Westport, Conn., Greenwood Press, 1986. 182p. index. (Annotated Bibliographies of Serials: A Subject Approach, no.10). $36.95. LC 86-19574. ISBN 0-313-23834-0.

In this work, 404 serial titles are organized under the broad areas of archaeology, cultural anthropology, linguistics, and physical anthropology, with a separate section for indexing and abstracting tools. The volume is similar in format and organization to other titles in the series. Bibliographic information for each publication indicates title changes, price, publisher, manuscript selection procedures, where title is indexed, circulation, and intended audience. Annotations average about 100 words and discuss focus, content, and physical description. There are geographic and subject indexes and an index by current and variant titles.

Dictionaries and Encyclopedias

100. Hunter, David E., and Phillip Whitten, eds. **Encyclopedia of Anthropology.** New York, Harper & Row, 1976. 411p. o.p. LC 75-41386. ISBN 0-06-047094-1.

This title provides brief definitions for the beginning anthropology student. Coverage is fairly evenly distributed among cultural and physical anthropology and linguistics, area studies and Western cultures, the discipline's historical development and its founders, and current research and researchers. Article length varies from as few as 25 words to about 3,000 words. Many of the 1,400 articles are accompanied by maps, charts, and photographs. There are lists of suggested readings for all but the briefest entries. The abundant cross-references compensate for the lack of a subject index.

HISTORY

Guides

101. Frick, Elizabeth. **Library Research Guide to History: Illustrated Search Strategy and Sources.** Ann Arbor, Mich., Pierian Press, 1980. 86p. index. (Library Research Guides Series, no.4). o.p. (hc.); $15.00pa. LC 80-83514. ISBN 0-87650-119-6; 0-87650-123-4pa.

Research guides in the discipline of history most often focus on specific areas or time periods. This is one of the few general guides to the discipline, and it is intended for undergraduate students new to the area. Introductory chapters discuss selecting and narrowing the research topic, finding and evaluating books, using major periodical indexes in the humanities and social sciences, and the role of government documents and guides to the literature. There is also a chapter on locating biographical information on historical figures and finding materials not available in the local library. Unfortunately, some chapters discuss sources in more depth than do others. However, similar to others in the series, this volume provides a good, basic introduction to specialized bibliographies, guides, indexes, and other reference tools of interest to the undergraduate and beginning graduate student. Most of these tools are grouped by geographical area or historical time period, with a section for general materials by format, such as book review sources, chronologies, newspaper indexes, and atlases.

102. Fritze, Ronald H., Brian E. Coutts, and Louis A. Vyhnanek. **Reference Sources in History: An Introductory Guide.** Santa Barbara, Calif., ABC-Clio, 1990. 319p. index. $49.50. LC 90-45169. ISBN 0-87436-164-8.

As noted in the preface, a guide that updated the well-regarded *Historian's Handbook* by Helen J. Poulton and Marguerite S. Howland (University of Oklahoma Press, 1972) was long overdue. Although most of the 685 citations to reference tools fall into traditional monograph formats, the authors accommodate alternate research sources, such as microformat collections of primary source material and fulltext newspapers online. There are also chapters listing publisher and trade associations, journal titles, and computerized bibliographic files.

Entries are hierarchically arranged according to 14 broad sections by reference format (e.g., guides and handbooks, statistics sources), subject matter (e.g., guides to special collections and archives), and source of publication (e.g., government documents). Most are further subdivided by geographic area. There is an author/title/subject index. The emphasis is on recent reference sources (up to the late 1980s), although unique and important retrospective publications are included.

Bibliographies

103. deMause, Lloyd, ed. **A Bibliography of Psychohistory.** New York, Garland, 1975. 81p. index. LC 75-5140. ISBN 0-8240-9999-0.

Psychohistory is defined by the editor as "the use of modern psychology in interpreting history" (p. 1), including studies on mass behavior and leadership qualities, childhood development and its impact on societies and individuals, and what has been referred to as "applied psychoanalysis" to explain the actions of individuals or nations. To this end, approximately 1,200 references to journal articles, books, book chapters, and conferences papers are listed under 6 categories: general works and methodology, the history of childhood, works on ancient history, medieval and Renaissance works, material from modern history, and Asian items. The unannotated citations represent literature through 1974 published in English and a variety of European languages. Primary works by Freud, Fromm, Erikson, and Bonaparte are included along with secondary works. The index is scant but might be helpful for locating works on specific individuals or geographic areas. An appendix annotates standard reference indexes, directories, handbooks, and other reference works in the social sciences, with emphasis on the history of childhood and the role of motivation patterns in the course of human history.

104. Gilmore, William J. **Psychohistorical Inquiry: A Comprehensive Research Bibliography**. New York, Garland, 1984. 317p. index. (Garland Reference Library of Social Science, v.156). price not reported. LC 82-49165. ISBN 0-8240-9167-1.

Gilmore provides a fine introduction to the history, development, methodology, and current issues in psychohistory. Over 4,000 citations to material produced through 1981 represent a comprehensive list of publications in English, with selective coverage of other languages and a focus on United States and European studies and psychohistory methodology. Sections 1 and 2 include general works, models, and methodology. The remaining eight sections encompass specific geographic locations. Although the literature on non-Western history affords some good cross-cultural coverage, the best coverage is of Europe and the United States. Subcategories divide the citations by chronological period, periods in the life span from infancy to old age and death, and psychobiography.

Most citations to English-language items are annotated, although the length of the annotations varies widely. Foreign-language items are not annotated. A variety of formats are covered: books and journal articles, a smattering of popular material, dissertations, conference papers, and unpublished research reports. The disciplines of history, psychology, sociology, and medicine are the most heavily represented. There are numerous cross-references among sections, and there is an author index.

Indexes and Abstracts

105. **America: History and Life**. Vol. 1- , No. 1- . Santa Barbara, Calif., ABC-Clio, 1964- . quarterly with cumulated index issue. price varies. ISSN 0002-7065.

106. **Historical Abstracts**. Vol. 1- , No. 1- . Santa Barbara, Calif., ABC-Clio, 1955- . quarterly with cumulated index issue. price varies. ISSN 0364-2717.

Produced by a major publisher of history reference sources, these indexes share a journal source list of over 1,600 journal titles that represent worldwide coverage of the literature in history, the humanities, and the social sciences. *America: History and Life* focuses on the United States and Canada, with citations to journal articles, book reviews, and dissertations organized under time period and geographic area. (Until volume 26, an annual set consisted of a bewildering array of issues, four dedicated to journal citations and the remainder to book reviews and dissertations.) *Historical Abstracts* cites the same publication formats and covers the remainder of the world from 1450 to the present, organizing material by geographical area, country, and time period. Both titles provide indexes by author, subject, book and audiovisual titles, and review authors. Each work contains citations to research in historical methodology and the interrelationship of history and other disciplines.

Obviously, this is a source for those conducting psychohistorical research. It should also be of interest to those taking a historical perspective to the study of the evolution and development of psychology as a discipline and such topics in social psychology as political behavior and social attitudes.

Handbooks

107. Lawton, Henry. **The Psychohistorian's Handbook.** New York, Psychohistory Press, 1988. 241p. $25.95. LC 88-20943. ISBN 0-914434-27-6.

Psychohistory, defined here as the application of psychoanalytic theory to the understanding of historical events, is well served by this handbook to theory, research, and teaching. Eight chapters discuss issues in methodology and interdisciplinary research, training and orientation of the psychohistorian, requisite psychoanalytic theory, and the publishing in and teaching of psychohistory. Three additional chapters cover childhood, psychobiography, and group psychohistory.

As appropriate to each chapter, Lawton combines an overview essay with a discussion of the area's literature, reference materials and primary sources, selected references to journal articles and books, and important journal titles and organizations. Most citations are accompanied by evaluative annotations. Lawton is cognizant of some controversy in both history and psychology; literature both supportive and critical of psychohistorical study is included. An appendix contains a bibliography of notable publications in the field.

108. Steiner, Dale R. **Historical Journals: A Handbook for Writers and Reviewers.** Santa Barbara, Calif., ABC-Clio, 1981. 213p. index. LC 80-26215. ISBN 0-87436-312-8.

Historical Journals is designed to assist prospective authors, whether amateur or professional, in selecting an appropriate publication for manuscript submission. Over 350 publications are represented, from those of American regional, state, or local interest to scholarly international journals, journals on regional studies, and journals dealing with the history of other disciplines.

Data were obtained from questionnaires and include general information (address, editor, frequency and circulation, intended audience, and pages per issue), manuscript submission requirements and the review process, and procedures for submitting book reviews and other materials. There is a subject index to the journals.

An introductory essay gives advice on writing an article, selecting a journal, and submitting a manuscript for publication. A second chapter talks about book reviewing. Each chapter is appended by a list of additional sources on preparing manuscripts and reviews, which is very informative for the nonhistorian hoping to break into print.

Dictionaries and Encyclopedias

109. **Dictionary of the History of Ideas: Studies of Selected Pivotal Ideas.** Philip P. Wiener, ed.-in-chief. New York, Scribner's, 1980. 5v. index. $67.50pa./set. LC 72-7943. ISBN 0-684-16418-3.

This set was originally published in 1973-1974. In it, essays by noted scholars investigate the historical and cultural contributions of selected theoretical concepts and movements in Western thought. Implications of scientific, economic, and legal institutions and social force ideologies are discussed along with philosophical, literary, and aesthetic movements. Approximately 300 lengthy, well-written articles are enhanced by bibliographies and cross-references, and a detailed subject index comprises the entire fifth volume.

An analytical table of contents divides articles under seven broad categories reflecting influences on the human endeavor (e.g., human nature, aesthetic theory, historical development of social and legal institutions). Of course, the Freudian, Jungian, and Adlerian schools of thought and their antecedents and influences are discussed, as are learning, the origins and impact of behaviorism and its adherents, influences of biology and environment on the individual, and the man-machine interface. Often, concepts are not only placed in a contemporary context but also are discussed as they were manifested from antiquity.

POLITICAL SCIENCE AND CRIMINAL JUSTICE

Guides

110. Holler, Frederick L. **Information Sources of Political Science**. 4th ed. Santa Barbara, Calif., ABC-Clio, 1986. 417p. index. $89.50. LC 85-11279. ISBN 0-87436-375-6.

This is more than a guide to research tools in political science and related social sciences. It also provides structure to a very disparate literature commensurate with the diverse needs of students and researchers in the discipline. Part 1, "Political Reference Theory," defines these needs, the literature search strategy, and resources. Part 2 lists 2,423 sources cited within chapters on general reference tools, works from other social science disciplines, U.S. government materials, international relations and organizations, comparative and area studies, political theory, and public administration. Individual chapters further define sources by format, intended use, or theoretical orientation. Abstracts are lengthy, descriptive, and evaluative. Publication formats include books and serials, microprint, and online sources in a variety of languages. There are author, title, subject, and format indexes. Of interest to researchers and students in psychology is the work's coverage of social control, social group behavior, social attitudes, and political behavior.

111. O'Block, Robert L. **Criminal Justice Research Sources**. Cincinnati, Ohio, Anderson Publishing, 1986. 183p. $17.95. LC 85-18629. ISBN 0-87084-664-7.

This title is designed to guide the undergraduate student in the use of basic tools in criminology and related areas, although some chapters are sufficiently focused to be of value to graduate students as well. Introductory chapters discuss basic book catalog use and provide lists of indexing and abstracting journals, scholarly research journals, and bibliographies. Later chapters introduce such sources as databases, directories, government documents, federal agencies, legal research tools, statistical data, and historical and nonprint material.

Almost all sources are discussed in an essay format or are annotated at length. Some assistance with research paper composition and the research process is provided, but the emphasis throughout is on literature sources. There is a separate chapter of selected tools from other social sciences and general reference sources, such as newspaper indexes, yearbooks, and encyclopedias.

Bibliographies

112. Denno, Deborah W., and Ruth M. Schwartz, comps. **Biological, Psychological, and Environmental Factors in Delinquency and Mental Disorder: An Interdisciplinary Bibliography**. Westport, Conn., Greenwood Press, 1985. 222p. index. (Bibliographies and Indexes in Sociology, no.4). $45.00. LC 85-5620. ISBN 0-313-24939-3.

This bibliography draws its strength from the broad range of disciplines from which the citations are drawn (e.g., medicine, sociology, criminal justice, psychiatry). It takes an interdisciplinary approach to the factors influencing the development of mental disorder and its manifestation as antisocial behavior, aggression, deviance, and criminal behavior. It also covers efforts to treat and rehabilitate offenders. Over 2,000 references are topically arranged according to subject headings provided in the appendix.

Indexes and Abstracts

113. **Criminal Justice Abstracts.** Vol. 1- , No. 1- . Monsey, N.Y., Willow Tree Press, 1968- . quarterly. $125.00/yr. ISSN 0146-9177.

Although it contains fewer items per year, *Criminal Justice Abstracts* is similar to *Criminology and Penology Abstracts* (see entry 114): It cites and abstracts public documents from a variety of sources, books, and journal articles, emphasizing English-language research material. One distinguishing feature is that each quarterly issue contains a review article on a topic of current interest in the field, such as children as homicide victims, youth gangs, and racial discrimination in sentencing.

Citations and abstracts are listed under six broad categories: "Crime, the Offender, and the Victim"; "Juvenile Justice and Delinquency"; "Police"; "Court and the Legal Process"; "Adult Corrections"; and "Crime Prevention and Control Strategies." The detailed subject/geographic area and author indexes cumulate annually.

114. **Criminology and Penology Abstracts.** Vol. 1- , No. 1- . Amsterdam, Netherlands, Kugler Publications, 1961- . bimonthly. $335.00/yr. ISSN 0166-6231.

Each issue cites and summarizes approximately 400 journal articles; publications of federal, state, and municipal governments; and books. Although there is some coverage of foreign-language material, including works from foreign governments and law enforcement agencies, the focus is on English-language research.

The 13 broad subject areas and 50-plus subtopics provide scanning access to the literature. For example, the broad heading that covers psychopathology and psychiatry contains subheadings for general literature, mental disorders and psychopathology, and specific approaches to treatment (e.g., psychoanalysis, psychotherapy, group psychotherapy). Of particular interest to psychologists is the coverage of psychopathology and deviance in antisocial and criminal behavior, prediction of criminal behavior, victimology, social problems (e.g., suicide, drug abuse), and the role of psychotherapists and social workers in dealing with criminal behavior and its effects. In addition to the detailed table of contents, each issue contains an extensive subject index and an author index, both of which cumulate annually.

Handbooks

115. **Sourcebook of Criminal Justice Statistics.** Vol. 1- .Washington, D.C., U.S. Department of Justice, Bureau of Justice Statistics, 1973- . annual. $32.00. ISSN 0360-3431. (SuDoc J 1.42/3:SD-SB-3)

This is a massive cumulation of statistical data from a wide variety of sources on the American criminal justice system, criminal activity, and the judicial process. Many of the statistical tables and brief explanatory abstracts are derived from federal, state, and local government documents and reporting sources. Others have been obtained from population polls and surveys, commercial publications, and documents from research centers and universities.

Statistical charts and tables are arranged within six chapters: "Characteristics of the Criminal Justice System," "Public Attitudes Toward Crime and Criminal Justice-related Topics," "Nature and Distribution of Known Offenses," "Characteristics and Distribution of Persons Arrested," "Judicial Processing of Defendants," and "Persons Under Correctional Supervision." Each section is preceded by a brief explanation of the coverage, and the table of contents lists the figures under each section. The 21 appendixes discuss methodology and definitional aspects of significant ongoing studies on crime and delinquency. There are a subject index to the data, a publisher directory, and an annotated list of federal published sources from which much of the data were derived.

Encyclopedias

116. **Encyclopedia of Crime and Justice**. Sanford H. Kadish, ed.-in-chief. New York, Free Press/Macmillan, 1983. 4v. index. $375.00/set. LC 83-7156. ISBN 0-02-918110-0.

Essays in this set address broad topics and issues, with an emphasis on legal aspects of criminal behavior and the judicial process. Each of the approximately 200 articles is about 10 pages long and addresses a conceptually broad topic, such as deterrence, dispute resolution programs, and women and crime. Some topics that defy a single approach are divided among several articles with different emphases. For example, the topics of eyewitness identification and rape are each covered by two essays, one concentrating on psychological aspects and the other on constitutional aspects. Each article is appended by a bibliography and cross-references to related articles.

The broad nature of the articles makes it necessary to consult the subject index in volume 4. This volume also contains a lengthy glossary of terms and a legal index that consists of a table of cases and an index by statute or document. Although behavioral aspects are discussed, legal and judicial approaches to criminal justice are the work's primary focus.

Part III

GENERAL PSYCHOLOGY REFERENCE SOURCES

GUIDES

117. Borchardt, D. H., and R. D. Francis. **How to Find Out in Psychology: A Guide to the Literature and Methods of Research.** Elmsford, N.Y., Pergamon Press, 1984. 189p. index. (How to Find Out Series). $23.00pa. LC 84-2827. ISBN 0-08-031280-2.

Intended for the advanced student, this book defines the discipline, introduces the varieties of reference sources, and discusses the basic steps in organizing information and using types of research methodology. Information is organized under 11 chapters: overviews of the field, historical and theoretical works, reference sources, indexes and union lists, bibliographic databases, a survey of subareas in the discipline, preparing for the literature search, maintaining a citation file, quantitative methods, presentation of research results, and the profession of psychology. Throughout the book there is a British bias, but it is not overwhelming.

"A Guide to Library Searches," appendix A, lists the types of common information needs and suggested sources. Appendix B presents the components of a sample empirical paper, and appendixes C and D give guidelines for evaluating published research. A final appendix is a directory of major national psychological societies. There is a complete bibliography of works cited and a subject index.

118. Douglas, Nancy E., and Nathan Baum. **Library Research Guide to Psychology: Illustrated Search Strategy and Sources.** Ann Arbor, Mich., Pierian Press, 1984. 65p. index. (Library Research Guides Series, no.7). $15.00pa. LC 84-60640. ISBN 0-87650-175-7.

Assuming that students know only of the card catalog and the *Readers' Guide to Periodical Literature*, this work introduces them to basic reference tools in psychology. Following information on how to choose a research topic, the authors discuss the *Library of Congress Subject Headings*, book catalog organization, *Annual Review of Psychology* (see entry 159), three indexing tools most relevant to psychology, *Current Contents* (see entry 18), using guides to the literature, and tapping the resources of other libraries.

Illustrations and sample search topics throughout make the text easy to use. Although a limited number of sources are covered in depth, more specialized sources and their use are discussed in the appendixes. Taking the "Library Knowledge Test" tells students if they have mastered the basics of the card catalog and the *Readers' Guide*, and a final appendix provides an outline for students to measure their literature search progress. There is an index to titles described in the text.

119. Klein, Barry T., ed. **Reference Encyclopedia of American Psychology and Psychiatry.** Rye, N.Y., Todd Publications, 1975. 459p. index. $30.00. LC 74-14938.

Klein presents a tremendous number of information sources across a very broad spectrum of formats. Entries are listed under type of source: professional associations and societies, research centers, journals and other serials, grant-giving foundations, special library collections, audiovisual material, psychiatric and mental health centers, and psychiatric training programs. Most entries are annotated and briefly describe the organization, publication, or audiovisual material. For publications (print and nonprint), purchase information is provided. In the case of organizations, addresses and contact information are supplied.

There is an index of sorts, called the "Subject/Category Index." Under each of 25 broad subject areas (e.g., psycholinguistics, industrial psychology, aging, abnormal psychology), names or titles listed in the main section are given.

120. McInnis, Raymond G. **Research Guide for Psychology**. Westport, Conn., Greenwood Press, 1982. 604p. index. (Reference Sources for the Social Sciences and Humanities, no. 1). $55.00. LC 81-1377. ISBN 0-313-21399-2.

Despite the publication of more current guides to the literature, this source remains the major bibliographic guide to psychology and related disciplines. Over 1,200 sources are discussed, evaluated, and compared in lengthy bibliographic essays. The 16 topical chapters and a general psychology chapter are based on the subject arrangement of *Psychological Abstracts* (see entry 129), with most chapters further subdivided under several narrower topics. Within each chapter and subchapter McInnis provides an overview of reference works, then discusses works by format, including research guides, handbooks, encyclopedic works, and retrospective and recurrent bibliographies and literature reviews. The section of general psychology sources is arranged primarily by format of publication or intended reference use.

McInnis does not limit sources to books. Serials, government publications, extensive review articles published in journals, ERIC and NTIS documents, and other research reports of limited circulation are described. Each source discussed is assigned an alphanumeric code that corresponds to the cumulated reference list in the back. There is a cumulated index by author, title, and subject. There is especially good coverage of topics in human and animal experimental psychology (e.g., perception, learning, memory, cognition) and in social psychology, although no area of the discipline is slighted.

This book is not intended as a guide for beginning students, as the few figures are intended to be illustrative, not instructive. Rather, it is a major retrospective and reference title to the discipline for advanced students, researchers, and librarians.

121. Reed, Jeffrey G., and Pam M. Baxter. **Library Use: A Handbook for Psychology**. 2d ed. Washington, D.C., American Psychological Association, 1992. 179p. index. $19.95pa. LC 91-31704. ISBN 1-55798-144-2.

Library Use introduces the literature search process for psychology undergraduate and beginning graduate students: where to begin; topic selection and definition; and refining a research topic by using handbooks, encyclopedias, and other reference tools. Most of the text is devoted to using a variety of sources to meet a particular information need, such as using a card catalog effectively to find books; searching *Psychological Abstracts* (see entry 129) and related periodical indexes in education, business, sociology, and medicine; citation searching and the *Social Sciences Citation Index* (see entry 25); and using bibliographic sources to find psychological tests. Additional chapters outline the purpose of interlibrary loan, initiating a computer search, and related reference tools for book reviews and biographical information. Chapters focus on a sample topic appropriate to the sources discussed.

Although a small number of sources are presented compared to other bibliographic guides, there is an abundance of illustrations and textual explanation for each tool. More specialized sources are listed in an appendix. A second appendix presents the basics of the search process, including what questions to consider. A third appendix contains brief descriptions of 14 sample topics, accompanied by a few important references, to illustrate well-defined topic definitions. A combined author, title, and subject index finishes the book.

122. Sternberg, Robert J. **The Psychologist's Companion: A Guide to Scientific Writing for Students and Researchers**. 2d ed. New York, Cambridge University Press, 1988. 208p. index. $32.50; $13.95pa. LC 87-22406. ISBN 0-521-34121-3; 0-521-34921-4pa.

Appropriate for undergraduate psychology students, this guide takes a step-by-step approach to constructing the research paper. It is composed of 10 chapters that cover the following categories: defining topics, researching, and writing library and experimental research papers; style conventions, such as APA guidelines; appropriate vocabulary; guides for references and data presentation;

how to evaluate published research papers; and submitting work to a journal. An appendix gives an example of a typical psychology paper, and there is a subject index.

The section on critical evaluation of published work is especially helpful for the beginning student, as is the discussion on the manner in which data are logically presented in a paper. For library research, "References for the Paper" lists and annotates major reference works and journals in psychology.

BIBLIOGRAPHIES

123. **Bibliographic Guide to Psychology**. Boston, G. K. Hall, 1975- . annual. $170.00. LC 76-642687. ISSN 0360-277X.

This is one of a series of subject-oriented guides to the collections of the New York Public Library (NYPL) Research Libraries. The core of material represented in this series has been gleaned from the Library of Congress MARC tapes, with selective NYPL acquisitions included. A severe limitation is that items cited are only from the Library of Congress BF classification section, the section generally representing psychology. This excludes most areas in applied psychology and clinical psychology, which are usually classed elsewhere in the LC system.

Nonetheless, there is substantial international, multilingual, and multiformat coverage of most experimental areas: personality and emotion, cognition and perception, sensation, volition, developmental psychology, and parapsychology. The format is in the form of a dictionary catalog. Entries for authors or main entries are afforded full bibliographic information, including all subject and added entry analytics. Subject and title entries are condensed, with no analytics but still a fairly complete record. Items represented in the 1990 volume include cataloging records for material added from September 1, 1989, to August 31, 1990. This is an especially worthwhile guide for the international access it provides to book literature, pamphlets, audiovisual material, and other items that are cataloged by two of the nation's most exhaustive research collections, within the subject limitations indicated above.

124. **Harvard List of Books in Psychology**. 4th ed. Cambridge, Mass., Harvard University Press, 1971. 108p. index. $4.95pa. LC 71-15270. ISBN 0-674-37601-3.

First published in 1938, this list was intended as a guide to the most appropriate and authoritative books in the discipline for the beginning student. Subsequent editions have updated and supplemented the original list, so that it now contains 744 selected books, with emphasis on contemporary (i.e., 1960s) publications. Unfortunately, this edition is woefully out of date and now serves almost solely as a list of historical basic books for the undergraduate. Titles also represent literature from psychology only, with few titles from interdisciplinary areas or related fields.

Books are listed under one of 31 categories. Aside from the three sections for reference books, texts and handbooks, and popular works, the categories are subject- or concept-oriented, sometimes coinciding with the *Psychological Abstracts* (see entry 129) subject arrangement. Annotations are consistently brief, generally descriptive, and occasionally evaluative, although the very inclusion of a work indicates that it has value to the student. There is an author index.

125. Osier, Donald V., and Robert H. Wozniak. **A Century of Serial Publications in Psychology, 1850-1950: An International Bibliography**. Millwood, N.Y., Kraus International, 1984. 805p. index. (Bibliographies in the History of Psychology and Psychiatry, v.2). $100.00. LC 82-48989. ISBN 0-527-98196-6.

As an exhaustive, international list of serial publications, this bibliography chronicles the scientific publishing in psychology. The focus is on publications inaugurated between 1850 and 1950, although 41 titles from 1783-1849 are also included. A prefatory essay provides a comprehensive history of journal publishing in scientific psychology and complements the exhaustive nature of the bibliography. Entries are listed under the year started and thereunder by established title. Each of the 1,107 serials contains title (all variations and the transliterated title in the case of non-Roman alphabets), publishing history and frequency, publishers and editors during the life span of the title, and members of editorial boards and associate editors. Individual titles and authors or editors for volumes are included for monograph serials.

An additional 739 entries are listed in the appendix under 11 subject disciplines of related but tangential interest. Titles and years of publication are the only information supplied for these. There are indexes by established and variant titles in both sections, as well as one by name to all editors and authors.

126. Watson, Robert I., ed. **Eminent Contributors to Psychology**. New York, Springer Publishing, 1974-1976. 2v. index. LC 73-88108. ISBN 0-8261-1450-4(v.1); 0-8261-1780-5(v.2).

Volume 1, *A Bibliography of Primary References*, cites approximately 12,000 publications by over 500 people whose work is considered important to the evolution and development of psychology. Because one of the criteria for selection is that individuals had lived between 1600 and 1967, citations to works by famous psychologists are accompanied by those of philosophers, biologists, physicians, and researchers in many other disciplines. Along with English, German- and French-language publications are well represented, with a smattering of other languages.

The complementary volume, *A Bibliography of Secondary References*, contains about 55,000 references to lesser-known research of the eminent contributors cited in volume 1. Included as materials of secondary importance are translations of primary works, collections of letters or papers, book reviews, biographies and autobiographies, bibliographies of their work, and highly selective works from areas of scholarship that these individuals are not normally associated with. The name index for contributors in volume 2 is not truly a comprehensive name index but an index to the approximately 500 contributors who are cited in connection with the works of others.

INDEXING AND ABSTRACTING TOOLS

127. **Chicorel Index to Mental Health Book Reviews**. Vol. 1- . New York, Chicorel, 1974/1984. $125.00/v. ISSN 0149-4090.

The title of this set is misleading, because citations to reviews are derived from source journals in psychology and mental health. In fact, the scope of the books included is broad to the point where some have little relevance to psychology. The format of volumes has varied, from the annual publication that was suspended with the 1979 volume to the multiyear compilation that covered 1980 to 1984. Entries to books are accompanied by a short list of citations to published reviews in professional and scholarly journals. Some book entries are accompanied by short annotations that appear to be excerpts from one of the book reviews cited. There are usually indexes by title and subject.

The book review journal *Contemporary Psychology* (see entry 208), *Book Review Index* (see entry 12), and the review section of *Social Sciences Index* (see entry 156) afford more current and reliable coverage of the same literature. However, despite the irregular publication of this series and the idiosyncratic nature of the books included, *Chicorel* retains some small value due to its narrow subject focus and its unique coverage of reviews in journals not dealt with by other tools.

128. **PsycBOOKS: Books and Chapters in Psychology.** Arlington, Va., American Psychological Association, 1987-1991. 20v. price not reported. ISSN 1044-1514.

As an index to books and chapters in psychology, this is a unique source; it helped fill a gap when *Psychological Abstracts* (see entry 129) discontinued indexing books in 1980. Every annual set consists of five volumes. Each of the first four covers a group of subjects: basic and applied experimental psychology (including human factors and organizational behavior); developmental, personality, and social issues; clinical psychology, community psychology, law, and professional issues; and educational and health psychology. Volume 5 consists of the author index, a subject index that uses the *Thesaurus of Psychological Index Terms* (see entry 163) vocabulary, a title index, and a list of publishers' addresses and a publishers' index.

Each annual set contains abstracts for approximately 1,400 books and 7,000 chapters in edited works. Entries within each volume are organized under 5 to 12 broad subject classifications that usually have several subheadings. In the case of edited volumes, the content of chapters determines where they are listed, so that a book entry may be included in a subject volume completely separate from its chapters' entries. This arrangement makes the use of the subject index and cross-references essential. In addition to basic bibliographic information, each entry contains an ISBN and such details as pagination. Author or editor affiliation, a table of contents (in total or abbreviated), and descriptive material from the jacket or book is included.

PsycBOOKS was hampered by its brief publication history and annual publication schedule. The American Psychological Association has added the contents of the four-year publication to the CD-ROM database PsycLIT (see entry 155). Book and chapter indexing is now a feature of PsycLIT and, beginning with 1992 issues, of *Psychological Abstracts* (see entry 129).

129. **Psychological Abstracts.** Vol. 1- , No. 1- . Washington, D.C., American Psychological Association, 1927- . monthly. $995.00/yr. ISSN 0033-2887.

As the single most comprehensive printed indexing tool of the periodical literature in psychology, *Psychological Abstracts* (*PA*) indexes articles from approximately 1,200 English-language journals and technical report series, providing descriptive, nonevaluative abstracts. Content and indexing policy has varied since its inception. For example, the paucity of dedicated psychological journals in the past allowed many general-interest publications to be indexed along with journals from philosophy, medicine, and related areas. More recently, coverage of books and dissertations ceased in 1980, and citations to foreign-language journals were discontinued in 1988. (Information on books and chapters was resumed in 1992.) Access to these materials, however, is available through the PsycINFO database (see entry 154), of which *PA* is a printed subset.

Monthly issues contain approximately 3,000 citations organized under 17 subject categories. Many categories are further subdivided hierarchically. In each issue, there are a "Brief Subject Index," which uses terminology from the *Thesaurus of Psychological Index Terms* (see entry 163), and an author index; both indexes are cumulated annually. Multiple-year indexes by author and subject that covered 1927 to 1983 were published at varying intervals by G. K. Hall and the American Psychological Association, although no further indexes of this type will be published.

In general, *PA* provides excellent coverage of almost all areas of experimental psychology, abnormal and clinical psychology, human and animal development, social psychology, and the multitude of interdisciplinary publications in these areas. For applied areas, such as educational psychology, industrial and organizational behavior, ergonomics, and the neurosciences, the use of *PA* should be supplemented by more discipline-specific tools to ensure comprehensive coverage.

130. **Psychological Index.** Vols. 1-42. Washington, D.C., American Psychological Association, 1894-1935.

Now solely of historical interest, *Psychological Index* was the precursor of *Psychological Abstracts* (*PA*) (see entry 129). It was originally published as an annual bibliographic supplement to the journal *Psychological Review* and was discontinued when the American Psychological

Association decided to rely solely on *PA* as its indexing tool. It included citations to books, pamphlets, and journal articles and accessed a wide variety of European languages. It is an essential source for historical research on the foundations and evolution of early psychology.

131. **Social and Psychological Documents.** Vols. 16-18, no. 1. San Rafael, Calif., Select Press, 1986-1988. o.p. ISSN 0896-9140.

Similar to education's *Resources in Education* (see entry 52), this work provides abstracts of documents not otherwise considered suitable for publication in most of the discipline's journals: bibliographies, research questionnaires and surveys, lengthy articles or brief work-in-progress reports, collections of data, classroom materials, and negative replications of previous findings.

The accepted, refereed documents are announced and abstracted in the journal. Microfiche copies of documents are available by subscription, and fiche and hardcopy documents may still be purchased from the publisher. This abstract journal and associated document delivery service was provided by the American Psychological Association under the titles *Catalog of Selected Documents in Psychology* (1971-1983) and *Psychological Documents* (1983-1985).

ONLINE DATABASES

Directories

132. **Computer-Readable Databases: A Directory and Data Sourcebook.** 8th ed. Kathleen Young Marcaccio, ed. Detroit, Gale, 1992. 1691p. index. price not reported. ISBN 0-8103-2946-8.

Over 5,500 databases are listed in this volume, including those that have recently been discontinued or that are no longer publicly available. The types of files are varied and include statistics, fulltext files of reference works and periodicals, bibliographical information, and selected online bulletin boards. For each entry, extensive information about the composition, origin, and availability is provided: directory information for the producer; a basic description of size, years of coverage, and languages; vendors or distributors; availability of batch searching, diskette, or CD-ROM products; related products in print and nonprint formats; search aids; and prices. Indexes cover subjects and products for which there is a CD-ROM format; there is also a master index for database names, acronyms, variant names, and related products.

Vendors

133. **BRS Online Products, Maxwell Online.** 8000 Westpark Dr., McLean, VA 22102. (703) 442-0900, (800) 289-4277.

The BRS menu of approximately 150 databases covers all disciplines from the humanities to the sciences but has an emphasis on bibliographic files in the health sciences. It offers a number of files of particular interest to psychology, including the Mental Measurements Yearbook and DRUGINFO. In addition to its inclusive service, BRS offers two other services. BRS/After Dark allows user-friendly access to a selected core of popular databases at special rates during off hours, and BRS Colleague, designed for health care professionals, has biomedical bibliographic databases and entire selected key journals online. BRS offers special rates for users who subscribe at a minimum level of online usage, although the rates given are for no guaranteed minimum use.

134. **DIALOG Information Services, Inc.** 3460 Hillview Ave., Palo Alto, CA 94304. (415) 858-3810, (800) 334-2564.

DIALOG is the largest of the vendors listed here, with approximately 200 bibliographic and fulltext databases. Although files represent every conceivable discipline, its offerings are especially strong in the sciences, business, and law. One of its unique files in the social sciences is Mental Health Abstracts. In addition to its DIALOG service, Knowledge Index is a system designed for end users, using simplified search commands and providing access to about 100 databases during evening and weekend hours at a reduced rate. DIALOG also supports approximately 20 databases as CD-ROM products, called DIALOG Ondisc.

135. **WILSONLINE.** H. W. Wilson, 950 University Ave., Bronx, NY 10452. (212) 590-1617, (800) 367-6770.

Most of the approximately 30 WILSONLINE files correspond to the Wilson print indexes of the same name (e.g., *Book Review Digest*). The remainder are bibliographic files that originate from other producers but that use the WILSONLINE search software, such as the GPO Monthly Catalog and MLA International Bibliography. WILSONLINE offers special rates for libraries that already subscribe to the print indexes or that guarantee a specific level of online use.

Databases

136. **ABI/Inform**. Louisville, Ken., Data Courier, 1970- . DIALOG file #15 (1971- , weekly updates); $114.00/hr. BRS label: INFO (monthly updates); $95.00/hr.(open access).

Over 800 professional, trade, and academic periodicals are indexed in this database—primarily those of interest to practitioners and academics in business management and human resources. For psychologists the coverage of advertising and consumer behavior, organizational behavior, and human resource management and personnel issues is especially important. Coverage is international, and ABI/Inform has no print counterpart.

137. **Ageline**. Washington, D.C., American Association of Retired Persons, National Gerontology Resource Center, 1978- . bimonthly updates. BRS label: AARP; $50.00/hr.(open access).

This file attempts to cover the wide-ranging field of gerontology and specific areas of concern to the aged, such as economic and political issues, geriatrics and health care, and social and psychological concerns. Citations to books, documents, journal articles, and dissertations, and a directory of ongoing federal research projects comprise the database.

138. **BIOSIS Previews**. Philadelphia, Pa., BIOSIS, 1969- . DIALOG files #5, 55 (biweekly updates); $ 84.00/hr. BRS labels: BIOL, BIOB, BIOZ (merged file) (1970- , monthly updates); $75.00/hr.(open access).

Corresponding to the print *Biological Abstracts* (see entry 387) and *Biological Abstracts/RRM* BIOSIS provides comprehensive coverage of medicine, biology, and interdisciplinary areas of the life sciences. Over 9,000 journal titles, books, symposia, technical and government report series, and conferences are regularly indexed. Of special interest are studies in ethology, physiological psychology and intervention, and the neurosciences.

139. **Business Periodicals Index**. Bronx, N.Y., H. W. Wilson, 1982- . twice weekly updates. WILSONLINE file BPI; $65.00/hr.(nonsubscribers).

This is the online equivalent of the print index of the same name (see entry 63), with coverage from July 1982. Over 300 serials are indexed, with an emphasis on trade and professional magazines. Advertising, personnel, marketing and retailing, and business management publications are included to some degree, although coverage is considerably narrower than other online business files.

140. **Dissertation Abstracts Online.** Ann Arbor, Mich., University Microfilms International, 1861- . monthly updates. DIALOG file #35; $72.00/hr. BRS label: DISS; $65.00/hr.(open access).

This database has a comprehensive, multidisciplinary, and retrospective approach to an important body of unpublished research literature. It most closely corresponds to the print *Dissertation Abstracts International* (see entry 20), although abstracts have been added to the file only since 1980. It also contains citations comprising the printed *American Doctoral Dissertations* and *Comprehensive Dissertations Index* (see entry 17). References from UMI's *Masters Abstracts* since 1962 are included. Foreign dissertations have recently been added. UMI also produces a compact disc version of this database, Dissertation Abstracts Ondisc.

141. **DRUGINFO/Alcohol Use and Abuse.** Minneapolis, Minn., University of Minnesota, College of Pharmacy, Drug Information Services, 1968- . quarterly updates. BRS label: DRUG; $53.00/hr.(open access).

DRUGINFO is made up of two separate files best searched together: HAZE, a closed file (1968-1978) of alcohol addiction literature, and DRSC, which covers the social, psychological, and therapeutic aspects of substance abuse. Journal articles, books and pamphlets, conference papers, and instructional materials are included.

142. **ERIC.** Washington, D.C., Educational Resources Information Center, U.S. Department of Education, 1966- . monthly updates. DIALOG file #1; $30.00/hr. BRS label: ERIC; $31.00/hr.(open access).

ERIC encompasses the equivalent of two print indexes: *Resources in Education* (see entry 52) and *Current Index to Journals in Education* (see entry 49). The combined file indexes over 700 serials in every area of education as well as a diverse group of unpublished research reports, conference papers, books, and curriculum materials. There is excellent coverage of materials in vocational education, school and educational psychology, and all areas of counseling.

143. **Education Index.** Bronx, N.Y., H. W. Wilson, 1983- . twice weekly updates. WILSONLINE file EDI; $45.00/hr.(nonsubscribers).

This is the online equivalent of Wilson's *Education Index* (see entry 50), covering over 300 source journals and annual publications since June 1983. Although not as comprehensive as the ERIC database, this file does include basic coverage of educational psychology, counseling, child and adolescent psychology, special education, and the psychology of learning.

144. **Educational Testing Service Test Collection.** Princeton, N.J., Educational Testing Service, current and retrospective tests. quarterly updates. BRS label: ETSF; $50.00/hr.(open access).

As an index to the ETS Test Collection, this file provides access to an extensive body of educational measures for achievement, aptitude, attitudes, and skill levels. Records are searchable by a variety of access points, such as type of test, audience level, and availability.

145. **Exceptional Child Education Resources.** Reston, Va., Council for Exceptional Children, 1966- . monthly updates. DIALOG file #54; $45.00/hr. BRS label: ECER; $45.00/hr.(open access).

This database includes a variety of published and unpublished materials, such as books and journal articles, dissertations, conference papers, nonprint media, curriculum guides, and government publications. All aspects of the identification, diagnosis, education, rehabilitation, and development of handicapped and gifted children are covered. Coverage corresponds to the print source of the same name. Because the Council serves as an ERIC subject clearinghouse and processing center, approximately one-half of the citations are duplicated in the ERIC file (see entry 142).

146. **Family Resources**. St. Paul, Minn., National Council on Family Relations, 1970- . monthly updates. DIALOG file #291; $66.00 /hr. BRS label: NCFR; $60.00/hr.(open access).

Although journal articles are the most prevalent type of literature included, this file also lists books, nonprint material, dissertations, and newsletters. Additionally, it contains a directory of organizations and research institutes in all areas of marriage and family functioning and counseling. Its approximate equivalent is *Inventory of Marriage and Family Literature* (see entry 459).

147. **GPO Monthly Catalog**. Washington, D.C., U.S. Government Printing Office, 1976- . monthly updates. DIALOG file #66; $35.00/hr. BRS label: GPOM; $25.00/hr.(open access).

Corresponding to the print *Monthly Catalog of United States Government Publications* (see entry 24) from July 1976 forward, GPO cites the vast literature resulting from Congressional reports and hearings, bills and laws, judiciary and executive publications, and commission and regulatory reports. It provides citations to a wealth of information on public and social policy issues in virtually every discipline.

148. **Linguistics and Language Behavior Abstracts**. San Diego, Calif., Sociological Abstracts, 1973- . quarterly updates. DIALOG file #36; $66.00/hr. BRS label: LLBA; $53.00/hr.(open access).

This file corresponds to the print publication of the same name (see entry 406) and includes citations to journal articles, books and book reviews, and conference papers and proceedings. Verbal and nonverbal communication, psycholinguistics and sociolinguistics, language acquisition, and learning and language disabilities are among the literatures covered.

149. **Management Contents**. Belmont, Calif., Information Access Company, 1974- . monthly updates. DIALOG file #75; $102.00/hr. BRS label: MGMT, MGMB; $70.00/hr.(open access).

Primary coverage in this database is of approximately 1,200 journal titles, with some citations to conference proceedings, newsletters, and research reports in all areas of management. The file provides especially good coverage of literature on decision making, marketing, personnel management, and organizational behavior.

150. **MEDLINE**. Bethesda, Md., National Library of Medicine, 1966- . biweekly updates. DIALOG files #152, 153, 154, 155 (merged); $36.00/hr. BRS labels: MESH, MESB, MS85, MS80, MS70, MESZ (merged); $25.00/hr.(open access).

This gigantic file contains citations from over 3,000 journals published worldwide and corresponds to the combined *Index Medicus* (see entry 388), *Index to Dental Literature*, and *International Nursing Index*. Exhaustive coverage is provided for every aspect of biomedicine. Almost half of the records added since 1975 contain abstracts. The number, years of coverage, and names of the several files comprising MEDLINE change frequently due to the size of the file. MEDLINE provides excellent coverage of the literature in the neurosciences, psychopharmacology, psychiatric and physiological intervention, and public health care and social support programs.

151. **Mental Health Abstracts**. Alexandria, Va., Plenum Data Company, 1969- . monthly updates. DIALOG file #86; $111.00/hr.

Until 1982, this file was maintained by the National Institute of Mental Health. It contains citations to a variety of print and nonprint formats: journal articles, books and book chapters, conference proceedings, and audiovisual products. All aspects of mental health and illness are included, and the file has no absolute corresponding print equivalent. The variety of formats included makes it a valuable supplement to PsycINFO (see entry 154) and MEDLINE (see entry 150), especially in clinical psychology and psychiatry.

152. **Mental Measurements Yearbook.** Lincoln, Nebr., Buros Institute of Mental Measurements, University of Nebraska, 1972- . monthly updates. BRS label: MMYD; $55.00/hr.(open access).

Containing descriptive information on, and critical reviews of, tests and assessment tools, this database roughly corresponds to the 8th edition of the *Mental Measurements Yearbook* (*MMY*) (see entry 349) and all subsequent editions. Bibliographic information and the text of the critical reviews are included, although the lengthy reference lists in the print source are not. Updates include information and reviews destined for the next *MMY* edition, making it more current than the print version.

153. **NTIS.** Springfield, Va., National Technical Information Service, 1964- . biweekly updates. DIALOG file #6; $84.00/hr. BRS label: NTIS (1970- , monthly updates); $55.00/hr.(open access).

The NTIS file provides comprehensive access to unclassified reports from U.S. government sponsored research, plus documents submitted by federal agencies or their grantees. It is the equivalent of the printed source *Government Reports Announcements and Index* (see entry 22). Although reports are generally in the pure and applied sciences, such areas as human factors, management and personnel, and social issues and their public policy implications are covered. Citations include contract and report information, as well as lengthy abstracts.

154. **PsycINFO.** Washington, D.C., American Psychological Association, 1967- . monthly updates. DIALOG file #11; $55.00/hr. BRS label: PSYC; $50.00/hr.(open access).

PsycINFO is the single most comprehensive file for coverage of all areas of psychology, both experimental and applied, as well as the psychological aspects of many other disciplines. It indexes approximately 1,400 serial publications: journals, technical report series, and selected citations from *Dissertation Abstracts International* (see entry 20). The file no longer directly corresponds to the print *Psychological Abstracts* (see entry 129); citations to dissertations are unique to PsycINFO after 1980, and foreign-language citations are unique to it after 1988. Coverage is international and multilingual.

155. **PsycLIT.** Washington, D.C., American Psychological Association, 1974- . Dist. by Norwood, Mass., SilverPlatter Information, Inc. $4,495/single workstation. quarterly updates.

A compact disc (CD-ROM) reference tool, PsycLIT is a hybrid product of several sources intended for use by students, researchers, and practioners. It contains citations and abstracts to the English- and foreign-language journal literature for the years covered, as does PsycINFO (see entry 154), provides both the retrospective citations from *PsycBOOKS* (see entry 128) and the current book and chapter citations found in *Psychological Abstracts* (see entry 129), and contains a machine-readable version of the *Thesaurus of Psychological Index Terms* (see entry 163).

156. **Social Sciences Index.** Bronx, N.Y., H. W. Wilson, 1984- . twice weekly updates. WILSONLINE file SSI; $55.00/yr.(nonsubscriber).

This is the online equivalent of Wilson's index of the same name (see entry 26) beginning with February 1984. It is considerably smaller than the Social SCISEARCH database (see entry 157), both in terms of years covered and number of source journals. It does index the basic journals in psychology, political science, criminology, sociology, social work, and anthropology. Some titles in interdisciplinary areas, such as area studies, demographics, and gerontology, are also included.

157. **Social SCISEARCH.** Philadelphia, Pa., Institute for Scientific Information, 1972- . weekly updates. DIALOG file #7; $120.00/hr. BRS label: SSCI (weekly updates); $107.00/hr.(open access).

Corresponding to *Social Sciences Citation Index* (*SSCI*) (see entry 25), Social SCISEARCH indexes 1,500 journals and selected books in the social and behavioral sciences. Selected material from biomedical and physical science disciplines is also indexed. This file may be searched in much the same way as many other files (e.g., keyword-in-title, author, source journal, institutional affiliation), although the most valuable strategy to use is to search by cited references in the source document. Discounted access rates are available for subscribers to the print *SSCI.*

158. **Sociological Abstracts**. San Diego, Calif., Sociological Abstracts, 1963- . updated five times per year. DIALOG file #37; $69.00/hr. BRS labels: SOCA; $53.00/hr.(open access).

Roughly corresponding to the print *Sociological Abstracts* (see entry 72), this is a primary database for the social psychology literature, especially family relations, social relations and attitudes, sex roles, and aging. International journal coverage is supplemented by citations to published and unpublished conference papers. Book abstracts and citations to reviews and dissertations have been added since 1986.

HANDBOOKS AND YEARBOOKS

159. **Annual Review of Psychology**. Vol. 1- . Palo Alto, Calif., Annual Reviews, 1950- . annual. $38.00/year. ISSN 0066-4308.

Annual and biennial volumes that review research in specialized areas of psychology have proliferated since 1970, but this publication remains the most influential and heavily cited in the discipline. Approximately 20 review essays appear in each volume and are written by people with considerable expertise in their areas. Each essay summarizes and discusses the most influential research and consequent clinical, experimental, or psychology literature, accompanied by extensive reference lists.

Topics covered in recent volumes include reasoning, hemispheric asymmetry, cognitive science, and engineering psychology. Individual topics of the essays differ from year to year, and topics are re-reviewed if there have been significant recent contributions to the literature. Each volume has its own subject and author index.

160. Gilgen, Albert R., and Carol K. Gilgen, eds. **International Handbook of Psychology**. Westport, Conn., Greenwood Press, 1987. 629p. index. $79.95. LC 86-29457. ISBN 0-313-23832-4.

This is an excellent source for an international perspective on the discipline and profession of psychology. With so much psychological practice and theory dominated by English-language publication and Western thought, the value of this work lies in its discussion of contributions that flourish worldwide. Essays survey the development of, evolution of, and influences on psychology as a profession and as an academic discipline in 29 countries. Major research institutes, the education and training of psychologists, and significant publications are surveyed. More in-depth coverage is provided for each region, whereas Wolman's *International Directory of Psychology* (see entry 294) serves more of a directory function. There are name and subject indexes.

In large part, the reference lists accompanying each article reflect the literature of the countries themselves, and most contributors are professionally active in the countries about which they write. Although this detracts from in-depth discussion of some controversial topics, chapters are largely free of overt bias.

161. **Journals in Psychology: A Resource Listing for Authors**. 3d ed. Washington, D.C., American Psychological Association, 1990. 133p. index. $20.00. LC 90-657651. ISBN 1-55798-047-0.

This edition lists almost 300 professional and research journals and is aimed at psychologists seeking an appropriate publishing outlet for manuscripts. Only American publications are included, so important British and Canadian titles have been excluded, as well as those that originate in other countries. In addition to mainstream journals in experimental, clinical, and paranormal psychology, a considerable number of interdisciplinary titles from communications, sociology, management, and engineering are listed.

Each entry contains publisher and editorial addresses, statements of editorial policy, notes on the types of manuscripts appropriate for consideration, frequency, average number of articles and pages published per year, and number of subscribers. Recent years arrange entries by journal titles, with a separate list of titles under broad subject categories.

162. **Publication Manual of the American Psychological Association.** Washington, D.C., American Psychological Association, 1983. 208p. index. $16.50. LC 83-2521. ISBN 0-912704-57-8.

The most frequent use of this manual is as a guide to the APA style of manuscript preparation, specifically the method of citing resources used and preparation of the reference list. In addition, several chapters discuss general principles for preparing the manuscript, writing styles, the communication of ideas and research results, the presentation of graphic and statistical material, and proofreading techniques. The manual's emphasis is on preparing manuscripts for submission to journals, and there is a description of APA's journal publication program. An appendix provides advice on preparing selected nonjournal manuscripts. There is a combined title and subject index. Because APA style is commonly used in many social science disciplines, the work speaks to a wide audience of student, faculty, and professional users.

163. **Thesaurus of Psychological Index Terms.** 6th ed. Alvin Walker, Jr., ed. Washington, D.C., American Psychological Association, 1991. 332p. $65.00. LC 90-14520. ISBN 1-55798-111-6.

This work is a guide to the current, standardized lexicon of the discipline. Since the first edition was published in 1974, this thesaurus has supplied the terminology for *Psychological Abstracts* (see entry 129) and the PsycINFO database (see entry 154). New editions are published approximately every four years. This latest edition contains over 6,000 terms used as subject headings. Many have a brief scope note describing the use of the term, as well as suggested narrower, broader, and related terms. An entry also indicates when it was added and category codes used in searching the online database. Cross-reference terms, those in common usage but not part of the controlled vocabulary, account for about 2,000 additional entries.

Other features include a rotated descriptor display that lists each subject heading and cross-reference by their significant words, and a "clusters section." The latter arranges around half of the thesaurus subject headings under seven broad concept areas and over 61 subheadings, allowing one to browse for conceptually related terms.

164. Wang, Alvin Y. **Author's Guide to Journals in the Behavioral Sciences.** Hillsdale, N.J., Lawrence Erlbaum, 1989. 481p. index. $24.95pa.; $49.95(disk). LC 89-11664. ISBN 0-8058-0313-0pa.; 0-8058-0647-4(3.5" disk); 0-8058-0314-9(5.25" disk).

This title differs from the corresponding APA publication *Journals in Psychology* (see entry 161). Its scope is considerably broader; it covers over 400 journals titles published primarily in English throughout the world, and its entries contain more information. In addition to providing general editorial, address, and circulation information, the work details manuscript style requirements, the manuscript review process, acceptance rate of submissions, and the indexing and abstracting sources in which a title is included. There is also greater coverage of titles considered primary to other fields but of interest to psychologists and others in the behavioral sciences as publishing outlets, with particular emphasis on medicine, education, social work, and management.

Data were obtained from questionnaires mailed to journals included in *Psychological Abstracts* (see entry 129), and the few serious omissions are presumably due to nonresponse. Primary arrangement is by journal title, and there are title and keyword subject indexes.

165. Wolman, Benjamin B., ed. **Handbook of General Psychology**. Englewood Cliffs, N.J., Prentice-Hall, 1973. 1006p. index. price not reported. LC 74-166142. ISBN 0-13-378141-0.

This handbook attempts to encompass the entire discipline of psychology, from theory and history to methodology and applied research. Contributors include some distinguished names in the field, such as J. P. Guilford and Douglas Jackson. Its 45 chapters are organized under eight broad areas. In addition to theory and method, topics covered include "The Human Organism" (primarily the physiological and biological aspects of behavior), perception, learning, communication and intelligence, motivation and emotion, personality, and four topical chapters lumped under "Selected Areas." Unfortunately, the age of this volume limits many chapters to being sources of history or survey information.

DICTIONARIES AND ENCYCLOPEDIAS

166. **Baker Encyclopedia of Psychology**. David G. Benner, ed. Grand Rapids, Mich., Baker Book House, 1985. 1223p. (Baker Reference Library, v.2). $39.95. LC 85-70713. ISBN 0-8010-0865-4.

Although there are other excellent psychology encyclopedias, this one fills a niche by having several strengths not covered in such depth elsewhere. Given the publisher, it is no surprise that the psychology of religion is one of these areas. Mental disorders and treatment approaches are covered in approximately 500 individual articles. There are about 100 biographical entries, and some important assessment instruments receive individual treatment. Surveys on the areas of psychology (e.g., counseling, social psychology, parapsychology) are especially good. Articles are between half a page to several pages in length, and most place a concept, person, or instrument in a historical context. Preceding the encyclopedia proper is a topical grouping of articles. Cross-references and brief bibliographies are appended to most of the signed articles.

167. Bruno, Frank J. **Dictionary of Key Words in Psychology**. New York, Routledge, Chapman & Hall, 1986. 274p. index. $14.95pa. LC 85-2277. ISBN 0-7102-1394-8.

"The book does not seek to present an exhaustive catalog of psychological terms, but a selective list of key terms—terms that are used with very high levels of frequency" (p. ix). Its purpose is not only to define words but also to provide context to the vocabulary as used in the discipline, thereby seeking to curtail unbridled (and usually inaccurate) popular use of psychological terms. About a page in length, each entry begins with a working definition, followed by an example (e.g., an imaginary case study, an applied setting) and an explanation of how the concept fits into psychological theory and thought. Among the approximately 150 essays are biographies of major figures in the development of the discipline. Bruno also includes a selective bibliography of readings, a topical index listing entries under 18 broad categories, and name and subject indexes.

168. **Concise Encyclopedia of Psychology**. Raymond J. Corsini, ed. New York, John Wiley, 1987. 1242p. index. $99.95. LC 86-22392. ISBN 0-471-01068-5.

169. **Encyclopedia of Psychology**. Raymond J. Corsini, ed. New York, John Wiley, 1984. 4v. index. $310.00/set. LC 83-16814. ISBN 0-471-86594-X.

This four-volume set is among the best of the recent, comprehensive psychology encyclopedias. There are over 2,000 separate entries, and approximately one-third of them are devoted to biographies. Psychological concepts, important controversial issues in the development of psychology, and major testing instruments are also represented. As appropriate, cross-references and further readings are appended to articles, although a list of approximately 15,000 references cited within articles is cumulated in volume 4. This volume also contains name and subject indexes.

Articles vary in length from fewer than 200 to more than 9,000 words. Illustrations and figures are sparse but appropriately placed. All entries are signed, and the list of over 400 contributors attests to the quality of the set. Articles are well written and will be comprehensible to the educated layperson, although some background in psychology is assumed.

The *Concise Encyclopedia* is an abridgment. Although a few new entries have been added, the condensed version retains a substantial amount of the material and most of the other features of the 1984 set, including its own cumulated list of references and index.

170. **Encyclopedic Dictionary of Psychology.** Rom Harre and Roger Lamb, eds. Cambridge, Mass., MIT Press, 1983. 718p. index. $95.00. LC 83-920. ISBN 0-262-08135-0.

Over 250 authorities contributed to this concise but comprehensive work. Articles, ranging from fewer than 100 words to several pages in length, emphasize theories and concepts, although there are some biographical entries. The well-written essays are usually more descriptive than comparative or evaluative. There are liberal cross-references, relevant and timely reference lists, and a detailed subject index. Although not as comprehensive as Corsini's four-volume *Encyclopedia of Psychology* (see entry 169), this is a fine encyclopedia for the beginning psychology student and general user.

171. **Dictionary of Behavioral Science.** 2d ed. Benjamin B. Wolman, ed. San Diego, Calif., Academic Press, 1989. 370p. $39.95. LC 88-14128. ISBN 0-12-762455-4.

This work provides brief definitions for approximately 20,000 terms and individuals associated with psychology and related fields. Definitions are generally between 20 and 100 words long and include brief information on the theorist who devised the term or concept (if appropriate). Eponymous and brief biographical entries are provided for living and deceased individuals important in the history and development of the discipline. There are liberal *see* references but no bibliographic references. Formulas and graphs are included, albeit sparingly, to illustrate quantitative and statistical concepts. This is a current and comprehensive work for quick definitions of concepts and terms found in all areas of psychology.

172. **International Encyclopedia of Psychiatry, Psychology, Psychoanalysis, & Neurology.** Benjamin B. Wolman, ed. New York, Van Nostrand Reinhold for Aesculapius, 1977. 12v. index. $675.00/set. LC 76-54527. ISBN 0-918228-01-8.

173. **Progress Volume I.** New York, Aesculapius, 1983. 509p. index. $89.00. LC 83-2505. ISBN 0-918228-28-X.

As a source of comprehensive and authoritative information on most areas of psychology and related fields, this set is unequaled. A lengthy and international list of contributors, a broad and exhaustive approach to the disciplines and their schools of thought, and references to the seminal literature make this a research tool for both student and scholar.

Most articles are lengthy discussions of broad issues (e.g., aging, communication, sleep and dreaming) in which the breadth of theory, historical development, and professional opinion are presented. Entries for individuals concentrate on biographical information as opposed to their theories. The average bibliography contains 10 references, including the seminal works on the subject. Charts and tables are not abundant, and the paucity of cross-references makes use of the subject index in volume 12 essential. Both subject and name indexes are exhaustive.

The subject strengths of the *International Encyclopedia* are experimental and theoretical psychology, psychoanalysis, therapeutic approaches, and psychiatry. Less impressive is its coverage of the neurosciences and areas of applied psychology. The *Progress Volume* reflects these emphases, with slightly better (and updated) coverage of neuropsychology.

174. Kuper, Jessica, ed. **A Lexicon of Psychology, Psychiatry, and Psychoanalysis.** New York, Routledge, Chapman & Hall, 1988. 471p. (Social Science Lexicons). $19.95pa. LC 88-19884. ISBN 0-415-00233-8.

This is an encyclopedia in the sense that it has over 100 essays on broad topics, significant issues, or individuals important in the development of research and theory in psychology. Among the individuals profiled are Anna and Sigmund Freud, B. F. Skinner, Carl Jung, Carl Rogers, and Jerome Bruner. Topical essays focus on specific areas of current research rather than theory, and coverage is uneven rather than comprehensive. For example, an essay covers drug use but not alcoholism, and *free association* and *superego* warrant essays, but the entire area of sensation and perception is lumped into one essay. The essay on Harry Sullivan is almost three times the length of the Skinner essay. Lack of an index makes it more difficult to locate specific concepts, although there are cross-references among articles.

For the topics that are covered, reference lists and current citations to additional readings are helpful introductions to both current and seminal literature. On the topics covered, idiosyncratic as their inclusion is, this volumes will be helpful to the beginning student.

175. **Oxford Companion to the Mind.** Richard L. Gregory, ed. New York, Oxford University Press, 1987. 856p. index. $49.95. LC 87-1671. ISBN 0-19-866124-X.

This "companion" is really a one-volume encyclopedia of concepts, persons, and theories in psychology and related disciplines. Entries vary from just a few words that define a term to several pages for broad concepts. Also, the discipline is defined to include aspects of language and communication, biological and medical measurement of psychophysics and psychopathology, and philosophical antecedents of psychological theories and thought. Examples of this broad spectrum include articles on Chinese language and space psychology. Individuals from medicine, philosophy, biology, and physics as well as psychology are represented in the biographical entries.

For the amount of information in a one-volume reference, there is liberal use of illustrations, photographs, and tabular material. Cross-references are used among the entries, and additional access is allowed through the subject index. Reading lists at the end of longer articles draw from both classic and recent work.

176. Popplestone, John A., and Marion White McPherson. **Dictionary of Concepts in General Psychology**. Westport, Conn., Greenwood Press, 1988. 380p. index. (Reference Sources for the Social Sciences and Humanities, no.7). $65.00. LC 88-3120. ISBN 0-313-23190-7.

This work is both a dictionary and an encyclopedia. In dictionary style, an entry for a broad concept begins with a brief description, compares it with similar or related concepts, and defines it in the context of the areas of psychology in which it is frequently used. As in an encyclopedia, each concept is evaluated in a lengthy essay (about five pages), including discussion of early research, how it evolved and changed, and how it is reflected across the discipline. The list of cited references is followed by a substantial list of further research readings.

Because the work's emphasis is on concepts as opposed to subjects or terms, most essays cover broad topics (e.g., aggression, habituation, curiosity, ecological psychology, Gestalt). Throughout, experimental psychology is of greatest importance, especially phenomena in personality, cognition, perception, learning, and memory. There is little coverage of social, developmental, and clinical psychology; applied areas; or research methodology. Some entries represent wide research areas or theoretical approaches. As terms are not usually represented by entries, a more substantial index would have enhanced access, although there are cross-references among articles.

177. **Psychoanalytic Terms and Concepts**. Burness E. Moore and Bernard D. Fine, eds. New Haven, Conn., Yale University Press, 1990. 240p. $35.00; o.p.(pa.). LC 89-36223. ISBN 0-300-04577-8; 0-300-04701-0pa.

Copublished with the American Psychoanalytic Association, this is a revised version of the 1968 *Glossary of Psychoanalytic Terms and Concepts*. Terms are defined in about 1,000 words and accompanied by relevant references to both Sigmund Freud's work and more modern writings as appropriate. Definitions are clearly written and avoid (or at least define) technical terms, making the language accessible to the student and layperson. Psychoanalysis as a psychological theory is the book's major focus, but the therapeutic approach is not ignored. Overall, this is a clear presentation of what can be an ambiguous (and often misused) vocabulary.

178. Stratton, Peter, and Nicky Hayes. **A Student's Dictionary of Psychology**. London, Edward Arnold; distr., New York, Routledge, Chapman & Hall, 1988. 216p. $49.50; $13.95pa. ISBN 0-7131-6500-6; 0-7131-6501-4pa.

Stratton and Hayes focus on the vocabulary of psychology and its subdisciplines, largely excluding terms more commonly associated with other fields or found in general dictionaries. Definitions average about 60 words in length and include multiple definitions depending on context, such as *regression*. Where possible, examples are provided, and abundant cross-references are supplied. Line-drawing illustrations include flowcharts, tables, anatomical drawings, visual illusions, and explanations of theoretical concepts. Most are very useful, although a few are more entertaining than informative. There is a brief but not very helpful bibliography.

Student's Dictionary provides limited coverage of applied areas and parapsychology. It also contains no biographical entries, although eponyms are included. However, it is especially good for succinct yet informative definitions in clinical and experimental psychology, statistics, and psychological theory.

179. Sutherland, Stuart. **The International Dictionary of Psychology**. New York, Continuum, 1989. 491p. $49.95. LC 88-39340. ISBN 0-8264-0440-5.

This dictionary is similar to that of *A Student's Dictionary of Psychology* (see entry 178). It lists terms used in psychology but not those most commonly associated with other disciplines, provides brief, contextual definitions, and includes eponymous but not biographical entries. Its subject strengths are also similar, with good coverage of experimental, quantitative, clinical, and theoretical psychology and less detail on applied areas. It is especially strong for locating vocabulary associated with neuropsychophysiology and psychopharmacology.

Similar to Wolman's *Dictionary of Behavioral Science* (see entry 171), this work has few illustrations and brief definitions. (A few of the latter provide more humor than information.) Many cross-references and synonymous entries are given. Most illustrations are of visual illusions, and the five appendixes consist of anatomical drawings of the human brain.

180. **Trilingual Psychological Dictionary**. By International Union of Psychological Science. Hubert C. J. Duijker and Maria J. van Rijswijk, eds. Bern, Switzerland, Hans Huber, 1975. 3v. LC 75-511303. ISBN 3-456-30558-3.

This is strictly a dictionary of translations. No definitions are provided. Each volume lists over 15,000 terms and phrases commonly found in the psychological and psychiatric literature. Volume 1 lists terms in English, with accompanying French and German equivalents and their genders in a tabular format, making the dictionary extremely easy to use. There are no cross-references, and terms are sometimes listed under broader terms, with closely related terms listed alongside. For example, under *handwriting*, which is itself translated, *analyst* and *graphologist* are also listed with their equivalent terms. The last two terms, however, also have their own entries.

Volume 2, *Dictionnaire de Psychologie en Trois Langues*, lists the same terms with primary arrangement by the French, followed by the German and English. Volume 3, *Dreisprachiges Psychologisches Worterbuch*, follows a similar format for the German.

181. Zusne, Leonard. **Eponyms in Psychology: A Dictionary and Biographical Sourcebook.** Westport, Conn., Greenwood Press, 1987. 339p. index. $75.00. LC 87-255. ISBN 0-313-25750-7.

A large number of syndromes, theorems, mental measures, anatomical parts, complexes, and other phenomena in the psychological literature are named after persons or places. Therefore, this compilation of 852 eponymous terms is useful for both students and librarians. Entries are alphabetically listed by the test, concept, or syndrome (e.g., Mach bands, Cornell technique, Jastrow cylinders, Jocasta complex), followed by a paragraph about the person (real or mythological) or place. The published source in which the eponym first appeared is usually cited. References to other biographical works are provided by way of standard biographical dictionaries or references in psychology journals. There is also an index by eponym.

BIOGRAPHICAL SOURCES

182. **History of Psychology in Autobiography**. Carl Murchinson, ed. (Vols. 1-3) and Edwin G. Boring, et al., eds. (Vol. 4). New York, Russell & Russell, 1930-1952. 4v. index. (International University Series in Psychology). LC 30-20129. ISSN 0097-6091.

183. **History of Psychology in Autobiography. Volume 5**. Edwin G. Boring and Gardner Lindzey, eds. New York, Appleton-Century-Crofts, 1967. 449p. (Century Psychology Series). Reprint: Manchester, N. H., Irvington. $34.50. ISBN 0-89197-216-1.

184. **History of Psychology in Autobiography. Volume 6**. Gardner Lindzey, ed. Englewood Cliffs, N.J., Prentice-Hall, 1974. 420p. (Century Psychology Series). o.p. ISBN 0-13-392274-X.

185. **History of Psychology in Autobiography. Volume 7**. Gardner Lindzey, eds. San Francisco, Calif., W. H. Freeman, 1980. 472p. (International University Series in Psychology). o.p. ISBN 0-7167-1119-2; 0-7167-1120-6pa.

186. **History of Psychology in Autobiography. Volume 8**. Gardner Lindzey, ed. Stanford, Calif., Stanford University Press, 1989. 485p. index. $49.50. ISBN 0-8047-1492-4.

This set is an especially important source for those interested in the history of psychology. Approximately 13 individuals are profiled in each volume, representing researchers from every area of the discipline. Gordon Allport, Lee Cronbach, B. F. Skinner, and Eleanor Maccoby are only a few of those represented. Along with recollections of their youth, people discuss how their work evolved and developed over the course of their careers, how the work of others influenced their research, and how they perceive their contributions to the discipline. Lists of selected publications are appended to each essay.

187. Krawiec, T. S. **The Psychologists**. New York, Oxford University Press, 1972-1974. 2v. index. price not reported. LC 78-188293. Volume 3: Brandon, Vt., Clinical Psychology Publishing, 1978. 314p. $12.50pa. LC 78-188293. ISBN 0-88422-010-9.

This work has autobiographical essays of 35 psychologists, all significant contributors to the field by virtue of their teaching or research. Articles are usually lengthier and include more personal biographical details than those in *History of Psychology in Autobiography* (see entry 182), although far fewer individuals are included. Bibliographies of the contributors also tend to be longer.

The first two volumes contain a biographical index to important persons discussed in the essays, with a brief biography, their importance, and the pages on which they are discussed. Among those profiled are Raymond Cattell, Arthur Jensen, Gardner Murphy, Jerome Kagan, and Edwin Ghiselli.

188. O'Connell, Agnes N., and Nancy Felipe Russo, eds. **Models of Achievement: Reflections of Eminent Women in Psychology**. 2v. index. Volume 1: New York, Columbia University Press, 1983. $30.00; $16.00pa. LC 82-23583. ISBN 0-231-05312-6; 0-231-05313-4pa. Volume 2: Hillsdale, N.J., Lawrence Erlbaum, 1988. $59.95; $19.95pa. ISBN 0-8058-0083-2; 0-8058-0322-Xpa.

The autobiographical essays in this set discuss the influences of family, home, and education on the women, as well as their professional careers and research. However, many essays differ from those in other sources because the contributors talk about being female in social, educational, and research settings dominated by men and its effect on their careers. In addition to the 34 autobiographies, chapters by the editors deal with the role of women in the profession's history, differences and similarities of the women's experiences, and how each woman overcame barriers to attain recognition. There is a combined subject and name index.

189. Stevens, Gwendolyn, and Sheldon Gardner. **The Women of Psychology**. Cambridge, Mass., Schenkman Publishing, 1982. 2v. index. $18.95/set; $13.95pa./set. LC 81-14394. ISBN 0-87973-443-1; 0-87073-444-Xpa.(v.1); 0-87073-445-8; 0-87073-446-6pa.(v.2).

In response to scant coverage previously afforded women in biographical works, this set contains sketches of women who are difficult to locate in other biographical sources. Also included are women whose work contributed to psychological theory and research but who were not psychologists by training, such as Margaret Mead and Eleanor Touroff Glueck.

Volume I, *Pioneers and Innovators*, provides an excellent introductory essay on the roles of women in the discipline. Biographical essays for 37 women follow, with entries varying from half a page to over 10 pages. Most essays discuss the subjects' early lives and the difficulties they had getting their work recognized and being accepted in a male-dominated profession.

The second volume, *Expansion and Refinement*, lists 100 women who have considerably shorter entries of just a few pages for each. The biographies are grouped under the headings "Era of Acceptance" (women born between 1881 and 1900), "The Researchers" (women born between 1901 and 1910 who participated in all areas of scientific psychology), and "Women of Contemporary Psychology" (women born between 1911 and 1940, many of whom were active in the field at the time of publication). Each volume has its own subject and name index.

190. Zusne, Leonard. **Biographical Dictionary of Psychology**. Westport, Conn., Greenwood Press, 1984. 563p. index. $79.95. LC 83-18326. ISBN 0-313-24027-2.

This is a revised edition of Zusne's 1975 publication, *Names in the History of Psychology*. It is a sourcebook of information on nearly 600 deceased individuals whose thought and work contributed to the development of psychology. Included are individuals from practically every research area: naturalists and biologists, chemists and physicians, philosophers, sociologists, mathematicians, and, of course, psychologists and psychiatrists. The time frame is broad, covering the ancients (e.g., Thales, Galen) to contemporaries (e.g., Leta Hollingworth, David Rapaport). Basic information includes dates and places of birth and death, highest degrees awarded, and positions held. The contributions of each person are summarized in one or two paragraphs, and there is a list of additional biographical sources published in book form or in standard biographical reference works.

Appendixes list biographees chronologically by date of birth, rank the individuals according to the relative coverage afforded to each in selected texts on the history of psychology, and list nineteenth- and twentieth-century contributors by the academic or research institution with which they were affiliated. There is a combined index by name, book titles, and subjects.

JOURNALS

191. **APA Monitor**. Vol. 1- , No. 1- . Washington, D.C., American Psychological Association, 1970- . monthly. $25.00/yr.(institutions). ISSN 0001-2114.

Published in newspaper format, this is the APA's membership awareness forum. The publication concentrates on recent scientific developments in psychology, clinical practice, professional education, and psychology in the public interest. Position openings, continuing education opportunities, and Association news and issues are among the regular features.

192. **Acta Psychologica**. Vol. 1- , No. 1- . Amsterdam, Netherlands, Elsevier Science Publishing, 1936- . 9 issues/yr. in 3v. $380.00/yr.(institutions). ISSN 0001-6918.

In this journal, substantive experimental, theoretical, and review articles are published on all aspects of human experimental psychology. Between 5 and 10 papers appear in each issue.

193. **Aggressive Behavior**. Vol. 1- , No. 1- . New York, Alan R. Liss, 1974- . bimonthly. $205.00/yr.(institutions). ISSN 0096-140X.

The overall content of this journal is described by its subtitle: "A Multidisciplinary Journal Devoted to the Experimental and Observational Analysis of Conflict in Humans and Animals." Published on behalf of the International Society for Research on Aggression, each issue contains about five research reports, with an occasional book review section. Issues also contain a literature awareness section composed of citations derived from the Institute for Scientific Information citation indexes and five of its *Current Contents* (see entry 18) services.

194. **American Journal of Orthopsychiatry**. Vol. 1- , No. 1- . New York, American Orthopsychiatric Association, 1930- . quarterly. $45.00/yr.(institutions). ISSN

Each issue divides approximately 15 articles among sections on theory and review, research, clinical, and service delivery. Reflecting the purpose of the Association, papers focus on interdisciplinary matters, interprofessional strategies, and prevention of mental illness, with an emphasis on related social issues.

195. **American Journal of Psychiatry**. Vol. 78- , No. 1- . Washington, D.C., American Psychiatric Association, 1921- . monthly. $56.00/yr.(institutions). ISSN 0002-953X.

The preeminent journal of American psychiatry, this publication is of interest to a broad spectrum of practitioners and researchers in mental health. Articles cover clinical research, diagnosis, treatment, professional issues, and the influence of psychiatric theory and practice. Each issue has about 10 lengthy research articles, with several other contributions consisting of shorter reports and articles, official news of the association, and 15 book reviews. This title was previously published as *American Journal of Insanity*.

196. **American Journal of Psychology**. Vol. 1- , No. 1- . Champaign, Ill., University of Illinois Press, 1887- . quarterly. $48.00/yr.(institutions). ISSN 0002-9556.

Founded by G. Stanley Hall at Johns Hopkins University, this journal claims to be the longest continuously published journal devoted to psychology. The research-based articles (roughly 10 per issue) are devoted to all facets of experimental psychology, especially human. Several book reviews are included in each issue.

197. **American Journal of Psychotherapy.** Vol. 1- , No. 1- . New York, Association for the Advancement of Psychotherapy, 1947- . quarterly. $75.00/yr.(institutions). ISSN 0002-9564.

This journal should be of interest to advanced students and professionals in all mental health care settings. Articles deal with etiology, incidence, identification, and treatment of aberrant behavior without a specific theoretical orientation. Some 10 theoretical or empirical articles are in each issue, with a few case study reports and several book and media reviews.

198. **American Psychologist.** Vol. 1- , No. 1- . Washington, D.C., American Psychological Association, 1946- . monthly. $200.00/yr.(institutions). ISSN 0003-066X.

As the official journal of the association, the publication's content emphasizes psychology as a profession: education, training, professional interaction, public and social issues, and contributions of the profession. One month (usually June or July) is devoted to APA reports of and activities for that year. Other issues contain about 10 articles each, with brief commentary pieces and professional announcements.

199. **Applied Ergonomics.** Vol. 1- , No. 1- . Guilford, England, Butterworth Scientific, 1970- . quarterly. $304.00/yr.(institutions). ISSN 0003-6870.

This journal is published in cooperation with the Ergonomics Society, which also publishes the more theoretical journal *Ergonomics*. *Applied Ergonomics* focuses on the adaptation of equipment design and use to the psychological and physiological needs of people. Related areas include design and adaptation of the work environment and the employment and training of personnel. Survey pieces and articles on specific applications in a particular setting are the most numerous, with a few case studies in each issue.

200. **Behavior Research Methods, Instruments, & Computers.** Vol. 16- , No. 1- . Austin, Tex., Psychonomic Society, 1984- . bimonthly. $84.00/yr.(institutions). ISSN 0743-3808.

Published previously as *Behavior Research Methods & Instrumentation*, this publication is devoted to research, methods, design, techniques, and computer applications in experimental psychology. About 15 articles appear in each issue, accompanied by occasional shorter articles and book reviews. Almost every issue contains a section of brief articles on algorithms and computer programs that can be used in specific research situations.

201. **Behavior Therapy.** Vol. 1- , No. 1- . New York, Association for Advancement of Behavior Therapy, 1970- . quarterly. $110.00/yr. ISSN 0005-7894.

The emphasis of the approximately seven articles in each issue is the application and evaluation of behavior change therapy as represented in experimental or clinical settings. Empirically based research articles predominate, with some review, theoretical, and methodological pieces.

202. **British Journal of Psychology.** Vol. 1- , No. 1- . Leicester, England, British Psychological Association, 1904- . quarterly. $181.00/yr.(institutions). ISSN 0007-1269.

One of several journals published by the Society, its focus is on human experimental psychology. Empirical research studies, reviews, and discussions of theoretical issues are published, with about 10 substantial papers per issue and several book reviews.

203. **Bulletin of the Psychonomic Society.** Vol. 1- , No. 1- . Austin, Tex., Psychonomic Society, 1973- . bimonthly. $74.00/yr.(institutions). ISSN 0090-5054.

All contributors to this journal are members of, or have their work sponsored by, members of the Psychonomic Society, a scholarly organization devoted to research in experimental psychology. Because membership is restricted to established scholars, the approximately 25 brief articles in each issue represent the evolving research in experimental areas.

204. **Canadian Psychology. Psychologie Canadienne.** Vol. 21- , No. 1- . Old Chelsea, Quebec, Canadian Psychological Association, 1980- . quarterly. $67.00/yr.(institutions). ISSN 0708-5591.

Previously published as *Canadian Psychologist* and *Canadian Psychological Review*, this journal is analogous to the American Psychological Association's *American Psychologist* (see entry 198). Articles focus on issues, theories, and practices of interest to all psychologists and include official documents and information on transactions of the association. Complementary journal publications of the Association include *Canadian Journal of Psychology* and *Canadian Journal of Behavioural Science*, which respectively emphasize empirical and applied research.

205. **Child Abuse and Neglect**. Vol. 1- , No. 1- . Elmsford, N.Y., Pergamon Press, 1977- . quarterly. $195.00/yr.(institutions). ISSN 0145-2134.

This is the official journal of the International Society for Prevention of Child Abuse and Neglect. It is the primary research journal on the abuse, neglect, and exploitation of children, including related issues in identification, treatment, prevention of abuse, and implications for child development. Some 10 theoretical, review, or research articles appear in each issue, with a few brief reports, case studies, and book reviews.

206. **Cognitive Psychology**. Vol. 1- , No. 1- . San Diego, Calif., Academic Press, 1970- . quarterly. $129.00/yr.(institutions). ISSN 0010-0285.

About four articles appear in each issue of this journal devoted to human cognition, which also covers the processes of learning and memory, perception, language processing, and problem solving. Although empirically based research studies dominate, articles on methodological issues, critical literature reviews, and theoretical models are published occasionally.

207. **Cognitive Science**. Vol. 1- , No. 1- . Norwood, N.J., Ablex Publishing, 1977- . quarterly. $82.50/yr.(institutions). ISSN 0364-0213.

This is the official journal of the Cognitive Science Society. It stresses a multidisciplinary approach to the study of human cognition and covers original research; theoretical and methodological studies on the processes of knowing; problem solving; inference and decision making; and intersecting research areas in memory, perception, intelligence, and the neurosciences. An average of five articles appear in each issue, with an occasional book review section.

208. **Contemporary Psychology**. Vol. 1- , No. 1- . Arlington, Va., American Psychological Association, 1956- . monthly. $160.00/yr.(institutions). ISSN 0010-7549.

Subtitled "A Journal of Reviews," *Contemporary Psychology* consists of critical reviews of books and audiovisual materials. About 40 titles are reviewed in depth, with another 20 or so receiving briefer reviews. Coverage of the discipline is broad, encompassing experimental, applied, and clinical titles as well as instructional materials. Unfortunately, the complete and comparative nature of the reviews also dictates substantial time lags between book and review publication dates.

209. **Developmental Psychology**. Vol. 1- , No. 1- . Arlington, Va., American Psychological Association, 1969- . bimonthly. $200.00/yr.(institutions). ISSN 0012-1649.

This is the primary research journal in the broad area of developmental psychology. Although articles on development throughout the life span and nonhuman studies are accepted, most concern human development from birth through adolescence. Approximately 20 articles reflect empirical contributions, theoretical views, literature reviews, and social policy papers. All areas of development are considered, including personality, emotional, cognitive, communication, social, and familial.

210. **Genetic, Social, and General Psychology Monographs**. Vol. 111- , No. 1- . Washington, D.C., Heldref Publications, 1985- . quarterly. $57.00/yr.(institutions). ISSN 8756-7547.

Originally begun as *Genetic Psychology Monographs* in 1935, the intent of this journal has been to publish articles considered too lengthy for a typical journal format. Usually fewer than five articles are published per issue, most representing empirically based research and papers that discuss theoretical issues in biological, behavioral, and social psychology.

211. **Health Psychology**. Vol. 1- , No. 1- . Hillsdale, N.J., Lawrence Erlbaum, 1982- . bimonthly. $180.00/yr.(institutions). ISSN 0278-6133.

As the official journal of the APA Division of Health Psychology, this publication is "devoted to furthering an understanding of scientific relationships between behavioral principles . . . and physical health and illness . . . ." The breadth of this title makes it appropriate for a wide range of researchers and practitioners in the health sciences, mental health, and rehabilitation professions. Reports of empirical research dominate (with occasional review and "brief report" contributions).

212. **Infant Behavior & Development**. Vol. 1- , No. 1- . Norwood, N.J., Ablex Publishing, 1979- . quarterly. $84.50/yr.(institutions). ISSN 0163-6383.

This is one of the few journals devoted solely to research on infancy, with an emphasis on human studies. The contributions are multidisciplinary, including research on the influence of social and environmental factors on infant behavior and development, perception, learning, and other processes at this developmental stage. About 10 articles and a few research notes are published in each issue.

213. **International Journal of Clinical and Experimental Hypnosis**. Vol. 1- , No. 1- . Philadelphia, Pa., Society for Clinical and Experimental Hypnosis, 1953- . quarterly. $82.00/yr.(institutions). ISSN 0020-7144.

This title publishes research and substantive case studies on the clinical uses of hypnosis in psychology, psychiatry, medicine, dentistry, and related health care fields. Five articles generally appear in each issue, accompanied by a few book or media reviews.

214. **Journal of Abnormal Psychology**. Vol. 70- , No. 1- . Arlington, Va., American Psychological Association, 1965- . quarterly. $120.00/yr.(institutions). ISSN 0021-843X.

The scope of this journal encompasses the etiology and pathology of human behavior, although not diagnosis and treatment. Experimental studies of human subjects, including abnormal populations and normal populations that exhibit abnormal behavior, are included; single case studies are not. This journal has been published under a variety of titles since its inception in 1906, including *Journal of Abnormal Psychology and Social Psychology* and *Journal of Abnormal and Social Psychology*.

215. **Journal of Applied Psychology**. Vol. 1- , No. 1- . Arlington, Va., American Psychological Association, 1917- . quarterly. $200.00/yr.(institutions). ISSN 0021-9010.

This is one of the most important and influential journals in applied psychology. Although the scope of applied psychology is inherently broad, most of its content concerns industrial settings, organizational studies, and the psychology of work. About 20 articles appear in each issue. Most are research investigations, with occasional review articles. Briefer research reports and "monographs" (i.e., lengthy articles) are also included.

216. **Journal of Child Psychology and Psychiatry and Allied Disciplines**. Vol. 1- , No. 1- . Oxford, England, Pergamon Press, 1960- . bimonthly. $190.00/yr.(institutions). ISSN 0021-9630.

As the official journal of the Association for Child Psychology and Psychiatry, this title addresses the needs of researchers in child and adolescent psychopathology and developmental disorders. Roughly 15 articles appear in each issue; they represent empirical papers, research reviews, and case studies, as well as book reviews and software descriptions.

217. **Journal of Consulting and Clinical Psychology**. Vol. 33- , No. 1- . Washington, D.C., American Psychological Association, 1969- . bimonthly. $240.00/yr.(institutions). ISSN 0022-006X.

This publication complements *Journal of Abnormal Psychology* (see entry 214) by publishing research on the assessment, diagnosis, and treatment of abnormal behavior. About 15 substantial papers are in each issue, along with several brief reports that represent ongoing research. Occasionally, half of the contents are devoted to a series of papers on a single topic. This title was originally published as *Journal of Consulting Psychology*. Beginning in 1989, assessment has been covered by a complementary journal, *Psychological Assessment*.

218. **Journal of Counseling Psychology**. Vol. 1- , No. 1- . Washington, D.C., American Psychological Association, 1954- . quarterly. $100.00/yr.(institutions). ISSN 0022-0167.

The content of this title consists largely of research papers on intervention, assessment, and diagnosis in counseling that will be of interest to psychologists and counselors in a variety of settings. Some articles also cover professional issues and research methodology, and there are occasional special topic issues. Around 20 papers appear per issue, including short reports and an occasional lengthy monograph paper.

219. **Journal of Cross-Cultural Psychology**. Vol. 1- , No. 1- . Newbury Park, Calif., Sage, 1970- . quarterly. $104.00/yr.(institutions). ISSN 0022-0021.

This journal focuses on research reports in which individual differences can be measured as being influenced across cultural (as opposed to social) differences. Usually six articles and several book reviews are published in each issue, and special-topic issues are published on occasion.

220. **Journal of Educational Psychology**. Vol. 1- , No. 1- . Washington, D.C., American Psychological Association, 1910- . quarterly. $120.00/yr.(institutions). ISSN 0022-0663.

Learning and cognitive processes, particularly in instructional or developmental contexts, are represented in empirical and theoretical papers in this journal. Content is not restricted by population educational level or age group. About 15 papers are arranged under themes such as reading comprehension, teacher effectiveness, and early learning, with the categories changing from issue to issue.

221. **Journal of Experimental Child Psychology**. Vol. 1- , No. 1- . San Diego, Calif., Academic Press, 1964- . bimonthly. (2 vols./yr.). $240.00/yr.(institutions). ISSN 0022-0965.

This publication's scope includes almost all aspects of child psychology but excludes disorders and therapeutic intervention. Most articles represent empirically based research with occasional reviews and theoretical pieces. This is a primary journal in child psychology research.

222. **Journal of Experimental Psychology: Animal Behavior Processes**. Vol. 1- , No. 1- . Washington, D.C., American Psychological Association, 1975- . quarterly. $72.00/yr.(institutions). ISSN 0097-7403.

223. **Journal of Experimental Psychology: General**. Vol. 1- , No. 1- . Washington, D.C., American Psychological Association, 1975- . quarterly. $72.00/yr.(institutions). ISSN 0096-3445.

224. **Journal of Experimental Psychology: Human Perception and Performance**. Vol. 1- , No. 1- . Washington, D.C., American Psychological Association, 1975- . quarterly. $160.00/yr.(institutions). ISSN 0096-1523.

225. **Journal of Experimental Psychology: Learning, Memory, and Cognition.** Vol. 8- , No. 1- . Washington, D.C., American Psychological Association, 1982- . bimonthly. $200.00/yr.(institutions). ISSN 0278-7393.

Each journal continues, in part, *Journal of Experimental Psychology* (1916-1974). *General* is most closely related to the previous title and publishes research studies of potential interest to all experimental psychologists. Its emphasis is on human studies. Only five or six lengthy reports appear in each issue, with commentary on previous reports or brief research notes.

The scope of the other *JEPs* are explained sufficiently by their subtitles. Their contents conform to a format of approximately 10 research studies per issue, although there are occasional theoretical contributions. The only significant change has been the title of *Learning, Memory & Cognition*, which was previously published as *Journal of Experimental Psychology: Human Learning and Memory*.

226. **Journal of Humanistic Psychology**. Vol. 1- , No. 1- . Newbury Park, Calif., Sage, 1961- . quarterly. $90.00/yr.(institutions). ISSN 0022-1678.

In this, the official journal of the Association for Humanistic Psychology, articles generally reflect the holistic view toward psychological health, the vastness of human potential, self-actualization, humanistic and alternative approaches to psychotherapy, and the need for personal growth. Some 10 articles per year reflect experimental research, theoretical and personal viewpoints, and applications of the humanistic approach.

227. **Journal of Mathematical Psychology**. Vol. 1- , No. 1- . San Diego, Calif., Academic Press, 1964- . quarterly. $165.00/yr.(institutions). ISSN 0022-2496.

This is one of the few journals emphasizing research in quantitative approaches to experimental and theoretical psychology. It is published under the auspices of the Society for Mathematical Psychology. Five substantive papers generally appear in each issue, accompanied by one or two book reviews.

228. **Journal of Memory and Language.** Vol. 24- , No. 1- . San Diego, Calif., Academic Press, 1985- . bimonthly. $145.00/yr.(institutions). ISSN 0749-596X.

Formerly published under the title *Journal of Verbal Learning and Verbal Behavior* (1962-1984), this journal is devoted to human faculties and their relationship to language learning, retention, and use. There are usually no more than 10 research articles per issue.

229. **Journal of Personality**. Vol. 14- , No. 1- . Durham, N.C., Duke University Press, 1945- . quarterly. $52.00/yr.(institutions). ISSN 0022-3506.

This title was originally published as *Character and Personality*. About 10 articles per issue are devoted to experimental papers. The areas of personality assessment and testing are not included. Special-topic issues have been published more or less annually.

230. **Journal of Personality and Social Psychology**. Vol. 1- , No. 1- . Washington, D.C., American Psychological Association, 1965- . monthly (2 vols./yr.). $400.00/yr.(institutions). ISSN 0022-3514.

The contents of this journal are divided into three primary categories: social cognition and attitudes, interpersonal and group behavior, and personality and individual differences. An average of 15 articles are published in each issue, most falling in the personality section. Empirical research papers are the most numerous, but some theoretical, review, and methodological papers are also included.

231. **Learning and Motivation**. Vol. 1- , No. 1- . San Diego, Calif., Academic Press, 1970- . quarterly. $125.00/yr.(institutions). ISSN 0023-9690.

Issues generally contain five substantial research articles on learning and motivational processes. Articles on biological influences dominate, reporting research with human or animal subjects.

232. **Memory & Cognition**. Vol. 1- , No. 1- . Austin, Tex., Psychonomic Society, 1973- . bimonthly. $84.00/yr.(institutions). ISSN 0090-502X.

About 10 research-based articles appear in each issue of this title, although substantive literature reviews and theoretical contributions are also published. The scope is broad, encompassing almost all areas of investigation in human memory and cognitive processes.

233. **Organizational Behavior and Human Decision Processes**. Vol. 35- , No. 1- . San Diego, Calif., Academic Press, 1985- . bimonthly. (3 vols/yr.) $255.00/yr.(institutions). ISSN 0749-5978.

Originally published as *Organizational Behavior and Human Performance*, this title has about 10 substantial articles per issue. The emphasis is on empirical research and theoretical developments and their implications in all area of human behavior in organizations, judgment and decision-making processes, and performance in applied settings.

234. **Perception & Psychophysics**. Vol. 1- , No. 1- . Austin, Tex., Psychonomic Society, 1966- . monthly. $120.00/yr.(institutions). ISSN 0031-5117.

In this journal, around 10 articles are published per issue and are devoted to reporting research and theoretical investigations in sensory processes, perception, and psychophysics (the study of the relationship between sensory stimulation and response). Studies on human and animal subjects are represented, although human studies predominate. Issues usually contain a section of brief research notes or comments on previous contributions.

235. **Perceptual and Motor Skills**. Vol. 1- , No. 1- . Missoula, Mont., Perceptual and Motor Skills, 1949- . bimonthly (2 vols./yr.). $192.50/yr.(institutions). ISSN 0031-5125.

Although the subject scope is interpreted broadly in this title, the primary areas of interest are human perception and motor behavior, with occasional animal studies. A large number of brief articles are published in each issue, sometimes as many as 70 or 80, as well as a few short book reviews. Despite the uneven quality of the contributions, this is an important title.

236. **Personnel Psychology**. Vol. 1- , No. 1- . Houston, Tex., Personnel Psychology, 1948- . quarterly. $50.00/yr.(institutions). ISSN 0031-5826.

All aspects of psychology in the workplace are included: employee selection, training, and appraisal; job satisfaction and employee motivation; personnel management; and professional issues. Research-based studies, surveys, literature reviews, and case studies are included. Until 1965, the journal contained the "Validity Information Exchange," which consisted of contributed case studies of measurement programs and predictors for employee selection and assessment.

237. **Professional Psychology: Research and Practice**. Vol. 1- , No. 1- . Washington, D.C., American Psychological Association, 1969- . bimonthly. $140.00/yr.(institutions). ISSN 0735-7028.

Although there is some coverage of clinical assessment and treatment, the emphasis in this journal is on issues in professional education and practice: community prevention and treatment programs, public image of practitioners and the profession, education and supervision of students and interns, public policy and standards and their implications for practice, and work settings and environments of mental health practitioners. About 15 lengthy articles appear in each issue, with occasional briefer reports.

238. **Psychological Bulletin**. Vol. 1- , No. 1- . Washington, D.C., American Psychological Association, 1904- . bimonthly (2 vols./yr.). $200.00/yr.(institutions). ISSN 0033-2909.

This title publishes review and interpretive articles on methodological issues and major developments in psychology. In particular, the reviews attempt to survey and connect related areas of research in the discipline. Studies on quantitative methods survey and critique methodological approaches to research. Original research findings are not presented. Generally, 15 articles are published in each issue.

239. **Psychological Reports**. Vol. 1- , No. 1- . Missoula, Mont., Psychological Reports, 1955- . bimonthly. (2 vols./yr.). $192.50/yr.(institutions). ISSN 0033-2941.

From 60 to 70 articles in all areas of psychology are published per issue of this journal. Studies involving clinical or abnormal populations appear to dominate, although articles on theoretical and methodological issues, experimental and applied studies, review pieces, and single case studies are also published. Most articles are research-based. There is a book review section. The breadth and number of articles contribute to this journal's uneven quality, although it remains an important, heavily cited title.

240. **Psychological Review**. Vol. 1- , No. 1- . Washington, D.C., American Psychological Association, 1894- . quarterly. $120.00/yr.(institutions). ISSN 0033-295X.

The title of this journal can be misleading, as it is not devoted to review articles. Approximately 10 articles in each issue discuss theory in psychological thought, including comparisons and contradictions among theoretical models and approaches. A section of theoretical notes contains briefer discussions on contributions in previous issues.

241. **Psychology and Aging**. Vol. 1- , No. 1- . Washington, D.C., American Psychological Association, 1986- . quarterly. $120.00/yr.(institutions). ISSN 0882-7974.

Each issue contains around 15 research articles and brief reports representing all aspects of adult aging. The two most prominent areas of research concern life events and social issues (e.g., care-giving, stereotyping, stress, work and the older adult) and research on intellectual and sensory process changes associated with the aging process. Studies on the elderly and gerontological issues generally outnumber those on other adult populations.

242. **Psychology of Women Quarterly**. Vol. 1- , No. 1- . New York, Cambridge University Press, 1976- . quarterly. $80.00/yr.(institutions). ISSN 0361-6843.

This is the primary journal on the psychology of women. Its scope is wide enough to encompass almost any situation or influence relevant to the psychology of women: psychobiological factors, sex-related individual differences, sex-role development and change, career and social influences, life span development, and therapeutic processes and practices. About 10 substantive articles are in each issue, as well as a few book and media reviews.

243. **Psychotherapy**. Vol. 1- , No. 1- . Phoenix, Ariz., Psychotherapy, 1963- . quarterly. $75.00/yr.(institutions). ISSN 0033-3204.

This is the official journal of the American Psychological Association's Division of Psychotherapy. Its content emphasizes theory, practice, and training in psychotherapeutic intervention. About 20 articles are in each issue, mostly empirical, although case studies, issue-oriented articles, and book reviews are included. Occasional special-topic issues are published.

244. **Sex Roles**. Vol. 1- , No. 1- . New York, Plenum, 1975- . monthly. $175.00/yr.(institutions). ISSN 0360-0025.

The scope of this journal is broad, encompassing gender role socialization in children, the impact of sex roles in social and employment participation, self-image and self-perception, attitudes and stereotyping, and a spectrum of other areas. In general, 10 empirical research and theoretical articles appear in each issue, with occasional briefer articles and book reviews.

245. **Teaching of Psychology**. Vol. 1- , No. 1- . Hillsdale, N.J., Lawrence Erlbaum, 1974- . quarterly. $60.00/yr.(institutions). ISSN 0098-6283.

As the official journal of the American Psychological Association's division concerned with teaching, this publication is devoted to disseminating information on teaching methods, techniques, and issues. Issues include several lengthy articles and a faculty forum section devoted to shorter contributions. Although the focus is the teaching of psychology from secondary school to professional education, most articles focus on the undergraduate curriculum and coursework.

ORGANIZATIONS

Encyclopedias

246. **Encyclopedia of Associations**. Detroit, Gale, 1961- . 5v. annual. price varies. ISSN 0071-0202.

The exhaustiveness of this set makes it a complete guide to professional, trade, charitable, avocational, and fraternal organizations. Volume 1 lists vital information on over 20,000 American organizations, including membership, address and telephone numbers, budget, affiliated organizations or divisions, publications, meetings, and a brief description. Entries are organized under 18 subject areas and then by a keyword or phrase indicating the area of primary interest, so that similar organizations appear together. A separate volume contains a keyword subject and organization index, which also acts as an index to associations in several other Gale directories of organizations. Volume 2 indexes entries by geographic location and executive officers.

Although these parts constitute the basic set, Gale publishes similar directories which expand and update this work. "New Associations and Projects," published between *Encyclopedia of Associations* editions, contains new entries and updates others. Recent additions to the basic set include *International Organizations*; *Regional, State, and Local Organizations*; and *Association Periodicals*.

Organizations

247. **American Art Therapy Association**. 505 E. Hawley St., Mundelein, IL 60060. (312) 949-6064.

This organization produces the only substantial journal on the therapeutic uses of art, *Journal of Art Therapy*. Its 2,700 members include art therapists and others devoted to the development, advancement, and practice of this therapeutic approach. The organization has also established criteria for the training of art therapists.

248. **American Association for Counseling and Development**. 5999 Stevenson Ave., Alexandria, VA 22304. (703) 823-9800.

This association has a broad scope of interest and membership, including professionals in every educational, rehabilitative, and therapeutic setting and orientation. The interests of its 50,000-plus members are reflected in the number and diversity of its periodical publications, including substantial research journals reflecting the defined research and professional interests of its divisions.

249. **American Association for Marriage and Family Therapy.** 1717 K St., N.W., #407, Washington, DC 20006. (202) 429-1825.

As the major professional society of marital and family therapists, AAMFT has about 13,000 members. It maintains regional training centers for therapists and sponsors research awards and scholarships. Its journal, *Journal of Marital and Family Therapy*, is an important one in the field.

250. **American Association of Sex Educators, Counselors, and Therapists.** 11 Dupont Circle, N.W., Suite 220, Washington, DC 20036. (202) 462-1171.

As its name suggests, this is a professional society of sex educators, therapists, and counselors. In addition to its interest in professional training and service delivery standards, it provides programming and advisory services to educational and social service agencies concerned with sex education and counseling. It publishes a newsletter, a research journal, training manuals, and an annual directory of certified sex educators and therapists.

251. **American Association on Mental Deficiency.** 1719 Kalorama Rd., N.W., Washington, DC 20009. (202) 387-1968.

This association is composed of professionals in the medical sciences, psychology, social work, education, and other fields concerned with the causes and treatment of mental retardation. In addition to publishing two journals (*American Journal of Mental Deficiency* and *Mental Retardation*), its 13,000 members support educational programs. It is also involved in public policy and legal issues surrounding the treatment and encouragement of mentally retarded citizens.

252. **American Dance Therapy Association.** 2000 Century Plaza, Suite 108, Columbia, MD 21044. (301) 997-4040.

This organization of 1,000 members conducts workshops, develops guidelines for the training of dance therapists, and conducts outreach programs to promote this therapeutic approach. Among its publications is *American Journal of Dance Therapy*.

253. **American Group Psychotherapy Association.** 25 E. 21st St., 6th Floor, New York, NY 10010. (212) 477-2677.

As a professional group, AGPA sponsors research and educational efforts in group therapy. Its 3,500 members include psychiatrists, psychologists, social workers, and others involved in the provision of mental health services. It publishes a membership directory, a monograph series, and the quarterly *International Journal of Group Psychotherapy*, among other things.

254. **American Orthopsychiatric Association.** 19 W. 44th St., #1616, New York, NY 10036. (212) 354-5770.

With over 10,000 members, this organization represents professionals from a variety of interrelated disciplines: educators, social workers, psychologists, psychiatrists, nurses, and other allied professions. The focus is on interdisciplinary approaches to the study and treatment of disordered human behavior. It publishes the quarterly *American Journal of Orthopsychiatry*.

255. **American Psychiatric Association.** 1400 K. St., N.W., Washington, D.C. 20005. (202) 682-6000.

This is the primary professional organization of psychiatrists, regardless of treatment orientation. Founded in 1844 and having a current membership of over 30,000, its emphasis is on psychiatric education, research, and practice, as well as the legal and social issues surrounding mental illness and its treatment. An active publishing program includes the influential *American Journal of Psychiatry*.

256. **American Psychoanalytic Association.** 309 E. 49th St., New York, NY 10022. (212) 752-0450.

This is one of the largest professional organizations of psychoanalysts, including those who are attending or have attended an accredited psychoanalytic institute. It promotes psychoanalytic training and standards of practice, with a focus on the integration of psychoanalysis with all areas of medicine.

257. **American Psychological Association.** 1200 17th St., N.W., Washington, D.C. 20036. (202) 955-7600.

Founded in 1892, APA is composed of nearly 60,000 psychologists, and its 41 divisions represent almost every theoretical and therapeutic approach to psychology. Membership includes both academic mental health practitioners and those employed in applied settings. The association maintains advocacy programs concerned with professional education and training, social and legal issues of psychological research and practice, and public education efforts on the applications of psychological research. It establishes the standards for and the credentials of doctoral-level training programs. Its publishing division produces *Psychological Abstracts* (see entry 129), the PsycINFO databases (see entry 154), books and directories, and several research journals. Some divisions produce their own journals, which are published by commercial publishers.

258. **American Psychosomatic Society.** 1311A Dolley Madison Blvd., McLean, VA 22101. (703) 556-9222.

This society's eclectic membership of medical professionals, psychologists, and social scientists is devoted to sponsoring and presenting research on the interaction of physical and mental health and illness. There are about 1,000 members. APS publishes the journal *Psychosomatic Medicine*.

259. **American Society for Psychical Research.** 5 W. 73d St., New York, NY 10023. (212) 799-5050.

As one of the largest organizations concerned with the study of paranormal phenomena, this 2,000-member organization focuses on fostering communication among those involved in phenomena investigation. It publishes a newsletter and a quarterly journal, maintains a speakers bureau, and sponsors educational programs and meetings.

260. **American Society of Clinical Hypnosis.** 2250 E. Devon Ave., Suite 336, Des Plaines, IL 60018. (312) 297-3317.

This organization represents about 4,000 physicians, psychologists, and other health service professionals who employ hypnosis in patient care or who conduct research on its clinical applications. It establishes training standards, provides a variety of professional education opportunities for those qualified to practice clinical hypnosis, and publishes *American Journal of Clinical Hypnosis*.

261. **Association for the Advancement of Behavior Therapy.** 15 W. 36th St., New York, NY 10018. (212) 279-7970.

Psychologists and psychiatrists comprise most of the 3,600 members concerned with the development and practice of behavior modification techniques, particularly in clinical settings. The association supports a broad professional education program and publishes several periodicals and directories, including the journal *Behavior Therapy*.

262. **British Psychological Society.** 48 Princess Road East, Leicester LE1 7DR England (0533) 549568.

With a membership of approximately 11,000, this is the primary professional association for British psychologists. It has about 17 special-interest divisions or sections. In addition to a bulletin, it publishes seven research journals in clinical, developmental, mathematical, medical, social, occupational, and general psychology, and sponsors professional meetings and conferences.

263. **Canadian Psychological Association.** Vincent Rd., Old Chelsea, Quebec J0X 2N0. (819) 827-3927.

Established in 1939, the association currently has over 4,000 members. It sponsors education efforts for members, publishes three professional and scholarly journals, and lobbies for the interests of practitioners and researchers. In addition to the national organization, similar organizations function at the provincial level.

264. **Cognitive Science Society.** c/o Alan M. Lesgold, Learning Research and Development Center, University of Pittsburgh, Pittsburgh, PA 15260. (412) 624-7046.

The membership of this society, which represents psychology and areas of specialization in engineering, reflects the interdisciplinary nature of current research in cognitive science. The society seeks to promote research on the simulation of human reasoning faculties by computerized means. It publishes the quarterly journal *Cognitive Science* and the proceedings of its annual conference.

265. **Gerontological Society of America.** 1411 K St., N.W., Suite 300, Washington, DC 20005. (202) 393-1411.

About 6,000 professionals from the helping professions and researchers comprise this society's membership, including those from medicine and the health sciences, social work, psychology, nutrition, and economics. The society sponsors scientific research and educational efforts on the process of aging: geriatrics, public policy, and behavioral and social aspects. It fosters and disseminates research in its two journals: *The Gerontologist* and *Journals of Gerontology.*

266. **Human Factors Society.** P.O. Box 1369, Santa Monica, CA 90406. (213) 394-1811.

This is a professional association of over 4,000 members dedicated to the study of human factors in the development of work systems and instruments. Its membership includes psychologists, engineers, and others involved in workplace environment design. Its publications include the journal *Human Factors* and the proceedings of its annual conference.

267. **International Transactional Analysis Association.** 1772 Vallejo St., San Francisco, CA 94123. (415) 885-5992.

Founded by Eric Berne, the "father" of TA, the association has 5,000 members who are mostly mental health professionals who adhere to this "interactional" approach to therapy. It publishes the quarterly *Transactional Analysis Journal*, a primary source of scholarly research on TA.

268. **National Association for Music Therapy.** 505 11th St., S.E., Washington, DC 20003. (202) 543-6864.

This organization is composed of about 3,800 music therapists, psychologists, and others interested in the development and use of music in therapy. It formulates standards for training therapists in this specialty. Among its publications is the quarterly *Journal of Music Therapy.*

269. **National Association of School Psychologists.** 655 15th St., N.W., Washington, DC 20005. (202) 347-3965.

Representing 9,000 school psychologists, NASP conducts continuing education activities for professional development, such as workshops and an annual conference, and fosters public awareness on the practice of school psychology. Publications include *School Psychology Review*, books, and research reports.

270. **Psi Chi.** 1400 N. Uhle, Suite 702, Arlington, VA 22201. (703) 522-2538.

Affiliated with the American Psychological Association, Psi Chi is a national honor society in psychology. Its 165,000 members in over 600 chapters sponsor research competitions, awards, and conventions at regional and national levels.

271. **Psychometric Society**. c/o ACT, P.O. Box 168, 2201 N. Dodge St., Iowa City, IA 52243. (319) 354-0520.

This society's membership is composed almost entirely of academic psychologists interested in the development of quantitative and statistical models and methodology for psychological processes. It sponsors scientific meetings and publishes the quarterly journal *Psychometrika.*

272. **Psychonomic Society**. c/o Michael Rashotte, Department of Psychology, Florida State University, Tallahassee, FL 32306. (904) 644-3511.

This organization's purpose is to promote communication among its 2,400 members, who are engaged in scientific research in psychology and allied areas. Membership is limited to scholars who have produced substantive research and have an established record of scholarly achievement. The society publishes several scholarly journals in experimental psychology and sponsors an annual conference.

273. **Society for Research in Child Development**. University of Chicago Press, 5801 Ellis Ave., Chicago, IL 60637. (312) 962-7470.

This society fosters research on all aspects of child development and disseminates its results. A very active publication program includes the bimonthly journal *Child Development*, a monograph series, and *Child Development Abstracts and Bibliography*. Membership consists of 4,000 academics and professionals from the social sciences, education, and the health science disciplines.

PUBLISHERS

274. **Academic Press**. 1250 Sixth Avenue, San Diego, CA 92101. (619) 231-0926.

Although Academic Press is a multidisciplinary publisher, much of its book, journal, and annual review publishing activity is in experimental psychology: human development, cognition, perception, educational psychology, personality, and psychophysiology. It also publishes a significant number of titles in social psychology and clinical psychology and psychiatry, including client assessment and therapy.

275. **American Psychiatric Press**. 1400 K Street, N.W., Washington, DC 20005. (202) 682-6262.

Predictably, this publisher's material focuses on books that deal with the diagnosis and treatment of mental disorders. It produces annual review volumes, several journal titles, and basic professional tools, such as the *DSM-III-R* (see entry 543). Much of its publication list concerns medical psychology, social issues in mental health and illness, psychiatry as a profession, and clinical and theoretical literature in psychiatry.

276. **American Psychological Association**. 1200 17th St. N.W., Washington, DC 20036. (202) 955-7600.

APA's active journal program touches practically every area of the discipline but represents only part of its publishing efforts. The association produces reference tools such as *Psychological Abstracts* (see entry 129) and its machine-readable counterparts PsycINFO (see entry 154) and PsycLIT (see entry 155), *PsycBOOKS* (see entry 128), professional standards and guides, instructional and vocational materials for use at undergraduate and graduate levels, and book publications.

277. **Basic Books**. 10 E. 53d St., New York, NY 10022. (212) 207-7057.

Aside from its trade titles in psychology aimed at the lay public, Basic Books publishes widely in the behavioral sciences, including professional handbooks. Its psychology titles focus on professional practice and public issues in clinical and social psychology.

278. **Brunner/Mazel Publishers**. 19 Union Square West, New York, NY 10003. (212) 924-3344.

Brunner/Mazel publishes in most of the social sciences but specializes in clinical psychology and psychiatry. It has books on topics in mental health for adults, children, and adolescents. Its other publications are professional resources for clinicians, including titles in psychological assessment.

279. **Elsevier Science Publishing**. P.O. Box 882, Madison Square Station, New York, NY 10159. (212) 989-5800.

Along with its North Holland imprint, Elsevier is known primarily as a source of scientific and technical titles that publishes heavily in the areas of human factors, ergonomics, cognitive science, and neuropsychology. It produces several important experimental journals in psychology that are primarily of interest to psychobiologists. Among its noteworthy series are titles published under the auspices of the International Union of Psychological Science, Advances in Psychology, and other proceedings of international conferences in experimental psychology.

280. **Guilford Press**. 72 Spring St., New York, NY 10012. (212) 431-9800.

In addition to books, Guilford publishes professional journals and other materials in the social sciences. Its publishing efforts are particularly strong in the areas of clinical psychology, psychiatry, gender and family issues, and social psychology. Although some of its works are of the self-help variety, most are aimed at researchers and clinicians.

281. **Jossey-Bass**. 350 Sansome St., San Francisco, CA 94104-1310. (415) 433-1767.

Jossey-Bass is known for its coverage of the social sciences. Titles in educational and school psychology, child development, social psychology, mental health, and statistics and methodology are especially strong. Publication formats include audiotapes, professional journals, and books in series. Among its noteworthy monographic series are New Directions in Child Development, New Directions for Methodology of Social and Behavioral Science, and Health Series.

282. **Lawrence Erlbaum Associates**. 365 Broadway, Hillsdale, NJ 07642. (201) 666-4110.

Erlbaum is a major publisher that specializes in social science texts and journals at the research, practitioner, and advanced student levels. In particular, it publishes monographs, journals, and series in all areas of experimental, clinical, and social psychology; neuropsychology and cognitive science; school and educational psychology; quantitative methods; behavioral medicine; human development; communications; and industrial and vocational behavior.

283. **MIT Press**. 55 Hayward Street, Cambridge, MA 02142. (617) 253-5646.

In addition to its publications in the pure and applied sciences, MIT Press includes titles in cognitive science, information processing, human perception, and neuropsychology. It is especially strong in its publication of human information processing and artificial intelligence.

284. **Routledge, Chapman & Hall**. 29 W. 35th St., New York, NY 10001-2291. (212) 244-6412.

Routledge is a multidisciplinary publisher, with strengths in the social sciences and humanities. Within psychology, titles focus on clinical and social psychology, theoretical issues, history, and research methods. The publisher's titles span the entire discipline and audience levels, from undergraduate texts to professional references and scholarly treatises.

285. **Sage Publications.** 2455 Teller Rd. Newbury Park, CA 91320. (805) 499-0721.

Sage describes itself as "The Publishers of Professional Social Science" and emphasizes area studies, sociology, and psychology. It publishes several established journals and monograph series in research methodology and social, developmental, and clinical psychology.

286. **Springer Publishing.** 536 Broadway, New York, NY 10012-3955. (212) 431-4370.

In addition to scientific and biomedical titles, Springer is known for its publishing in clinical psychology and counseling, behavioral medicine, aging and development, and social and family psychology. It also sponsors journals in the areas of mental health, aging, and health behavior.

287. **John Wiley.** 605 3rd Ave., New York, NY 10158-0012. (212) 850-6000.

Wiley publishes in a wide variety of disciplines but specializes in books and research journals in the social sciences. Its titles in industrial and organizational psychology, psychiatry and behavioral medicine, the neurosciences, and statistical methods are particularly strong.

DIRECTORIES

288. American Psychiatric Association. **Biographical Directory.** Washington, D.C., American Psychiatric Association, 1989. 1943p. index. $125.00; $85.00pa. LC 85-645241. ISBN 0-89042-186-2; 0-89042-185-4PA.

Considered by psychologists to be "the other APA," this directory of American Psychiatric Association members lists over 35,000 practicing psychiatrists and psychiatric researchers. New editions usually appear at six-year intervals.

As in other association directories, a brief history, lists of past officers, and additional information about the association is provided. Most entries for individuals include location, education and postgraduate training, language expertise, publications, professional services offered, and other professional affiliations. There are geographic area and foreign-language indexes.

289. American Psychological Association. **Directory.** Washington, D.C., American Psychological Association, 1989. 2v. index. $70.00. LC 49-3998. ISBN 0-912704-99-3.

290. American Psychological Association. **Membership Register.** Washington, D.C., American Psychological Association, 1982- . annual. $35.00. LC 72-623170. ISSN 0737-1446.

Together, these works comprise the largest single directory of living American clinical, applied, and research psychologists. The directory, currently published every four years, is an alphabetical list of approximately 70,000 individuals. Each entry contains current address and telephone number, educational background, areas of research or practice specialization, APA membership status and divisional affiliation, employment history, and licensure or other practitioner status. There are indexes by geographic location and divisional membership. Most of the important documents of the association are reprinted here, including "Guidelines for Providers of Psychological Services," the bylaws, a list of officers, and the code of ethics. There is also a useful chart delineating state requirements for licensing or certification of psychologists.

The membership register, published annually in years when there is no directory, serves to update the other title. Individual entries contain only mailing addresses, telephone numbers, membership status, and APA division affiliation, and there is a supplemental listing by APA division. It has been published under various titles since 1916.

291. **American Psychological Association's Guide to Research Support.** 3d ed. Kenneth Lee Herring, ed. Washington, D.C., American Psychological Association, 1987. 176p. index. $30.00pa. LC 87-17460. ISBN 0-912704-83-7.

This directory identifies sources of funding from federal agencies and private and charitable foundations that support basic and applied behavioral science research. Over 180 sources of federal support are listed under the executive department or administration, then hierarchically under the office, department, or division responsible for a grant's administration. A second section lists 70 private foundation and other nonprofit funding sources.

Information for entries includes names and addresses for contact persons, the areas of research supported by the agency, the types of awards and eligible grantees, approximate funds available, and general information on the application and review of proposals. A separate section lists additional directories and guides to funding. There are indexes by individual programs, subjects, and fellowships.

292. **International Directory of Psychologists, Exclusive of the U.S.A.** 4th ed. Kurt Pawlik, ed. New York, Elsevier Science Publishing, 1985. 1181p. $94.75. LC 85-10163. ISBN 0-444-87774-6.

This directory was published under the auspices of the International Union of Psychological Science. Data were gathered by the national psychology societies in each country. Individuals are listed alphabetically by country, and information includes their areas of specialization, a brief biography, and a mailing address. New editions are published every seven years, on the average. The breadth of coverage and completeness of individual entries vary widely. Predictably, representation among the 51 countries is heavily European and North American, as these are countries with established academic and professional traditions in psychology and organized professional associations. However, this is an important source for locating foreign psychologists who are not listed in other printed works.

293. **National Register of Health Service Providers in Psychology.** Washington, D.C., Council for the National Register of Health Service Providers in Psychology, 1975- . biennial. $110.00 (includes supplements). ISSN 0099-2151.

This register is published every two years with two intervening supplements. The 1989 edition lists approximately 16,000 psychologists in the United States who requested inclusion and met stated criteria. Foremost among these criteria are that they be licensed or certified by their states for the independent practice of clinical psychology, that they hold a doctorate from an accredited university, and that they have at least two years of supervised experience.

Although it contains a fairly extensive list of licensed practitioners, this directory is by no means comprehensive, because the individuals included are self-selected. For most, entries include address and telephone number, state in which certified to practice, theoretical orientation of the therapist (e.g., eclectic, humanistic, behavioral), ages served, and types of services offered (e.g., biofeedback, marital therapy, hypnosis).

294. Wolman, Benjamin B. **International Directory of Psychology: A Guide to People, Places, and Policies.** New York, Plenum, 1979. 279p. $45.00. LC 78-27868. ISBN 0-306-40209-2.

Although similar to *International Handbook of Psychology* (see entry 160), this title serves more of a directory function. Information for each country was compiled from questionnaires completed by national organizations of psychologists and other sources. Sixty-four countries are represented, and there are general surveys for sub-Saharan Africa and the Ukraine. The length and completeness of entries vary. Countries with well-established psychological organizations are represented by long essays; smaller nations (e.g., Nepal, Malta) have briefer ones. Included are names and descriptions of the major professional associations, the number and membership affiliations of psychologists, education and training opportunities in psychology, important research facilities and institutes, areas in which psychologists are employed, primary journal publications, and opportunities open to foreign psychologists for research and teaching.

295. **Graduate Study in Psychology and Associated Fields.** Washington, D.C., American Psychological Association, 1983- . annual. index. $18.50. ISSN 0742-7220.

Over 600 graduate programs in the United States are represented in this directory. Not all are in psychology departments. Many represent programs in schools of education, counseling and rehabilitation, and family and child studies. Entries are arranged in four separate sections: doctoral programs in psychology departments that hold accreditation from the American Psychological Association, other doctoral programs, psychology programs that offer less than the doctorate, and related departments that award degrees below the doctoral level. Program information includes number and composition of the faculty and the student body, admission and degree requirements, costs and financial aid, areas of specialization, and other information supplied by the departments. Introductory essays provide advice on applying to graduate programs in the field, examples of licensing procedures, and APA policies.

This directory was previously published as *Graduate Study in Psychology* (1968/1969-1983/1984). However, the current title reflects the broader program coverage.

Part IV

SPECIAL TOPICS IN PSYCHOLOGY

HISTORY AND THEORY

Guides

296. Arraj, James, and Tyra Arraj, comps. **A Jungian Psychology Resource Guide**. Chiloquin, Oreg., Tools for Inner Growth, 1987. 136p. index. $11.95pa. LC 87-25557. ISBN 0-914073-05-2.

This current and complete guide and directory to all things Jungian is intended for students and all those interested in his thought. Sources of information and services are divided into 10 chapters. There are two lists of print sources about Jung and his work: an annotated list of over 20 journals and newsletters in a variety of languages, and a basic list of almost 100 books and films. Two chapters describe professional groups, societies, and interest groups in the United States and around the world. There are a resource list of publishers and organizations with an interest in Jung's theory of psychology type, a list of professional conferences, book publishers and mail-order bookstores, specialized library collections and library reference tools, and a list of training programs in Jungian analysis. Most publications, organizations, and collections are described in some detail. There is an index of sources listed.

297. Gottsegen, Gloria Behar, and Abby J. Gottsegen. **Humanistic Psychology: A Guide to Information Sources**. Detroit, Gale, 1980. 185p. index. (Psychology Information Guide Series, v.6). $68.00. LC 80-16204. ISBN 0-8103-1462-2.

This is an excellent guide to an alternative to classical psychoanalysis and the behavioral school of thought. The authors define humanistic psychology as a movement concerned with the "self-awareness and interpersonal growth" of an individual, including interpersonal and social interactions.

The first nine chapters cite and descriptively annotate approximately 500 published books in the following areas: historical and theoretical works, texts and general works, affective education, encounter and sensitivity groups, nontraditional therapies, experimental approaches, industrial applications, applied settings, and reference sources. Some are further subdivided by subject area, as appropriate. Most items represented were published from the mid-1960s to the mid-1970s. Two additional chapters list and annotate periodicals and organizations. There are author, title, and subject indexes.

298. Sokal, Michael M., and Patrice A. Rafial. **A Guide to Manuscript Collections in the History of Psychology and Related Areas**. Millwood, N.Y., Kraus International, 1982. 212p. index. (Bibliographies in the History of Psychology and Psychiatry). $50.00. LC 81-17189. ISBN 0-527-84420-9.

The largest category in this volume, the guide to manuscripts, lists the personal papers and business correspondence of living and deceased individuals, professional associations and journals, and organizations whose activities were influential in the history of psychology. Individuals are the most heavily represented among the 501 entries. Each listing includes information on the collection's composition and size, a description of contributions to the profession, literary rights and restrictions on access, and other information on the manuscript repository. Listings are limited to U.S. manuscripts, whether in microform or paper. Paper collections of theorists outside the discipline but important to its development, such as David Hume and John Dewey, are listed. Coverage is uneven, despite reliance on the *National Union Catalog of Manuscript Collections*. A guide to manuscript repositories describes 15 major manuscript and oral history collections on the history of psychology, including information on using the collections effectively. There are a list of sources consulted and indexes by personal name/institution, repository, and subject.

299. Vincie, Joseph F., and Margreta Rathbauer-Vincie. **C. J. Jung and Analytical Psychology: A Comprehensive Bibliography**. New York, Garland, 1977. 297p. index. (Garland Reference Library of Social Science, v.38). price not reported. LC 76-52695. ISBN 0-8240-9874-9.

This is an extensive, international bibliography of substantive works on Jung, his work, and analytical psychology in general. Works by him are not included. The 3,687 citations to books and their chapters, journal articles, and doctoral dissertations are arranged chronologically, from 1906 to 1976. In addition, there are 344 references to book reviews of Jung's work, again drawing heavily on foreign-language materials and arranged chronologically. Although a few popular works are referenced, most are at the level of the advanced student and researcher. As might be expected, a large percentage are non-English publications, primarily in German, Italian, and French. If translated, the citations to the original work and the translations are cross-referenced. There are an author index and a detailed subject index.

300. Viney, Wayne, Michael Wertheimer, and Marilyn Lou Wertheimer. **History of Psychology: A Guide to Information Sources**. Detroit, Gale, 1979. 502p. index. (Psychology Information Guide Series, v.1) $68.00. LC 79-9044. ISBN 0-8103-1442-8.

Even in this bibliography of approximately 3,000 references (one-third annotated), selectivity was mandatory, as the authors have compiled books, book chapters, and articles on the breadth of the history of psychology. The first chapter lists reference works: directories, biographical directories, and other such works in general psychology and its subareas. The remaining sections list citations under a hierarchical arrangement. For example, the section on the general history of psychology provides several subcategories by geographic regions, specialized histories, and historiography. Other sections list systems and schools of psychological thought; subareas of the discipline; and histories of such related fields as education, psychiatry, and biology. The authors include works instrumental to and that reflect the development of psychological thought, not just historical surveys of the discipline. International contributions to the development of psychology are well covered, despite the exclusion of foreign-language material. Most items were published after 1940, although earlier classic works are also cited.

Bibliographies

301. Grenstein, Alexander. **The Index of Psychoanalytic Writings**. New York, International Universities Press, 1956-1971. 14v. $150.00(vols. I-V); $150.00(vols. VI-IX); $150.00(vols. X-XIV). LC 56-8932. ISBN 0-8236-8400-8(vols. I-V); 0-8236-8401-6(vols.VI-IX); 0-8236-8402-4(vols. X-XIV).

This is an exhaustive, international bibliography to the literature of psychoanalysis. The first five volumes include items published between 1900 and 1952; volumes 6 to 9 cover 1953 to 1959; and volumes 10 to 14 deal with material from 1960 to 1969. Each set consists of the basic arrangement of references by primary author (with cross-references provided for joint authors), followed by separate listings of anonymous or unsigned works and a wonderfully detailed subject index. The first and last set of volumes also have additions and corrections to references in the basic listing. The earliest set contains sections of references to reports and proceedings of psychoanalytic associations as well as an index to reviews of nonanalytic books appearing in psychoanalytic journals.

In total, the whole set includes more than 200,000 references to published books, abstracts, reviews, pamphlets, and articles. It is without parallel for complete and comprehensive coverage of the literature on the origins, development, and impact of psychoanalysis as a theory and therapy.

302. Mosak, Harold H., and Birdie Mosak. **A Bibliography of Adlerian Psychology**. Washington, D.C., Hemisphere; distr., New York, Halsted Press, 1975. 320p. index. price not reported. LC 74-26938. ISBN 0-470-61852-3.

Alfred Adler's post-Freudian associations spawned the school of individual psychology and its emphasis on the uniqueness of the self. They also resulted in a prolific literature that is partially represented in this comprehensive bibliography. Approximately 10,000 references cite articles, reviews, books, and chapters about Adler and his thought, on topics of interest to students of Adler by non-Adlerian writers, and by Adlerians on non-Adlerian topics. Although a variety of languages are represented, German and English works dominate the references, with many works listed under both the original and any translations. References extend from Adler's earliest work to the early 1970s.

The primary arrangement is under author, including multiple listings for coauthors and translators. An addendum of additional citations and a detailed subject index are provided.

303. Vande Kemp, Hendrika. **Psychology and Theology in Western Thought, 1672-1965: A Historical and Annotated Bibliography**. Millwood, N.Y., Kraus International, 1984. 367p. index. (Bibliographies in the History of Psychology and Psychiatry, 3). $75.00. LC 82-49045. ISBN 0-527-92779-1.

The core of this work consists of citations to 1,000 books and pamphlets on the integration of psychology and theology in the Western Judeo-Christian tradition. Supplemental lists include books in series, an annotated list of institutions and professional organizations concerned with psycho-theology, and a list of journals devoted to this topic. There are name, institution, title, and subject indexes.

The citations are topically arranged and encompass the historical basis for the integration of the disciplines, Biblical and theological underpinnings, the psychology of religion, pastoral counseling and Christian psychotherapies, issues in personality theory, and psychiatric and psychoanalytic perspectives. There is an abundance of foreign material cited, much of it in translation.

304. Watson, Robert I., Sr. **The History of Psychology and the Behavioral Sciences: A Bibliographic Guide**. New York, Springer Publishing, 1978. 241p. price not reported. LC 77-17371. ISBN 0-8261-2080-6; 0-8261-2081-4pa.

Watson cites almost 800 published works on the history, development, and structure of psychology. Most references represent books, with some book chapters and journal articles included. There is no restriction by language: English-language material dominates, but French and German works are also common. Most publications are from the twentieth century.

Items are listed under the following broad areas (each area is further subdivided, for a total of 45 categories): general works, including reference tools; historical accounts, divided by subdisciplines in psychology and related disciplines; historical methods; historigraphic fields; and historigraphic theories, works that take a more historical, philosophical approach to scientific discovery and psychology. The liberal cross-references are important as there are no name or author indexes. Similarly, the lack of a subject index makes it difficult to pinpoint specific theoretical orientations (e.g., behaviorism) or subdisciplines (e.g., memory).

Handbooks

305. Hillner, Kenneth P. **History and Systems of Modern Psychology: A Conceptual Approach**. New York, Gardner, 1984. 348p. index. $32.50. LC 83-5596. ISBN 0-89876-030-5.

Hillner postulates that "the history of psychology over the past century can be viewed as a progression of a basic set of dominant or highly influential systems" (p. xxvi). These systems are divided between classical (pre-1930) and contemporary periods. His introduction defines the concepts of system and theory and generally outlines the psychological systems represented in the volume.

Chapters cover structuralism; functionalism; gestalt; behaviorism; Watsonian, Skinnerian, and cognitive behaviorism; depth psychology (psychoanalysis); humanism and phenomenology; and dialectical psychology. Each section follows a common organization that makes the systems easy to compare: basic premises, acceptable research methodologies, historical origins, chief figures, primary areas of research, and contemporary significance to the disciplines. A concluding chapter defines the intellectual linkages among systems, followed by a selected bibliography of primary and other seminal sources and a subject index.

306. Kimble, Gregory A., and Kurt Schlesinger, eds. **Topics in the History of Psychology**. Hillsdale, N.J., Lawrence Erlbaum, 1985. 2v. index. $39.95/vol. LC 84-24709. ISBN 0-89859-311-5(v.1); 0-89859-312-3(v.2).

Unlike similar works, which tend to focus on the schools or philosophical theories in psychology, this set surveys research and theoretical trends within specific areas of psychology. Introductory chapters in each volume discuss the chronology of and trends in psychology's history. However, the remaining 17 chapters consider the issues specific to various fields of study, such as ethology, sensation, learning and memory, conditioning, testing, human development, psychopathology and therapy, behavioral genetics, sleep and dreams, and personality theory.

The contributed chapters are lucidly written and, with few exceptions, comprehensible by students. The essays acquaint students with basic knowledge of an area and researchers with an area outside their specialization. Reference lists introduce beginners to the seminal literature in an area of study. Illustrations, mostly line drawings, are sparse but appropriate. There are name and subject indexes.

307. Lawry, John D. **Guide to the History of Psychology**. Lanham, Md., University Press of America, 1990. 114p. index. $15.95pa. LC 90-41777. ISBN 0-8191-7851-9.

This little guide is hardly comprehensive but is a handy reference companion nonetheless. The first of its five sections provides biographical sketches of 118 major contributors to the theoretical development of psychology as a science, from antiquity to the mid-twentieth century. The focus in each biography is the unique and outstanding contribution of the individual and that person's impact on the development of psychology. The "Innovations" section lists significant firsts in psychology, such as the first person to use a specific experimental approach and the first journal established. There is a glossary of about 50 philosophical terms, primarily of mind-body theories and related areas. The last two sections cite important primary and secondary publications. The former is especially important because each citation is accompanied by a brief phrase on the importance of that publication. The list of secondary publications consists of survey works and biographies. There are name and subject indexes. This is a reprint edition of a Littlefield, Adams 1981 publication.

308. Neel, Ann. **Theories of Psychology: A Handbook**. rev. ed. New York, Schenkman, 1977. 699p. index. price not reported. LC 76-39778. ISBN 0-470-98968-8; 0-470-98969-6pa.

In her preface, Neel describes the theories selected for inclusion as "matured theories," or seminal research accepted and incorporated into the corpus of the discipline's knowledge. For this reason, some areas receive greater coverage than others. For example, lengthy chapters are devoted to behaviorist and analytic theories, but there is limited coverage of topics in applied psychology, sensation, and perception. Also, the discussion of developmental psychology is almost exclusively devoted to Piaget.

Within these limitations, Neel conveys an appreciation of the contributions of various schools of thought. Aside from the introductory section and the two last update sections, the remaining eight follow a consistent format by describing relevant research, highlighting the most important issues, and providing classified reading and reference lists. There is a subject index.

309. Sahakian, William S. **History and Systems of Psychology**. New York, Schenkman, 1975. 494p. index. o.p. LC 74-26354. ISBN 0-470-74975-X; 0-470-74977-6pa.

Until the mid-1900s, the history and development of psychology was often seen as a system of schools of thought that were associated with a particular institution and that evolved according to the contributions of those associated with it. Using this approach, Sahakian highlights major theorists and researchers, stretching back to antiquity and covering contributions from non-Western traditions.

Chapters are divided under one of seven broad sections: antiquity through the Renaissance, British psychology, German psychology, schools of Paris and Vienna, the American tradition, Soviet psychology, and the Orient and Latin America. Each chapter reflects a particular school; for example, the section on Germany discusses the rise of physiological psychology at Berlin, the rise of experimental psychology at Leipzig, and Gestalt psychology. Individuals are afforded brief biographies, discussions of their theories and contributions, and some excerpts from pertinent works. Most importantly, the contributions of each are discussed in the contexts of how the disciplines evolved. There are subject and name indexes.

310. Watson, Robert I., Sr. and Rand B. Evans. **The Great Psychologists: A History of Psychological Thought**. 5th ed. New York, HarperCollins, 1991. 658p. index. $51.50. LC 90-39371. ISBN 0-06-041919-9.

Contrary to what the title implies, this is not a biographical work. Instead, it concentrates on the origins, contributions, and implications of philosophies and methodologies in the discipline. Beginning with Thales and moving through Hippocrates, Plato, Galen, and Acquinas, early chapters discuss the contributions of ancient philosophers and scientists. Most of the remaining chapters focus on the influence of individuals or the schools they inspired: Decartes, Locke, and Kant; Binet and French psychology; Wertheimer and Gestalt; Watson and behaviorism; Freud and psychoanalysis; Ebbinghaus and memory; and Hall, Cattell, and the flowering of American psychology.

Other chapters focus on recent international developments in the discipline. Throughout, biographical information is supplied for individuals but not emphasized. Chapters are well written and do not assume considerable knowledge of the disciplines. There are indexes of names and subjects.

RESEARCH METHODS

Handbooks

311. Andrews, Frank M., et al. **A Guide for Selecting Statistical Techniques for Analyzing Social Science Data**. 2d ed. Ann Arbor, Institute for Social Research, University of Michigan, 1981. 70p. $8.00pa. LC 81-7082. ISBN 0-87944-274-3.

This is not a handbook that contains chapters, nor a guide to statistical techniques and their use. Rather, it is focused on a 28-page "decision tree" designed to help advanced students and researchers select a statistic or statistical technique to meet a specific experimental need. By responding to a series of hierarchical questions about the data available and its use, the chart directs users to appropriate techniques or statistics.

Use of the charts assumes a certain level of psychometric sophistication, but the book contains several features to assist the novice. Appendix A consists of a page-by-page list of statistics and statistical techniques; it provides appropriate citations for additional information, with a complete set of references provided at the end of the book. Tables that match a given calculation or specific technique with a software package or program are supplied as appendix B. Appendix C briefly describes new or seldom-used statistical techniques. There is a short glossary.

312. Ferguson, George A., and Yoshio Takane. **Statistical Analysis in Psychology and Education**. 6th ed. New York, McGraw-Hill, 1989. 587p. index. (McGraw-Hill Series in Psychology). $37.80. LC 88-27126. ISBN 0-07-020485-3.

The authors designed this volume as a text for advanced students, as is evidenced by the list of basic terms and exercises appended to each chapter. However, it also serves as a handbook to the analysis and interpretation of experimental data in psychology and education. The 28 chapters are divided into four parts. The first introduces the use and representation of standard statistical methodology, such as statistical notation, sampling, regression and correlation, and probability. Part 2 focuses on experimental design and the analysis of variance and covariance. Part 3 contains chapters on nonparametric statistics, variables with unknown distribution, and the statistics of rank. Part 4 consists of six chapters on psychological test construction, including error, multiple regression, and factor analysis. Thirteen appendixes contain statistical reference tables and charts, and there is a subject index.

313. Rossi, Peter H., James D. Wright, and Andy B. Anderson, eds. **Handbook of Survey Research**. San Diego, Calif., Academic Press, c1983, 1985. 755p. index. (Quantitative Studies in Social Relations). o.p.(hc.); $49.95pa. LC 83-3869. ISBN 0-12-598226-7; 0-12-598227-5pa.

This work will be most commonly consulted for its coverage of techniques on construction, administration, and analysis of surveys and questionnaires. Several chapters address population definition and sampling, writing survey questions, measurement and scaling techniques, response effects, and the issues of incomplete and missing data. A variety of social survey methods are covered, including telephone, mail, and interview. Most chapters include sample case studies or examples to illustrate data-gathering principles and problems. Remaining chapters discuss the development, evolution, and uses of sample surveys; the uses of computers in survey research (the information is still valuable despite its dated content); and the pitfalls associated with the use of surveys as indicators of social trends. A subject index is included.

314. Udinsky, B. Flavian, Steven J. Osterlind, and Samuel W. Lynch. **Evaluation Resource Handbook: Gathering, Analyzing, Reporting Data**. San Diego, Calif., EdITS, 1981. 250p. index $17.95; $13.95pa. LC 81-065479. ISBN 0-912736-24-0; 0-912736-26-7pa.

Thirty-nine articles discuss techniques, issues, and approaches commonly used in the social sciences, particularly in the behavioral sciences. Chapters are topically arranged and cover issues and ethics; problem-solving approaches, such as the Delphi technique, Q-sort, and task analysis; data classification, such as sampling and factor analysis; the quality control of data; data-gathering techniques; scales and measurements, such as semantic differentials and the Likert scale; issues and techniques in data analysis; and the reporting of results. Each chapter defines the technique and its applications, strategies for using the technique, pre- and post-design considerations, and its limitations. Charts, graphs, and examples illustrating applications are plentiful. A brief, selective bibliography is appended to each chapter, primarily listing books and professional standards. There is a selective, cumulated bibliography to additional materials, as well as name and subject indexes.

The volume is intended as a resource for a broad audience, from students to practitioners. Chapters are relatively jargon-free and will be comprehensible to persons as yet unversed in statistical research and evaluation.

315. Yaremko, R. M., et al. **Reference Handbook of Research and Statistical Methods in Psychology: For Students and Professionals**. New York, Harper & Row, 1982. 335p. o.p. LC 81-6556. ISBN 0-06-047332-0.

Part dictionary, part handbook, this is a very handy guide to terms and concepts frequently employed in behavioral research. An outline to the areas covered in the work defines the scope of the entries to follow, which include titles on experimental design, statistical methods, psychometrics, and procedures employed in empirical studies of psychological phenomena. The dictionary section contains brief definitions, often with examples and cross-references to other terms. Graphs, illustrations, and charts are provided as needed, but the authors' emphasis is on providing brief, workable definitions for the student.

In the book's function as a handbook, a series of appendixes provides statistical charts and tables frequently consulted in behavioral science research. One appendix consists of 23 tables for quick reference (e.g., critical values of 14 statistical tests, tables of the binomial distribution, standard normal curve). Four other appendixes provide a table of random numbers, metric symbols and conversion values, Greek symbols, and a flow chart to aid in statistical analysis.

Dictionaries and Encyclopedias

316. Wilkening, Howard E. **The Psychology Almanac: A Handbook for Students**. Monterey, Calif., Brooks/Cole, 1973. 241p. o.p. LC 72-86775. ISBN 0-8185-0020-4.

This title is both a dictionary and a statistical sourcebook. The dictionary section lists individuals, concepts, and all words (whether common or scientific) normally found in psychology. Definitions, from 10 to over 200 words long, are often accompanied by line drawings of tables, physiological phenomena, formulas, and graphs. Next there are over 70 pages of common statistical terms and symbols, graphs, and tables commonly used or referred to in behavioral research literature (e.g., arcs in transformation, orthogonal Latin squares, tables of squares and cube roots).

Among other features are descriptions of selected journals in psychology and of symbols used in statistics. Although there are a number of good, current dictionaries and encyclopedias covering general areas of psychology, this work retains its value as a statistical reference.

Directories

317. **Computer Use in Psychology: A Directory of Software**. Michael L. Stoloff and James V. Couch, eds. 3d ed. Washington, D.C., American Psychological Association, 1992. 363p. index. $29.95pa. ISBN 1-55798-173-6.

The 869 computer software products listed in this directory fall into four categories: simulations and tutorials for use in psychology instruction, software for use in clinical practice and applied settings, programs for statistics and data manipulation and other research uses, and programs for administering and interpreting psychological assessment instruments (this is the largest section, with 363 listings). Most are designed for use with personal computers. The products listed are representative rather than exhaustive.

Each entry briefly discusses the purpose and intended use of the software, availability, cost, and hardware requirements. There are software author and title indexes and separate subject indexes to each of the four usage categories noted above.

318. **Psychware Sourcebook.** Samuel E. Krug, comp. and ed. 3d ed. Kansas City, Mo., Test Corporation of America, 1988. 613p. index. $85.00; $45.00pa. LC 88-8639. ISBN 0-933701-27-6; 0-933701-26-8pa.

Subtitled "A Reference Guide to Computer-based Products for Assessment in Psychology, Education, and Business," *Psychware* describes the features of and uses for 451 software products. Among the types of tests represented are vocational, ability, interest/attitude, motivation, neuropsychological, personality, and self-administered questionnaires. Most are intended for computerized test interpretation and clinical report generation, although some represent test administration products.

The software is listed alphabetically by title. An appendix reproduces computer-generated reports for over half of the software listed, to a maximum of four pages per product. The test title index lists all software intended for use with its parallel print measure (e.g., Halstead-Reitan, Rorschach), which is especially helpful if the test name is not mentioned in the software name. There are also indexes by producer, product category, intended applications, support services, and hardware requirements.

TEST CONSTRUCTION AND PSYCHOLOGICAL MEASUREMENT

Handbooks

319. Goldstein, Gerald, and Michel Hersen, eds. **Handbook of Psychological Assessment**. 2d ed. Elmsford, N.Y., Pergamon Press, 1990. 650p. index. (Pergamon General Psychology Series, v.131) $90.00. LC 89-27356. ISBN 0-08-035866-7.

The research literature of psychological assessment is at once so broad and so specialized that a truly comprehensive handbook on all its aspects is practically impossible. This volume attempts to survey and organize the broad and sprawling base of knowledge. Each chapter covers a considerable amount of intellectual territory of interest to the graduate student and professional. Following an introductory historical essay on psychological testing and chapters on test construction and scaling, several sections examine various types of assessment: intelligence; achievement, interest, and aptitude; neuropsychological; behavioral; and personality. There are also sections that cover psychiatric interviewing and the use of assessment tools and procedures in treatment and intervention. Social and legal controversies receive less attention. Author and subject indexes are supplied.

319a. **Standards for Educational and Psychological Testing**. By Committee to Develop Standards for Educational and Psychological Testing. Washington, D.C., American Psychological Association, 1985. 100p. index. $23.00. LC 85-071493. ISBN 0-912704-95-0.

Developed jointly by APA, the American Educational Research Association, and the National Council of Measurement in Education, these standards can be applied in any testing situation or setting. They should be of interest to test authors, publishers, and users. Technical standards cover validity, reliability, norms, and other elements of test construction and publication. "Standards for Professional Use" addresses specific test applications or uses with certain populations, such as employment or clinical settings, testing in schools, program evaluation, and occupational certification and licensure. A separate section covers the considerations of linguistic minorities and the handicapped. The final section deals with test administration and scoring, the rights of test takers, and the use of scores obtained. Each standard is accompanied by brief commentary on how it might be applied in practice. There are a glossary of testing terms, a bibliography of related testing standards, and a subject index.

Bibliographies of Measures

320. Beere, Carole A. **Gender Roles: A Handbook of Tests and Measures.** Westport, Conn., Greenwood Press, 1990. 575p. index. $75.00. LC 89-17033. ISBN 0-313-26278-0.

321. Beere, Carole A. **Sex and Gender Issues: A Handbook of Tests and Measures.** Westport, Conn., Greenwood Press, 1990. 605p. index. $85.00. LC 90-32466. ISBN 0-313-27462-2.

322. Beere, Carole A. **Women and Women's Issues: A Handbook of Tests and Measures.** San Francisco, Jossey-Bass, 1979. 550p. index. (Jossey-Bass Social and Behavioral Science Series). $52.95. LC 79-88106. ISBN 0-87589-418-6.

Women and Women's Issues, Beere's original volume, contains descriptions of 235 published and unpublished instruments that measure variables pertinent to women's issues, including attitudes, somatic and sexual issues, sex roles and stereotypes, and gender knowledge. These measures cover both experimental (unpublished) and commercially published tests produced from the 1920s to 1977.

Beere's effort to update the 1979 volume uncovered a wealth of new and improved instruments that resulted in the two subsequent handbooks. *Gender Roles* covers 211 measures produced from 1977 to mid-1988, with emphasis on gender roles and related attitudes. Work and employment, marriage, parenting, and child-rearing are some of the topics explored. Sixty-seven measures appear in both *Gender Roles* and *Women and Women's Issues*. The 197 instruments represented in *Sex and Gender Issues* are intended to measure some aspect of or attitude toward interpersonal relationships and sexuality, such as contraception and abortion, dating, homosexuality, rape and family violence, body image and eating disorders, and menstruation and menopause.

Tests in each volume are arranged under broad subject categories. Each entry for a measure follows a standard format and includes bibliographic information, a description of the instrument, intended uses, reliability and statistical data, administration and development of the test, evaluative comments, studies in which it had been used, and a bibliography of items on the test. There are indexes by test titles, test authors, variables measured, and study authors.

The extent and quality of Beere's commentary is outstanding. The number and importance of measures concerning women's issues make these essential research sources in gender issues.

323. Chun, Ki-Taek, Sidney Cobb, and John R. P. French. **Measures for Psychological Assessment: A Guide to 3,000 Original Sources and Their Applications**. Ann Arbor, Mich., Survey Research Center, Institute for Social Research, 1975. 664p. index. $40.00. LC 74-620127. ISBN 0-87944-168-2.

This is a comprehensive bibliography of experimental (unpublished) mental health measures; its intent is to make these instruments accessible to students and researchers. The items cited appeared in 26 journals in psychology and sociology between 1960 and 1970. Articles in which measures were first described and used are listed in the section on primary references. Each of the 3,000 citations includes author, test title, and basic bibliographic information. Most also provide normative data, validity, other information specific to the instrument, and at least one reference to citations in the book's applications section. This section lists 6,600 articles in which the scales were used. Despite the cross-references between the two sections, the most effective method of locating measures is by using the author or subject indexes that precede the primary references.

324. Comrey, Andrew L., Thomas E. Backer, and Edward M. Glaser. **A Sourcebook for Mental Health Measures**. Los Angeles, Calif., Human Interaction Research Institute, 1973. 462p. index. price not reported.

This compilation of psychological measures was produced as a joint effort of the Human Interaction Research Institute, the Institute for Social Research at the University of Michigan, and the National Clearinghouse for Mental Health Information. Although many of the 1,100 unpublished measures were culled from research reported in the journal literature, others represent in-house questionnaires, surveys, rating scales, and inventories used at research institutes and mental health services.

Coverage is not limited to mental health and psychopathology scales, although a significant number concern alcohol and drug abuse, therapeutic processes and outcomes, aspects of psychological functioning, and the like. Among the 45 broad categories are those covering mental health service delivery, marital and family interaction, social and educational attitude surveys, educational adjustment, and vocational guidance. Each test entry indicates where it was developed; lists the authors and their addresses; and provides a 300-word abstract describing the content, construction, use, and availability of the measure. Citations to relevant journal articles are included as appropriate. There are author and title indexes. Although many test bibliographies have been published since this pioneering effort, the sourcebook remains a valuable source of information about little-known, seldom-cited measures.

325. Cook, John D., et al. **The Experience of Work: A Compendium and Review of 249 Measures and Their Use**. San Diego, Calif., Academic Press, 1981. 335p. index. (Organizational and Occupational Psychology Series). $96.00. LC 81-66680. ISBN 0-12-187050-2.

This volume cites experimental measures of work attitudes, values, and perceptions as published in the journal literature from 1974 to mid-1980. Instruments are organized under eight broad categories that cover such areas as job satisfaction and commitment, occupational mental health, motivation, work values, work roles, and leadership styles.

Some 100 inventories, questionnaires, scales, and surveys are reprinted in full, with scoring procedures, reliability and validity data, and similar information, as well as applications recorded in the 15 source journals searched by the authors. The remaining 149 items are represented by descriptions of the instruments and summaries of their research applications. Rounding out the book are an extensive list of works cited and an index to the scales and subscales.

326. Corcoran, Kevin, and Joel Fischer. **Measures for Clinical Practice: A Sourcebook**. New York, Free Press/Macmillan, 1987. 482p. index. $35.00. LC 86-25819. ISBN 0-02-906681-6.

The limitations of copyright and concerns for statistical integrity mean that few volumes reproduce testing instruments. This volume describes and presents 127 instruments intended to monitor client progress with problems frequently seen in clinical practice. They consist of rapid assessment instruments—brief questionnaires to be completed by the client that do not require extensive expertise to score and interpret. Over one-half are intended for use with adults and families. In addition to the measure and related bibliographic information, each entry contains a brief description of its intended use, scoring, and statistical data. The excellent introductory chapters discuss basic principles of testing, the importance and hazards of using assessment tools, and selecting and administering instruments. A subject index provides access to the material.

327. Eliot, John, and Ian Macfarlane Smith. **An International Directory of Spatial Tests**. Berkshire, England, NFER-Nelson, 1983. 458p. index. ISBN 0-7005-0517-2.

This is a directory of pencil-and-paper tests that are designed to measure spatial ability, including the perception and retention of visual forms and manipulation of visual shapes. Almost 400 tests are listed, arranged under 13 categories that represent the tasks involved (e.g., maze, embedded figures, figural rotations). Each entry provides a sample test item, instructions, availability status (commercially available, out-of-print, or unpublished research measure), bibliographic information, intended uses, and a brief description of content and scoring procedures. Some entries give statistical data on reliability and validity. The cited references are primarily to *Mental Measurements Yearbook* (see entry 349) or *Tests in Print* volumes (see entry 350), with a smattering of other references. Preliminary chapters discuss the history and classification of spatial tests, and a concluding chapter details factors for test selection. There are author and test title indexes.

328. **The ETS Test Collection Catalog. Volume 1: Achievement Tests and Measurement Device.** Compiled by Test Collection, Educational Testing Service. Phoenix, Ariz., Oryx Press, 1986. 286p. index. $49.50pa. LC 86-678. ISBN 0-89774-286-6.

329. **The ETS Test Collection Catalog. Volume 2: Vocational Tests and Measurement Devices.** Compiled by Test Collection, Educational Testing Service. Phoenix, Ariz., Oryx Press, 1988. 160p. index. $39.50pa. LC 86-678. ISBN 0-89774-439-X.

330. **The ETS Test Collection Catalog. Volume 3: Tests for Special Populations.** Compiled by Test Collection, Educational Testing Service. Phoenix, Ariz., Oryx Press, 1989. 202p. index. $49.50pa. LC 86-678. ISBN 0-89774-477-2.

331. **The ETS Test Collection Catalog. Volume 4: Cognitive Aptitude and Intelligence Tests.** Compiled by Test Collection, Educational Testing Service. Phoenix, Ariz., Oryx Press, 1990. 158p. index. $42.50pa. LC 86-678. ISBN 0-89774-558-2.

332. **The ETS Test Collection Catalog. Volume 5: Attitude Tests.** Compiled by Test Collection, Educational Testing Service. Phoenix, Ariz., Oryx Press, 1991. 130p. index. $45.00pa. LC 86-678. ISBN 0-89774-617-1.

333. **The ETS Test Collection Catalog. Volume 6: Affective Measures and Personality Tests.** Compiled by Test Collection, Educational Testing Service. Phoenix, Ariz., Oryx Press, 1992. 165p. index. $49.50pa. LC 86-678. ISBN 0-89774-692-9.

This set acts as an indexing tool to the ETS collection of research instruments of limited distribution. They are available as ERIC documents, reproduced in journal articles as research instruments, and published commercially. Each volume supplies bibliographic information on approximately 1,000 tests, including a brief annotation, the availability of subtests/subscores, and the target audience. Availability is also provided, consisting of publisher's address, journal citation, the ETS *Tests in Microfiche* research collection, ERIC (see entry 142), or other source as appropriate.

The format of all volumes emulates the ERIC indexes, including the assignment of major and minor descriptors and identifiers. Accordingly, subject indexes use the controlled vocabulary of *Thesaurus of ERIC Descriptors* (see entry 53). There are title and author indexes.

334. Fredman, Norman, and Robert Sherman. **Handbook of Measurements for Marriage and Family Therapy.** New York, Brunner/Mazel, 1987. 218p. $28.95. LC 87-9417. ISBN 0-87630-466-8.

Other volumes that cover marriage and family assessment contain information on more tests, but this volumes focuses on unpublished measures. It is also designed for novices in the field of measurement. For example, the introductory chapter provides useful advice for the student about selecting an appropriate test, discussing such basic issues as how tests are constructed, how to evaluate a test in terms of the situation to be evaluated, and the meaning and importance of statistical reliability.

One chapter briefly describes 11 "clinically popular" published tests (e.g., the Myers-Briggs Type Indicator, Rorschach) and their value to marriage and family therapists. Another discusses four observation instruments. Thirty-one scales are grouped within four remaining chapters that cover marital satisfaction and adjustment, communication and intimacy, special family assessment measures (most are attitude scales), and a series of family scales developed at the University of Minnesota. Each test is introduced by a brief description (history, construction, and subscales), information on validity and reliability, administration, a short critical evaluation, and its availability (bibliographic citation to the journal or publication information for the test). For most, either the entire measure or several sample items are reproduced, allowing a brief look at the test to determine its appropriateness.

335. Goldman, Bert Arthur, and John L. Saunders. **Directory of Unpublished Experimental Mental Measures. Volume 1**. New York, Human Sciences Press, 1974. 223p. index. $34.95. LC 73-17342. ISBN 0-87705-130-5.

336. Goldman, Bert Arthur, and John Christian Busch. **Directory of Unpublished Experimental Mental Measures. Volumes 2-3**. New York, Human Sciences Press, 1978-1982. 2v. index. $44.95/v. LC 73-17342. ISBN 0-87705-300-6(v.2), 0-89885-095-9(v.3).

337. Goldman, Bert Arthur, and William Larry Osborne. **Directory of Unpublished Experimental Mental Measures. Volume 4**. New York, Human Sciences Press, 1985. 423p. index. $44.95. LC 73-17342. ISBN 0-89885-100-9.

338. Goldman, Bert Arthur, and David F. Mitchell. **Directory of Unpublished Experimental Mental Measures. Volume 5**. Dubuque, Iowa, Wm. C. Brown, 1990. 441p. index. $44.95. LC 73-17342. ISBN 0-697-11490-2.

These volumes cite unpublished, experimental tests appearing in journals in psychology, sociology, education, and interdisciplinary areas in the social sciences. Coverage is almost exclusively of U.S. journal titles. Each entry gives a brief description of the test and a reference to the journal in which it and related information appeared.

Each volume covers a year or group of years, beginning with volume 1 for 1970 journal issues and concluding with volume 5, which has tests appearing between 1981 and 1985. The later volumes have cumulative indexes to the books in the series. Within each volume, instruments are categorized by general type (e.g., attitude, personality, vocational interest), supplemented by author and subject indexes.

339. Grotevant, H. D., and C. I. Carlson. **Family Assessment: A Guide to Methods and Measures**. New York, Guilford Press, 1989. 500p. index. $45.00. LC 88-12041. ISBN 0-89862-733-8.

The first three sections of this work discuss and compare specific groups of measures in the aggregate. An introductory chapter covers issues in and types of family assessment, observational measures, and the use of self-reported measures of family functioning. The remaining five sections group 70 measures under type of measure, including interaction coding schemes, rating scales, and self-report questionnaires (family functioning, stress and coping, and parent-child relationships). Each test is expounded in a five-page summary that focuses on a description of purpose, theoretical approach, and availability; a physical description, including scales and psychometric characteristics; administrative and scoring procedures; an evaluation; and a list of references. Each of the three sections is accompanied by critical evaluations of the tests' strengths and weaknesses, a summary evaluation, and a list of references. The primary author of each measure has supplied a brief author's response, with comments that can include future work on and plans for the measures, a rebuttal of the evaluation, and the opportunity to elucidate on the purpose or use of the measure.

There is some duplication with *Handbook of Measurements for Marriage and Family Therapy* (see entry 334), but Grotevant and Carlson focus on family functioning and its assessment. They do not include projective, experimental, structured interview, or behavior self-report measures. There are indexes by measure titles, authors, and variables.

340. Hersen, Michel, and Alan S. Bellack, eds. **Dictionary of Behavioral Assessment Techniques**. Elmsford, N.Y., Pergamon Press, 1988. 519p. index. (Pergamon General Psychology Series, v.147). $100.00. LC 86-25352. ISBN 0-08-031975-0.

This volume suffers from a title that implies brief definitions of concepts, terms, and instruments associated with measuring behaviors. However, it is really an alphabetical list of approximately 300 measurement techniques used in clinical and research settings. Most represent unpublished or published administered or observational instruments, with an emphasis on social skills and interaction, measurement of abnormal behavior, and personality disorders. Others represent apparati or techniques for measuring physiological responses, such as the cold pressor test, the Pain Cuff, and electromyography.

Critical, evaluative essays average three pages in length and follow a consistent format, including the description and purpose of the measure/technique and its development and psychometric characteristics, clinical and experimental uses, and other potential uses. Lists of cited references are short but include the core literature for each item. The author index lists both test authors and authors of cited references. A "Source of Entries" section lists the original source of each technique, which can include a journal citation reference, the researcher's name and address, or publisher name, as appropriate. A helpful user's guide is provided in the form of an alphabetical list of item or characteristic measured (e.g., marital distress) with an appropriate assessment device or technique (e.g., problem list) and the type of assessment it represents (e.g., spouse rating).

341. Johnson, Orval G. **Tests and Measurements in Child Development: Handbook II**. San Francisco, Jossey-Bass, 1976. 2v. index. (Jossey-Bass Behavioral Science Series). $95.00/set. LC 76-11890. ISBN 0-87589-278-7(v.1), 0-87589-279-5(v.2).

342. Johnson, Orval G., and James W. Bommarito. **Tests and Measurements in Child Development: A Handbook**. San Francisco, Jossey-Bass, 1971. 518p. index. (Jossey-Bass Behavioral Science Series). $47.50. LC 78-110636. ISBN 0-87589-090-3.

The original handbook includes measures that appeared in journals from 1950 to 1965 and that were intended for use with children from birth through age 12. *Handbook II* cites tests that were published from 1966 to 1974 and extends its testing population through age 18. Entries are arranged under categories that tests seek to measure, such as self-concept, sensory and motor perception, cognitive processes, and social interaction. Each test has a description, reliability and validity data, and a list of references. Indexes by test author, title, and subject appear in both books.

343. Levy, Philip, and Harvey Goldstein, comps. **Tests in Education: A Book of Critical Reviews**. London, Academic Press, 1984. 718p. index. o.p. LC 83-73142. ISBN 0-12-445880-7.

This volume displays an obvious British bias. All of the test reviewers are from Great Britain or the Commonwealth, and the tests reviewed are primarily used in the British education system. However, Levy and Goldstein evaluate about 200 instruments used in settings from preschool to secondary school. U.S. tests are included when they are available through U.K. publishers or distributors. Instruments are given a brief evaluation averaging two or three pages, a description of overall purpose and content, and reliability and validity information. The only index is by test title.

344. Robinson, John P., Jerrold G. Rusk, and Kendra B. Head. **Measures of Political Attitudes.** Ann Arbor, Mich., Survey Research Center, 1968. 712p. o.p. index. LC 68-65537.

345. Robinson, John P., Phillip R. Shaver, and Lawrence S. Wrightsman, eds. **Measures of Personality and Social Psychological Attitudes**. San Diego, Calif., Academic Press, 1991. 753p. (Measures of Social Psychological Attitudes, v.1). $89.95; $44.95pa. LC 90-91. ISBN 0-12-590241-7; 0-12-590244-1pa.

346. Robinson, John P., Robert Athanasou, and Kendra B. Head. **Measures of Occupational Attitudes and Occupational Characteristics**. Ann Arbor, Mich., Survey Research Center, Institute for Social Research, 1969. 460p. o.p. LC 75-627966. ISBN 0-87944-051-1.

These sourcebooks provide descriptive information for a wide range of experimental attitude measures. The intent of the two original volumes was to provide comprehensive coverage of experimental instruments on attitudes for researchers and students. The 1991 publication, a revision of *Measures of Social Psychological Attitudes* (1973), is more selective in the tests included for review essays.

The works are not limited to measures that were published in journal articles; many appear as parts of books, dissertations, and research reports of limited distribution. Approximately 150 measures are included in each volume. An introduction preceding each instrument describes the intent of the test; provides sample, reliability, and validity data; and supplies information on where the tools are available, additional references, and evaluative comments. In most cases, either the entire measure or some sample items are reproduced.

347. Shaw, Marvin E., and Jack M. Wright. **Scales for the Measurement of Attitudes**. New York, McGraw-Hill, 1967. 604p. index. (McGraw-Hill Series in Psychology). price not reported. LC 66-22791.

Shaw and Wright list approximately 175 experimental attitude measures, and the value of this volume is that, unlike many sources, the measures are reproduced. Three chapters review the nature and history of attitude research and measurement. The rest of the chapters group instruments under broad concepts areas, each discussing the applications and contributions of the body of tests to a particular area of study, such as social practice and institutions, social issues, attitudes toward significant others, and abstract concepts. In addition to reproductions of tests, scoring, statistical data, and evaluative comments are provided. The material is accessible through name and subject indexes.

348. Sweetland, Richard C., and Daniel J. Keyser, eds. **Tests: A Comprehensive Reference for Assessments in Psychology, Education, and Business**. 3d ed. Austin, Tex., Pro-Ed, 1991. 1250p. index. $69.00; $44.00pa. LC 89-78495. ISBN 0-89079-255-0; 0-89079-256-9pa.

This reference is designed for quick identification of a test to meet a specific need. Unlike other test guides, it does not provide evaluations. Over 3,000 published English-language assessment instruments are listed under three broad subject categories (psychology, education, and business) and 87 subsections. Each entry provides the purpose of each measure, a description, the intended population, administration and scoring, and cost and availability. A variety of indexes provides access by test publisher, title, author, out-of-print instruments, availability of computer scoring, and tests composed or adapted for special populations (e.g., the visually impaired, non-English speakers).

349. **Mental Measurements Yearbook**. Lincoln, Nebr., Buros Institute of Mental Measurements; distr., Lincoln, Nebr., University of Nebraska Press, 1985- . index. $125.00. LC 39-3422. ISBN varies.

350. **Tests in Print III: An Index to Tests, Test Reviews, and the Literature on Specific Tests.** James V. Mitchell, ed. Lincoln, Nebr., Buros Institute of Mental Measurements, University of Nebraska, 1983. 714p. index. $85.00. LC 83-18866. ISBN 0-910674-52-3.

Published from 1938 to 1949 by Rutgers University Press, and published by Gryphon Press between 1953 and 1978, the *Mental Measurements Yearbook* (*MMY*) series furnishes exhaustive coverage of published standardized tests commercially available in the English language. Volumes provide factual information on tests, critical reviews of most tests, and substantial bibliographies of references on the tests listed. Oscar K. Buros compiled the first *MMY* in 1938 and continued as compiler through the eighth in 1978; recent volumes have been edited by Jack Kramer and Jane Close Conoley. The editions have had an irregular revision schedule since then, with new editions appearing every 8 to 10 years. Beginning with the 9th edition in 1985, the Buros Institute has attempted a biennial publication schedule for its yearbooks, with paper supplements produced in the alternate years. The editions supplement each other; succeeding volumes include only new or substantially revised tests, new information about previously reviewed instruments, and (ever since the supplements appeared in 1988) the contents of the supplement published since the preceding *MMY*. Therefore, for comprehensive and historical coverage of a particular test, all volumes must be consulted. The latest edition, the eleventh (1992), contains information on 477 tests with 703 critical reviews. Abundant indexes include those by authors (of tests, test reviews, and reference citations), titles and acronyms, publishers, and subject categories. Recent editions include a helpful score index to supplement the broad access afforded by its subject index.

The *Tests in Print* (*TIP*) series has expanded considerably since publication of the first volume in 1961. This volume is "a comprehensive bibliography of commercially available tests for use with English-speaking subjects" (preface). As such, it acts as an exhaustive list of tests currently available for purchase. It also serves as a cumulative index to the reference lists and reviews for in-print tests appearing in all *MMY*s through the eighth (published in 1978), making it a valuable retrospective tool. Most entries contain bibliographic references (or citations to bibliographies in *MMY* editions) related to the construction, validity, or use of the tests. Tests are listed alphabetically by title and are supplemented by indexes of test titles (including titles in *TIP2* and tests that have recently gone out of print), subjects (the arrangement is hierarchical and classified), publishers (including addresses), and authors/names (not only test authors but also authors as cited in the lists of references). Unfortunately, *TIP* has a less-regular publication schedule than *MMY*, so its primary usefulness is as a retrospective index. A fourth edition is planned for 1993.

351. **Test Critiques.** Volume 1- . Daniel J. Keyser and Richard C. Sweetland, eds. Austin, Tex., Pro-Ed, 1991- . index. $85.00/vol. LC 84-26895. ISBN varies.

Each volume of this series, originally published by Test Corporation of America, contains approximately 100 critical reviews of commercially available tests, generally the most frequently used tests in psychological assessment, education, and business. Within each volume, primary arrangement is by test title. Beginning with volume 3, test title, test publisher, author/reviewer, and subject indexes cumulate. At present, volumes are published at the rate of one or two per year. The review essays follow a consistent format: a description of the development and applications of the test, technical data, a critique of about 10 pages, and a list of references.

There is significant, but not complete, duplication with the *Mental Measurements Yearbook* (see entry 349) volumes. Therefore, this series should be used as a supplement to those books.

352. Touliatos, John, Barry F. Perlmutter, and Murray A. Straus. **Handbook of Family Measurement Techniques.** Newbury Park, Calif., Sage Publishing, 1990. 797p. index. $65.00. LC 89-10542. ISBN 0-8039-3121-2.

This is the most extensive of several test bibliographies on devices that measure family functioning. The 976 tests, most of which were developed after 1975, are arranged according to the aspects the instruments are intended to measure: "Dimensions of Marital and

Family Interaction," "Intimacy and Family Values," "Parenthood," "Roles and Power," and "Adjustment." Each entry includes test availability, authorship, type of instrument, summaries describing the instrument, brief comments on the use of the test, and up to four bibliographic references to publications where the test is available or to material on its use or development. Most entries include a sample item from the measure. A separate section, "Abbreviated Abstracts of Instruments," provides briefer information about older (mostly pre-1975) measures.

Each abstract is assigned a classification code that reflects a more specific subcategory than the six noted above, the level of interaction the item is intended to measure, and the primary focus of the study. For example, a code may indicate that a test is located in the section on marital adjustment and that it concerns family stress between husband and wife, with focus on the child. This code is used to group tests in the classification index to locate items that meet a specific evaluation need.

Each section is preceded by a brief essay on the types of measures in each area and how they developed. These essays, in addition to the introductory one on the general area of family measurement, make this a handbook as well as a test bibliography.

Bibliographies on Tests and Testing

353. Lang, Alfred, ed. **Rorschach-Bibliographie/Bibliographie Rorschach/Rorschach-Bibliography: 1921-1964**. Bern, Verlag Hans Huber, 1966. 191p. index. price not reported. LC 67-104969.

This is an unannotated list of 3,855 references to books and articles published on the development and use of one of the most heavily administered and cited projective personality tests. References are listed under the following categories: manuals and texts on the test, methods and settings for use of the test (e.g., scoring, reliability, utility in specialized situations), modifications employed, interpretation, applications with general populations, and applications with disordered populations. Coverage is international, with good representation of foreign-language material.

354. O'Brien, Nancy Patricia, comp. **Test Construction: A Bibliography of Selected Resources**. Westport, Conn., Greenwood Press, 1988. 299p. index. $39.95. LC 87-25119. ISBN 0-313-23435-3.

This work contains a comprehensive, unannotated list of 2,759 items on test construction, design and item construction, and related methodologies. The areas of questionnaire and survey design are not included, nor are test validity, bias, and reliability (unless related to test construction). Citations were drawn from a large number of sources: ERIC documents, reports, dissertations, books, and journal literature. They are organized under the scheme used in the *Mental Measurements Yearbook* (see entry349) (e.g., achievement, sensory-motor, by subject disciplines); combined with the subcategories, there is a total of 63 categories. All items were published from the early 1900s to 1986, with the 1983 to 1986 citations included in a separate addendum. In addition to an author index, there is a subject index to locate more specific concepts and particular test names.

355. Taulbee, Earl S., H. Wilkes Wright, and David E. Stenmark. **The Minnesota Multiphasic Personality Inventory (MMPI): A Comprehensive, Annotated Bibliography (1940-1965)**. Troy, N.Y., Whitston Publishing, 1977. 603p. index. $35.00. LC 72-87108. ISBN 0-87875-037-1.

The MMPI is one of the most frequently used and cited assessment instruments. The authors selected the years covered by this bibliography as pivotal ones in the direction and influence of personality testing. Citations were derived from *Psychological Abstracts* (see entry 129), the *Mental Measurements Yearbook* series (see entry 349), and other sources. The 2,144 references are listed by format of publication: annotated citations to articles (1,310 citations); additional unannotated references to articles; unannotated references on manifest anxiety; foreign references; doctoral dissertations; masters' theses and unpublished studies; and books, reviews, and related material. There are author and subject indexes and location tables, the last especially useful for finding applications with certain populations; correlations with other tests; and information on scales, subscales, and scoring procedures.

PERCEPTION

Bibliographies

356. Emmett, Kathleen, and Peter Machamer. **Perception: An Annotated Bibliography**. New York, Garland, 1976. 177p. index. price not reported. LC 75-24086. ISBN 0-8240-9966-4.

In this work, Emmett and Machamer emphasize the philosophical and theoretical literature on the psychology of perception, including the psychology of mind and cognition. The 1,485 citations represent research in books and journals published from 1935 to 1974. Most are in English. Arrangement is by first author, and a subject index (not very detailed) is provided. Evaluative annotations are included for some entries and vary greatly in length.

Although the emphasis is on philosophical approaches to perception, there is some coverage of psychological literature and early journal titles in the sciences. Because the literature on what is now an experimental area of psychology was spread among that of several disciplines during this time, this bibliography is especially useful for its historical approach and coverage.

357. **Music Therapy Index. Volume 1, 1976**. Dallas, Tex., National Association for Music Therapy, 1976. 224p. o.p. LC 77-640629. ISSN 0145-6164.

358. **Music Psychology Index. Volume 2, 1978**. Dallas, Tex., Institute for Therapeutics Research, 1978. 278p. o.p. LC 79-644194. ISSN 0195-5802.

359. **Music Psychology Index. Volume 3**. Charles T. Eagle, Jr., and John J. Miniter, eds. Phoenix, Ariz., Oryx Press, 1984. 269p. o.p. LC 79-644194. ISBN 0-89774-144-7.

Each of these volumes contains approximately 2,000 citations selectively indexed from 400 journals in health and medicine, clinical psychology and psychiatry, education, perception, and physiology and the neurosciences. Also included are citations to secondary sources, such as *Dissertation Abstracts International* (see entry 20). Coverage is international and multilingual. Primary access is by subject and author, with extensive cross-references throughout the index. Respectively, references in the volumes cover 1960-1975, 1976-1977, and 1978-1980. Despite the titles, citations to works on the use of music in psychotherapy constitute a small percentage of the overall content, particularly in the last two volumes. There is excellent coverage of the perception of music, aural perception and psychoacoustics, the influence of music on behavior, and production of voice and sound among both human and animal populations.

360. Zelkind, Irving, and Joseph Sprug. **Time Research: 1172 Studies**. Metuchen, N.J., Scarecrow, 1974. 248p. index. $19.00. LC 74-14970. ISBN 0-8108-0768-8.

This is a comprehensive list of books, journal articles, and dissertations on time perception published in English between 1886 and 1973. Citations are listed by primary author, with *see* references provided for secondary authors. Entries are not annotated, but for each citation the independent variable, dependent variable, or other relevant variables present in the research are indicated. Inclusion is restricted to material that reports the results of empirical research or research that has theoretical implications. Complete access to the contents is provided by indexes to frequency of citation (as indicated by being cited four or more times in 300 selected bibliographies), monographs, dissertations, journal titles in which studies appeared (the most numerous publication type), dates of publication, and subjects (an index composed largely of keywords that make up the variables noted after citations).

Handbooks

361. Boff, Kenneth R., Lloyd Kaufman, and James P. Thomas, eds. **Handbook of Perception and Human Performance**. New York, John Wiley, 1986. 2v. index. $199.95. LC 85-20375. ISBN 0-471-85061-6.

This set has complete coverage of human perception, information processing, and motor performance. Volume 1, *Sensory Processes and Perception*, arranges 25 chapters under the categories "Theory and Methods" and "Space and Motor Perception," as well as within two sections that cover the basic senses. Volume 2, *Cognitive Processes and Performance*, includes 20 chapters on the general areas of information processing, cognition, and topics in performance (e.g., workload, vigilance, monitoring).

A lot of information is packed into the 45 chapters, which are aimed at the researcher and graduate student. Outlines preceding each chapter and the detailed subject indexes help pinpoint specific issues and topics. Overall, this is an outstanding, comprehensive handbook in experimental psychology.

362. **Handbook of Perception**. Edward C. Carterette and Morton P. Friedman, eds. New York, Academic Press, 1973-1978. 11v. index. $538.00/set. LC varies. ISBN varies.

Each volume of this work has its own title and index and can stand alone. As a set, it encompasses every aspect of perception theory, research, and application. Volumes 4 through 7 concern the senses: hearing (4), vision (5), taste and smell (6A), touch (6B), and language and speech (7). Others cover measurement of perception and judgment (2), historical and theoretical origins of perception (1), sensory physiology (3), information processing and coding (8), attention and perceptual processing (9), and interaction with the environment (10). Within each, an average of 10 chapters survey and review the history, evolution, and research trends in each area and supply lengthy bibliographies.

This is a reprint edition of the original 18-volume set published in 1968. The age of these volumes requires users to pursue more recent information in other sources. However, each remains as an excellent handbook on every area of perception.

COGNITION, LEARNING, AND MEMORY

Bibliographies

363. Arasteh, A. Reza, and Josephine D. Arasteh. **Creativity in Human Development: An Interpretive and Annotated Bibliography**. New York, Schenkman, 1976. 154p. price not reported. LC 76-26678. ISBN 0-470-98933-5.

The first three sections in this work cover creativity in the young child, in adolescence, and in adulthood, focusing on normal populations. Each section begins with an extensive literature review essay that defines the scope and research trends, followed by descriptive annotations of approximately 200 additional references to books, journal articles, government documents, research reports, and dissertations, most from the 1960s and 1970s. The last section, "A Unitary Theory of Creativity and Happiness," contains a short essay on the authors' theory of creativity and a brief selected bibliography on the nature and scope of creativity.

364. Hill, Claire Conley. **Problem Solving: Learning and Teaching. An Annotated Bibliography.** London, Frances Pinter, 1979. 143p. index. £20.00. ISBN 0-89397-069-7.

Hill approaches problem solving from two points of view: effecting increased learning and performance in the fields of mathematics and the sciences, and the interest of philosophers and psychologists in the processes of creativity, information processing, and reasoning. Both are well represented here, with emphasis on the learning and teaching processes of problem solving.

Most of the literature cited is derived from the journal, book, and dissertation literature in psychology, education, and mathematics teaching. The 296 references represent English-language references published in the 1960s and 1970s, with selected earlier coverage. Most of the annotations are descriptive and evaluative. Citations are arranged under 13 categories (e.g., teaching styles, creativity, the effect of individual differences on learning, the use of associations), most preceded by a brief discussion of the scope of the literature. There is an author index.

365. Razik, Taher A. **Bibliography of Creativity Studies and Related Areas.** Buffalo, N.Y., State University of New York, 1965. 451p. index. price not reported. LC 65-5813.

This work affords excellent retrospective coverage of the published and fugitive literature in creativity and its genesis, manifestations, and measurement. A total of 4,176 unannotated citations represent several languages, usually English. According to the preface, published items deal with material between 1744 and 1964. Books and articles from scholarly journals are the most common works cited, although dissertations, theses, technical reports, and unpublished lectures and speeches are also covered. Citations are drawn not only from philosophy, psychology, and education literature but also from the applied arts and sciences, literature, management, theology, and the spectrum of the social sciences.

There are author and title (for anonymous references) indexes. Subject access is provided by the table of contents. All items are classed under headings for nature (manifestations of creativity), nurture (environmental, biological, and other external factors), measurement, and miscellaneous material, with several subcategories.

366. Rothenberg, Albert, and Betty Greenberg. **The Index of Scientific Writings and Creativity: General, 1566-1974.** Hamden, Conn., Shoe String Press, 1976. 274p. index. price not reported. LC 75-31699. ISBN 0-208-01148-9.

The authors take a broad view of the research literature to include all elements of the creative process in this work—the person as agent, the process itself, creativity as a phenomenon, the role of imagination and intuition—all from a variety of disciplines, from the social sciences to the pure and applied sciences. Works from modern philosophy and the humanities and the substantial body of literature on aesthetics are excluded. Scientific studies on personality factors, aptitudes, and thought processes in the creative process are well represented, as are works of philosophers before 1925 (as precursors of modern psychology). After this date, works with empirical bases or pertaining to psychological factors dominate.

The unannotated references demonstrate a multilingual approach and are organized under eight broad categories: general works; psychopathology and creativity; developmental studies; creativity in the fine arts, sciences, industry and business, and women; and facilitating creativity. Most of these areas further subdivide their citations. An unclassified addendum for the most recent items (e.g., journal articles, books, conference papers, dissertations, master's theses) brings the total number of citations to 6,823. There are author and subject indexes.

367. Wasserman, Paul, with Fred S. Silander. **Decision-Making: An Annotated Bibliography**. Ithaca, N.Y., Graduate School of Business and Public Administration, Cornell University, 1958. 111p. index. (McKinsey Foundation Annotated Bibliography). price not reported. LC 58-4160.

368. Wasserman, Paul, and Fred S. Silander. **Decision-Making: An Annotated Bibliography Supplement, 1958-1963**. Ithaca, N.Y., Graduate School of Business and Public Administration, 1964. 178p. index. price not reported. LC 58-4160.

The original bibliography contains approximately 400 English-language references, most published between 1945 and 1957. The supplement contains over 600 additional citations. Acknowledging the volume and breadth of literature, the lists are selective and contain lengthy, descriptive abstracts. The references to journal articles, books, dissertations, and government publications reflect a spectrum of disciplines. However, although most of the applications deal with the spheres of management, economics, and politics, much of the research literature is drawn from social and quantitative psychology and sociology. The remainder represent contributions from economics, human factors, operations research, and business. Citations are listed under broad subject areas, with some variation of organization between volumes: general and theoretical, values and ethics, leadership, psychological factors and behavioral decision theory, small group decision making, community decision making, communications and information handling, statistical and mathematical implications, cases, and applications. Each volume contains author and title indexes.

369. Young, Morris N. **Bibliography of Memory**. Philadelphia, Chilton, 1961. 463p. $62.50. LC 61-9021.

Young provides an exhaustive, comprehensive list to works encompassing all aspects of mnemonics in a bibliography that meets a historical need. References are not limited by time period or language of publication and extend from the ancients (e.g., Pliny) to modern thinkers (e.g., William James); works of Europe, Great Britain, and the Americas predominate. Most citations represent published works, but other formats include conference papers, pamphlets, circulars, and similar fugitive items. Along with academic research materials, some popular self-improvement works are included. Applications in such areas as advertising and education are also covered.

Arrangement is by primary author, followed by anonymous works. There are liberal cross-references for secondary authors and variant name forms, but there is no subject access.

Handbooks

370. Glover, John A., Royce R. Ronning, and Cecil R. Reynolds, eds. **Handbook of Creativity**. New York, Plenum, 1989. 447p. index. (Perspectives on Individual Differences). $60.00. LC 89-16002. ISBN 0-306-43160-2.

Twenty-four chapters help codify what can be an ill-defined area of research. Part 1 consists of six chapters addressing the nature, measurement, and origins of creativity, including issues in individual differences, nature-nurture, and intelligence. The four chapters in part 3 discuss personality and situation variables, the role of the self, and creativity's association with mental illness. These are the best sections of the handbook. The other two parts cover cognitive models (cognitive processes, perception, memory, metacognition, and reasoning) and applications of research, here dealing with writing and literature, problem solving in the educational context, and creativity in intellectual productivity. There is a subject index.

371. **Stevens' Handbook of Experimental Psychology**. Richard C. Atkinson et al., eds. 2d ed. New York, John Wiley, 1988. 2v. index. $190.00/set. LC 87-31637. ISBN 0-471-61625-7.

This is an update and revision of the classic 1951 work by Stanley Stevens. It encompasses all aspects of human perception, learning, and cognition. Chapters are well written at a very advanced level. In volume 1, *Perception and Motivation*, nine chapters discuss all aspects of sensation (e.g., taste, audition, vision) and their measurement. The remaining chapters cover the biological basis of motivation, behavioral genetics, the roles of emotion and adaptation, and comparative studies. Volume 2, *Learning and Cognition*, encompasses all aspects of learning and memory: choice, representation in memory, psycholinguistics, biological influences and individual differences, problem solving, and decision making. Each volume contains a cumulated subject and author index.

Dictionaries and Encyclopedias

372. Eysenck, Michael W., ed. **The Blackwell Dictionary of Cognitive Psychology**. Cambridge, Mass., Basil Blackwell, 1990. 390p. index. $69.95. LC 90-34225. ISBN 0-631-15682-8.

Eysenck interprets human cognition as encompassing "attention, perception, learning, memory, language, thinking, and problem solving," and he also considers topics in such applied areas as artificial intelligence, eyewitness testimony, and study skills. Although most articles focus on concepts, theories, or research methodologies, some are biographical.

In some ways, this work is similar to Corsini's *Encyclopedia of Psychology* (see entry 169). For example, the length of the articles, which average five pages, makes them more substantial than the term *dictionary* implies. They are written with a minimum of technical language, but not simplistically, and they review basic precepts, present examples, and discuss important classic research associated with each concept or theory. Most references cited are current. There are a few charts, tables, and figures; cross-references; and a subject index.

INTELLIGENCE

Guides

373. Aby, Stephen H., comp. **The IQ Debate: A Selective Guide to the Literature**. Westport, Conn., Greenwood Press, 1990. 228p. index. (Bibliographies and Indexes in Psychology, no.8). $45.00. LC 90-13986. ISBN 0-313-26440-6.

This is an excellent guide to the IQ debate, especially as reflected in the education and psychology literature. Most of the 408 citations represent books, book chapters, articles in scholarly and popular periodicals, ERIC and research documents, substantive articles from major newspapers, and nonprint media published between 1969 and 1990, primarily from the disciplines of psychology and education. A lengthy descriptive annotation accompanies each citation.

Aby's introduction nicely summarizes the critical and often controversial issues surrounding IQ, such as genetic versus environmental determinants of intelligence, the fallibility of standardized testing instruments, and cultural bias in intelligence testing. Part 1 consists of reference sources, subdivided by publication format: bibliographies, indexes and databases, handbooks, and encyclopedias. Part 2, nonreference sources, contains citations again divided by publication type, such as magazine articles and professional journal articles. A brief but helpful glossary of terms and name and subject indexes round out the volume.

Bibliographies

374. Wright, Logan. **Bibliography on Human Intelligence: An Extensive Bibliography.** Washington, D.C., National Clearinghouse for Mental Health Information, National Institute of Mental Health, 1969. 222p. index. (Public Health Service Publication, no. 1839). o.p. (SuDoc HE 20.2417:H 88).

This title consists of approximately 6,700 citations, primarily to English-language books and journal articles but with scattered coverage of dissertations, conference papers, and foreign-language publications. Animal studies are cited if they have implications for the study of human intelligence. Most works are drawn from the disciplines of education and psychology, with learning, memory, the measurement of intelligence, intellectual development, and intellectual impairments (e.g., mental retardation) having the most citations.

Wright limits coverage of issues concerning nature/nurture, the validity of intelligence testing and related social and legal controversies, and most references to individual testing instruments. Even given these exclusions, the bibliography's scope is broad, covering historical and theoretical issues, the nature of intelligence, the educational context, coexisting factors (e.g., culture and physiology), and measurement of intelligence. Citations are listed topically within a hierarchical outline format, with supplemental subject and topical indexes.

Handbooks

375. Sternberg, Robert J., ed. **Handbook of Human Intelligence.** New York, Cambridge University Press, 1982. 1031p. index. $92.50; $34.50pa. LC 82-1160. ISBN 0-521-22870-0; 0-521-29687-0pa.

Sternberg and the other contributors take a comprehensive, wide-ranging view of intelligence, drawing on all areas of psychology for their influence and perspective. As the preface indicates, the purpose of chapters is to provide an introduction to issues and an evaluative review, rather than exhaustive literature surveys.

Fourteen chapters are grouped under four broad categories: the nature and measurement of intelligence; aspects of intelligence drawn from personality, learning and memory, the processes of reasoning and problem solving, attention and perception, and artificial intelligence; the roles of social policy, education, and environment in defining and interpreting intelligence; and the role of evolution, genetics, and human development. A final chapter summarizes the theoretical approaches, including their evolution and limitations. There are name and subject indexes.

The contributors assume considerable knowledge of psychology and a general understanding of intelligence on the part of the user, although the essays are generally accessible by students. There is better coverage of some topics, such as artificial intelligence and the intersection with other areas of the disciplines, than is provided by *Handbook of Intelligence* (see entry 376).

376. Wolman, Benjamin B., ed. **Handbook of Intelligence: Theories, Measurements, and Applications.** New York, John Wiley, 1985. 985p. index. $78.50. LC 85-3355. ISBN 0-471-89738-8.

The 23 contributed chapters in this book are grouped under three broad categories: theoretical and conceptual approaches to intelligence, measurement methods, and applications of related principles in the applied areas of clinical and educational psychology and mental health. There are name and subject indexes.

This is very much a handbook for the researcher, as opposed to the student or practitioner. The articles are comprehensive, in-depth, and well written, but a few concentrate on relatively narrow areas of interest. Those covering broader, issue-oriented topics (e.g., environmental influences, infant assessment, the neurological basis of intelligence) presuppose considerable knowledge of psychological principles in general and the foundations of intelligence in particular.

MOTIVATION

Bibliographies

377. Cofer, Charles N. **Human Motivation: A Guide to Information Sources**. Detroit, Gale, 1980. 176p. index. (Psychology Information Guide Series, v.4). $68.00. LC 80-14341. ISBN 0-8103-1418-5.

Cofer cites and briefly annotates approximately 1,000 sources, primarily from academic journals and books, published in English from the early twentieth century through the late 1970s. After a section that lists general guides to the literature and reference sources, the following 11 sections are divided into broad categories: instinct and ethology, biological rhythms and instincts, biological functions and influences, learning theory, curiosity and stimulus-seeking, emotion, conflict and stress, theoretical approaches to personality and motivation, derived and social motives, social motivation and attitudes, and applications of motivation theories. Most sections further classify citations in a hierarchical arrangement. There are author, title, and subject indexes.

378. Faunce, Patricia Spencer. **Women and Ambition: A Bibliography**. Metuchen, N.J., Scarecrow, 1980. 695p. index. $45.00. LC 79-18347. ISBN 0-8108-1242-8.

This excellent bibliography focuses on women's achievement motivation, ambition, and success from cultural, social, psychological, and environmental viewpoints. An introduction discusses the historical, theoretical, and practical issues surrounding the expectations and achievements of women. The bibliography contains works produced from 1960 to 1977. Although most are references to journal articles and books, also included are doctoral and masters' theses, ERIC and other microformat documents, unpublished reports and symposium papers, and popular periodical and newspaper articles. The book is comprehensive, but there is especially good coverage of literature in the broad areas of sociology, education, and psychology, and interdisciplinary areas such as women's and minority studies, business management and personnel, and criminology and the law. An author index is provided.

Approximately 7,500 citations are divided among broad subject categories: background literature, social forces, psychological factors, counseling, the educational environment, occupational and career factors, and minority women. Hierarchical subdivisions afford the volume's only subject access. For example, the substantial section on psychological aspects covers factors in personality and values, self-concept and self-esteem, expectations and control.

ATTENTION AND CONSCIOUS STATES

Bibliographies

379. Caputi, Natalino. **Unconscious: A Guide to the Sources**. Metuchen, N. J., American Theological Library Association and Scarecrow Press, 1985. 151p. index. (ATLA Bibliography Series, no.16). $20.00. LC 85-1979. ISBN 0-8108-1798-5.

Caputi has selected 821 citations that reflect one or more typologies, or theories of the unconscious: bio-physical, psycho-personal, socio-cultural, and transpersonal-spiritual.

References are listed by author, and a majority are accompanied by brief annotations and the approach represented (from the four typologies above). A considerable number of foreign-language citations are included, mostly from German and French sources, with the titles translated. Journal articles are the most numerous format type, supplemented by books, essays, dissertations, and a few popular works, most published between 1900 and the early 1980s.

Most citations reflect the psycho-personal approach, with emphasis on Freudian, Jungian, and Adlerian influences. Least numerous are references associated with the bio-physical approach. Although the introduction recognizes the distinction between the unconscious and the subconscious, the terms (if not the concepts) are used interchangeably in the bibliography. There is no list of citations by the typology used, although there is a detailed subject index.

380. Miletich, John J., comp. **States of Awareness: An Annotated Bibliography**. Westport, Conn., Greenwood Press, 1988. 292p. index. (Bibliographies and Indexes in Psychology, no.5). $39.95. LC 88-24733. ISBN 0-313-26194-6.

Miletich provides retrospective and comprehensive coverage of English-language books, scholarly and professional articles, dissertations, and conference proceedings published from the late 1800s to early 1988. Almost 1,100 items are organized under the following categories: depersonalization, sleepwalking, amnesia, anesthesia, thyroid disorders, near-death experiences, deja vu, out-of-body experiences, and sensory deprivation. Annotations are lengthy and descriptive. Along with subject, author, and personal name indexes, there is a list of commonly used acronyms.

The actual coverage in this work is altered states, not the entire realm of conscious states as implied by the title. Because of this parameter, its greatest audience will be among students of clinical psychology, psychiatry, medicine, and psychical research.

381. Parsifal-Charles, Nancy. **The Dream: 4,000 Years of Theory and Practice. A Critical, Descriptive, and Encyclopedic Bibliography**. West Cornwall, Conn., Locust Hill Press, 1986. 2v. index. $59.95/set. LC 86-15335. ISBN 0-933951-07-8.

Over 700 books on dreams, dream theory, and dream interpretation are cited and critically evaluated in lengthy abstracts in this book. Despite the subtitle, twentieth-century works published before 1986 are the most completely represented, along with publications from the nineteenth century. Many European languages are represented, with English materials by far the most numerous. Most are works of scholarship, with some coverage of popular books. A very detailed subject index and a name index are included in the second volume.

The compiler's background in comparative literature explains, at least in part, the emphasis of the items selected for inclusion. Works on the meaning and interpretation of dreams in literature and folklore, cross-cultural perspectives, and philosophical and analytical explanations of the subconscious from Aristotle to Adler are covered extremely well. The inclusion of nothing but book literature limits coverage of much of the physiological and empirical literature on dreaming (e.g., REM sleep and dream measurement) in psychology, psychiatry, and physiology. However, this work is comprehensive within the parameters indicated.

382. **Sleep Research**. Vol. 1- . Los Angeles, Calif., University of California, Brain Information Service, Brain Research Institute, 1972- . annual. $85.00.

The content of *Sleep Research* has varied since 1972. It now consists of "Current Claims," brief descriptions of papers presented at the annual meeting of the Association of Professional Sleep Societies; abstracts of papers from the same annual meeting; "Sleep Bibliography"; a rotated keyword index to the bibliography; and an author index to the abstracts and bibliography sections.

The bibliography, usually containing about 1,700 unannotated entries, begins with a section citing books and review articles, then all other research articles, arranging them under approximately 20 subject categories. All aspects of sleep are represented, such as biochemistry and neurology, dreaming, stimulus and environmental effects, personality, sleep disorders, sleep behavior, and instrumentation and measurement. Coverage is international and multilingual, with translated titles provided for non-English citations. Citations draw heavily from journals in the neurosciences, medicine, related biomedical disciplines, and physiology, less so from clinical and experimental psychology and psychiatry.

Handbooks

383. Wolman, Benjamin B., and Montague Ullman, eds. **Handbook of States of Consciousness.** New York, Van Nostrand Reinhold, 1986. 672p. index. $62.95. LC 85-7432. ISBN 0-442-29456-5.

In this book, 20 chapters are organized under three broad categories. Those on theory focus on the historical contexts of research into the conscious or unconscious states. Essays on manifestations generally deal with the phenomenon of altered states. There are also essays on accessibility of altered states and the unconscious to outside stimuli and investigation. Because the scope of the essays can be very narrow (e.g., "Protoconscious and Psychopathology") to relatively broad (e.g., "Drug-Induced States"), one must use the subject or name indexes to find discussion on a concept or theorist.

Dictionaries and Encyclopedias

384. Thorpy, Michael J., and Jan Yager. **The Encyclopedia of Sleep and Sleep Disorders.** New York, Facts on File, 1991. 298p. index. $45.00. LC 89-71520. ISBN 0-8160-1870-7.

Thorpy and Yager's unique volume focuses on sleep as a state of physical rest and as a state of unconsciousness, covering the biological and psychological influences on human sleep, sleep disorders, and the treatment of abnormal sleep patterns. Most articles are topical and vary from a paragraph to a few pages, discussing theories and concepts associated with sleep and sleep research. Others describe the work of prominent researchers, organizations, the impact of drugs and medications, journal titles, and associations and research centers. About half of the articles are appended by a few references to journal or popular articles and books, although some topics that would have benefited from a supporting reference lack this feature. This, coupled with uneven coverage of some topics, means that students will find the book more useful as a browsing tool and source of definitions rather than as a springboard for a research topic.

Introductory essays discuss the history of sleep research and the interrelatedness of psychology and sleep. In addition to a bibliography and a subject index, appendixes include directories of information clearinghouses and research centers, sleep disorder facilities, and two diagnostic classification schemes devised by the Association of Sleep Disorder Centers.

PHYSIOLOGICAL PSYCHOLOGY AND PHYSIOLOGICAL INTERVENTION

Bibliographies

385. Butler, Francine. **Biofeedback: A Survey of the Literature.** New York, IFI/Plenum, 1978. 340p. index. price not reported. LC 78-6159. ISBN 0-306-65173-4.

386. Butler, Francine, and Johann Stoyva, eds. **Biofeedback and Self-Control: A Bibliography.** Denver, Colo., Biofeedback Research Society, 1973. 113p. index. price not reported. LC 73-175239.

Together, these volumes list over 3,300 references on practically all aspects of biofeedback as a physiological phenomenon, as a relationship between mind and body, and as a therapeutic approach. Although there is some duplication between the two volumes, their contents are complementary. Years covered are usually from the late 1950s to the mid-1970s, but work from early in the century is also included. Citations are drawn from the English-language book, journal, conference, and dissertation literature. Materials from a variety of disciplines are represented: medicine, biological sciences, and neurology; research and clinical perspectives from psychiatry and psychology; and rehabilitative services and social work. The earlier title contains more references from basic psychophysiology and works on behavior therapy than the 1978 publication. Separate sections in the later edition provide a list of conference papers presented at annual meetings of the Biofeedback Society of America, a list of publications of the society, and a description of the organization. There is a keyword index. Arrangement in the 1973 bibliography is topical under 19 categories, with an author index. The later volume relies on an author arrangement, supplemented by a keyword-in-title index.

Indexes and Abstracts

387. **Biological Abstracts**. Vol. 1- , No. 1- . Philadelphia, Biosciences Information Service, 1926- . biweekly (2 volumes/yr.). $3,975.00/yr.(institutions). ISSN 0006-3169.

Biological Abstracts (*BA*) affords exhaustive coverage from the literatures of biology and its associated fields, such as biomedicine, neurology, physiology and anatomy, agriculture, and zoology. International and multilingual in scope, it indexes over 8,000 serial publications. It should be a primary resource when seeking research literature on any aspect of physiological psychology, especially ethology, comparative psychology, and physiological aspects of psychiatric disorders. It is also helpful for locating animal studies in any area of psychology. A companion publication, *Biological Abstracts/RRM* ("reports, reviews, meetings") indexes symposia, technical reports, conference papers, books, and review articles.

The size and composition of the indexes are daunting. Although citations and lengthy summaries are categorized under more than 80 broad categories and numerous subheadings, the number of citations makes this "concept" searching unmanageable. Entries in the subject index consist of a rotated string of significant words derived from the title of each citation and supplemented by additional significant words from the abstract. Every item is represented several times in the subject index under each significant word, surrounded by other words in the string to afford some subject context. Other indexes include those by organism (biosystematic and generic) and author. All indexes cumulate semiannually.

388. **Index Medicus**. Vol. 1- , No. 1- . Bethesda, Md., National Library of Medicine; distr., Washington, D.C., U.S. Government Printing Office, 1960- . monthly. $310.00/yr. ISSN 0019-3879. (SuDoc HE 20.3612).

389. **Abridged Index Medicus**. Vol. 1- , No. 1- . Bethesda, Md., National Library of Medicine; distr., Washington, D.C., U.S. Government Printing Office, 1980- . monthly. $50.00. ISSN 0001-3331. (SuDoc HE 20.3612/2)

As the primary journal index in medicine, biomedicine, nursing, and the health sciences, *Index Medicus* (*IM*) exhaustively indexes almost every contribution (including brief reports and letters) appearing in 3,000 journal and annual publications published worldwide and in practically all languages. (The source journals are listed in *List of Journals Indexed in Index Medicus*, an annual publication received as part of *IM*.) It is essential for any topic in health psychology or psychological aspects of illness, mental illness and psychiatric treatment, psychopharmacology, neuropsychology, and animal and human physiological studies.

Citations are indexed according to the *Medical Subject Headings List*, revised and published annually as a supplement to the January issue. Most subject headings provide narrower access under approximately 50 standardized subheadings as appropriate to the concept, such as complications, psychology, and surgery. Although there are no abstracts, the specificity and level of indexing is excellent. One drawback of the subject approach is that many concepts dealing with mental health and illness, psychiatric treatment, and life-span development are too broad and result in an overwhelming number of entries. Separate author and subject listings are published concurrently, with another separate section for literature reviews.

The entire publication is cumulated and republished as *Cumulated Index Medicus* and includes the annual subject headings list. *Abridged Index Medicus* (and the annual *Cumulated Abridged Index Medicus*) is intended for smaller libraries and indexes approximately 100 prominent English-language journals.

390. **Psychopharmacology Abstracts**. Vols. 1-19. Bethesda, Md., U.S. Department of Health, Education, and Welfare, Public Health Service, 1961-1982. quarterly. price not reported. ISSN 0033-2166.

Last produced under the auspices of the National Clearinghouse for Mental Health Information, *Psychopharmacology Abstracts* indexes the worldwide literature on the behavioral and mental effects of drugs. Article citations and abstracts are categorized under 17 subjects, although there are keyword and title indexes that cumulate semiannually. This index is also part of the Mental Health Abstracts bibliographic database (see entry 151), accessible through DIALOG. Since the demise of this publication, *Index Medicus* has provided similar coverage of this area.

Handbooks and Yearbooks

391. Gazzaniga, Michael S., and Colin Blakemore, eds. **Handbook of Psychobiology**. New York, Academic Press, 1975. 639p. index. $59.00. LC 74-10193. ISBN 0-122-78656-4.

As noted in the preface, psychobiology is an exceptionally broad field, incorporating many subareas of psychology, biochemistry, and neurology. Despite its age, this handbook is still a single-volume, authoritative source in the area. The 21 contributed chapters are divided among four sections. Part 1 encompasses elementary processes and foundations, primarily by looking at nonhuman species and elementary brain development and functions. Part 2 focuses on neurochemical influences on behavior, and part 3 covers sensory and motor functions in higher vertebrates (e.g., visual perception, the auditory system, coordination and reflexes). Integrative functions are covered in part 4, including the role of psychobiological processes in learning, attention, emotion, communication and language, and dreaming in humans and animals. There is a subject index.

Dictionaries and Encyclopedias

392. **Dictionary of Physiological and Clinical Psychology**. Rom Harre and Roger Lamb, eds. Cambridge, Mass., MIT Press, 1986. 314p. index. $12.50pa. LC 86-14379. ISBN 0-262-58075-6.

Articles from this work were selected from the editors' *Encyclopedic Dictionary of Psychology* (see entry 170). Some were updated and revised; others appear identical to those in the parent volume. The book's emphasis is on physiological processes and their effects on human and animal behavior, biographies of famous psychologists, and behavioral phenomena in abnormal psychology. In addition to physical aspects of abnormal behavior, physiological topics in perception, movement, and other areas of psychology are included. Articles run from half a column to about two pages. Slight coverage is provided on testing as it relates to clinical assessment. Similarly, there is little material on treatment and therapy within the realm of clinical psychology. The brief, selective bibliographies reflect late 1970s and early 1980s publications and in some cases are updated from the corresponding *Encyclopedic Dictionary* entry even if the article is not. There is a subject index.

393. **Encyclopedia of Neuroscience**. George Adelman, ed. Boston, Birkhauser, 1987. 2v. index. $150.00/set. LC 86-14779. ISBN 0-8176-3335-9.

Neurosciences, defined in the preface as "including all those fields involved in trying to understand how the brain and nervous system work," is made more accessible by the 700-plus articles in this volume. This specialized source is all the more important because neurophysiology and neuropsychology are not well covered in more comprehensive works, such as *International Encyclopedia of Psychiatry, Psychology, Psychoanalysis, and Neurology* (see entry 172). Although readable, the essays presuppose some knowledge of terminology associated with the brain, nervous system, and their behavioral influences.

Articles average two pages, often provide cross-references to related articles, and conclude with lists of current and classic suggested readings. Drawings, photographs, and other illustrations are plentiful. Appendixes include drawings of the human brain, a statement on the use of animals in research, and brief biographies of prominent contributors to neuroscience and related areas. There are a name index and a detailed subject index.

394. Goodwin, D. M. **A Dictionary of Neuropsychology**. New York, Springer-Verlag, 1989. 325p. $39.00. LC 89-21704. ISBN 0-387-97123-8.

This is a useful supplement to the more comprehensive and advanced *Encyclopedia of Neuroscience* (see entry 393). It is, in part, a medical dictionary, providing definitions for terms, syndromes, symptoms, and abbreviations used in medicine and neuroanatomy. However, definitions of concepts specific to brain structure and dysfunction and their diagnosis make this source more useful for students of physiological psychology. Of particular interest are descriptions of research methodologies, instrumentation, and approaches to treatment.

Definitions vary in length from a sentence to a few paragraphs. Although there is no index, entries provide many cross-references. A 40-page list of references cited in the definitions follows the dictionary.

PSYCHOLOGY OF VERBAL AND NONVERBAL BEHAVIOR

Guides

395. Key, Mary Ritchie. **Nonverbal Communication: A Research Guide and Bibliography**. Metuchen, N.J., Scarecrow, 1977. 439p. index. price not reported. LC 76-53024. ISBN 0-8108-1014-X.

Key starts her guide with a series of seven essays on the scope, issues, and multidisciplinary contributions to the study of nonverbal behavior. Some topics most relevant to psychology are relationships with neurological and brain functions, innate and learned behaviors in animals and humans, tactile and proxemic influences, patterned group and individual behavior, and mimicry. The bibliography portion cites books and chapters, dissertations, research reports, and journal and magazine articles in a variety of languages. Although some items refer to essays from as early as the sixteenth century, most reflect research and popular publications from the 1950s through the mid-1970s. Coverage reflects the content of the preceding essays. Unfortunately, arrangement is by author, and the volume's index does not cover the bibliography section, making the 3,000-plus citations difficult to access.

Bibliographies

396. Davis, Martha. **Understanding Body Movement: An Annotated Bibliography**. New York, Arno Press, 1972. 190p. index. $21.00. LC 73-37652. ISBN 0-405-00286-6.

397. Davis, Martha, and Janet Skupien, eds. **Body Movement and Nonverbal Communication: An Annotated Bibliography, 1971-1981**. Bloomington, Ind., Indiana University Press, 1982. 294p. index. (Advances in Semiotics). $29.50. LC 81-7881. ISBN 0-253-34101-9.

The scope of these bibliographies is, according to the earlier volume, "the anthropology and psychology of physical body movement, including nonverbal communication, body language, and psychological aspects of movement" (p. vii). The 1982 publication expands coverage to include dance therapy, motor learning and physiology, and related areas in physical education and recreation. Both have good prefatory chapters on the history, development, and direction of movement research. Animal studies that contribute to the understanding of human behavior are included.

Over 2,300 works are listed and descriptively annotated, most representing published literature such as journal articles, annual reviews, books and book chapters, government publications, and conference proceedings. The remainder cite doctoral dissertations, unpublished manuscripts, and research reports. The first volume covers only English-language works;the majority appeared from 1900 to mid-1971, but there are selected earlier items. The later book has some foreign-language coverage. Citations are listed by primary author and supported by subject indexes. The 1982 publication has a supplemental author index and an appendix that lists research journals important in human movement research.

398. Dingwall, William Orr. **Language and the Brain: A Bibliography and Guide**. New York, Garland, 1981. 2v. index. (Garland Reference Library of Social Science, v.73). price not reported. LC 80-8491. ISBN 0-8240-9495-6.

Dingwall provides a guide to the literature for general students and an in-depth bibliography to the international literature for researchers. The citations are categorized under five broad areas: general works and philosophical issues, language functions in the brain, neurological disorders, development of language, and the evolution of the brain and communicative behavior. Each topic area is preceded by an introduction, a list of suggested readings for students, charts, and a variety of explanatory material. The heart of the work however, is the 5,746 bibliographic references listed under the broad categories above and subdivided under narrower content areas. The major topical areas are historical background, experimental research on neurological disorders, and language development, with less coverage of clinical and applied topics. The literature cited is not limited to English-language sources. Most references were published after 1960, with selected earlier coverage. In addition to subject and author indexes, there are supplemental lists of bibliographies, societies, journals, and series that regularly publish relevant research.

399. Duker, Sam. **Listening Bibliography**. 2d ed. Metuchen, N.J., Scarecrow, 1968. 316p. index. $16.50. LC 68-12630. ISBN 0-8108-0085-3.

Duker defines listening as "the major receptive skill in the human communication process" (p. viii); that is, of verbal communication. English-language books, theses, published proceedings, technical reports, and articles from research and professional journals are cited. Although a liberal number of references are drawn from the literatures of education, language arts, linguistics, and communication, the book's primary concern is experimental studies from the psychological literature on the interrelated processes of listening, comprehension, and learning. Selected articles from trade periodicals in management, retailing, and the sciences are also cited. Unpublished papers and manuscripts, textbooks, and curriculum materials are excluded, as are items on the physiology of hearing and auditory processes, communication skills and theory, and mass media, and most literature on music listening.

Entries are arranged by author and supplemented by subject and author indexes. Annotations are brief and descriptive. Most of the 1,332 citations were published from the 1950s to the mid-1960s. Although the age of this publication lessens its value, it remains a comprehensive retrospective source.

400. Gitter, A. George, and Robert Grunin. **Communication: A Guide to Information Sources.** Detroit, Gale, 1980. 157p. index. (Psychology Information Guide Series, v.3). $68.00. LC 79-26529. ISBN 0-8103-1443-6.

Much of this bibliography covers topics in mass communication, communication research methods and theory, and international and cross-cultural communication. Two substantial sections deal with interpersonal communication (speech, small group, and nonverbal) and the influence of communication attitudes (e.g., persuasion, deception, compliance). A separate section contains annotated reference works, primarily those concerned with mass media.

The 723 annotated citations represent books, book chapters, and articles from the late 1960s through the late 1970s that will be of interest to mass media professionals, researchers, and students. Because coverage of the communication, speech, and media literature predominates, it is a good volume for relevant references outside the discipline of psychology.

401. Henley, Nancy, and Barrie Thorne, comps. **She Said/He Said: An Annotated Bibliography of Sex Differences in Language, Speech, and Nonverbal Communication.** Pittsburgh, Pa., Know, 1975. 311p. index. $3.50. ISBN 0-912786-36-1.

Henley and Thorne survey the literature on the influence of sex roles and differences on self-expression, verbal and nonverbal interaction, and communication as a reflection of those same roles and differences. Most citations represent journal and book literature, with limited coverage of unpublished conference papers and popular magazines.

The factors of limited time coverage (much material dating from the late 1960s) and the relatively small number of citations (about 150) limit the utility of this work. Still, this is a useful source of retrospective material on sex roles and communication styles. Citations and their lengthy descriptive annotations are arranged hierarchically under nine broad subject areas: general works on language and speech, vocabulary, phonology, patterns of conversation, dialectical differences of men and women, ethnic groups, language acquisitions, verbal ability, and nonverbal communication and behavior. An author index is supplied.

402. Jarrard, Mary E. W., and Phyllis R. Randall. **Women Speaking: An Annotated Bibliography of Verbal and Nonverbal Communication, 1970-1980.** New York, Garland, 1982. 478p. index. (Garland Reference Library of Social Science, v.108). price not reported. LC 82-15737. ISBN 0-8240-9281-3.

Jarrard and Randall focus on a decade of publishing in psychology, anthropology, sociology, linguistics and speech communication, business, and political science. The only relevant area not covered is the broad one of mass communication. Most of the 1,327 citations and their long, descriptive annotations are listed under three categories: communication settings, communication characteristics, and communication means. A fourth section lists comprehensive works. The numerous subheadings in the first three categories are indicative of the broad subject scope. The first part encompasses self-perception and communication styles and relationships with others and groups, within family and organization settings, and in public. Part 2, "Characteristics of Communication," incorporates leadership, listening, persuasion, and self-disclosure. Part 3 covers verbal and nonverbal communication, including language, word choice, and syntax; gestures, eye contact, and facial expressions; and touch and proxemics. English-language books and journal articles predominate, and popular works have been excluded. Material is accessible through a subject index and an abundance of cross-references.

403. Obudho, Constance, comp. **Human Nonverbal Behavior: An Annotated Bibliography**. Westport, Conn., Greenwood Press, 1979. 196p. index. $36.95. LC 79-7586. ISBN 0-313-21094-2.

This is a very good retrospective tool to the substantive research literature on nonverbal communication and interaction. It is primarily a list of 536 citations to academic and professional journals, books, and doctoral dissertations, with a smattering of unpublished research and conference papers and published proceedings. All were published between 1940 and 1978. The brief introduction reviews the scope and history of research on nonverbal behavior. The bibliography is divided into two parts: studies with normal individuals and studies with psychiatric subjects. Because the citations draw primarily from the English-language journal literature of psychology, sociology, and cultural anthropology, coverage of applied research is limited. Most references are accompanied by descriptive and lengthy annotations. There are author and subject indexes.

404. Slobin, Dan Isaac. **Leopold's Bibliography of Child Language**. Bloomington, Ind., Indiana University Press; repr., Ann Arbor, Mich., UMI Books on Demand, 1972. 202p. index. $41.80. LC 79-184526. ISBN 0-253-33340-7.

Slobin has revised Werner F. Leopold's 1952 *Bibliography of Child Language* and has substantially updated coverage to 1967. Consistent with the original volume, there is considerable coverage of the literature on language acquisition, learning, and development, including speech pathology, cross-linguistics, and linguistic structure. Particularly excellent is the coverage of foreign-language material, especially German, Russian, and French.

There are indexes by language spoken by the child and by subject; there is also a combined cross-reference index of these two elements. This work will be of particular interest to researchers in psycho- and sociolinguistics and child development.

Indexes and Abstracts

405. **Communications Abstracts**. Vol. 1- , No. 1- . Newbury Park, Calif., Sage, 1978- . bimonthly. $297.00/yr.(institutions). ISSN 0162-2811.

This title, published quarterly until the 1990 volume, is produced in cooperation with the Temple University School of Communications and Theater. Articles are selected from approximately 170 journal titles in law and public policy, management, psychology, sociology, and communications. Interdisciplinary journals are especially well covered. Issues in mass media receive the most solid coverage, including its effects on individual and group behaviors and attitudes. Other emphases are sex roles, stereotyping, and organizational behavior and communication. Journal citations are followed by references to books and book chapters, and both formats are accompanied by lengthy, nonevaluative abstracts. Issues contain author and subject indexes that cumulate annually.

406. **Linguistics and Language Behavior Abstracts**. Vol. 19, No. 1- . La Jolla, Calif., Sociological Abstracts, 1985- . quarterly. $200.00/yr. ISSN 0888-8027.

Each issue contains over 2,000 citations and nonevaluative abstracts for articles that represent a broad range of disciplines: education, speech and communications, medicine, anthropology, ethnology and cultural studies, linguistics, acoustics and speech, and psychology. There is considerable foreign-language coverage. Citations are hierarchically arranged according to 29 broad subject areas, most with narrower subcategories. For example, the section for psycholinguistics incorporates nine subareas, including verbal learning, neurolinguistics, and psychoacoustics. In addition to psycholinguistics, the service has important international coverage of auditory perception, communication and interpersonal behavior, nonverbal communication, and learning and developmental disabilities. Beginning with 1990 issues, it has incorporated citations to book reviews in linguistics.

Each issue includes author, subject, and source journal indexes, which cumulate annually. Volumes for 1967 through 1984 were published under the title *Language and Language Behavior Abstracts*.

Handbooks

407. Knapp, Mark K., and Gerald R. Miller, eds. **Handbook of Interpersonal Communication**. Newbury Park, Calif., Sage, 1985. 768p. index. $55.00. LC 85-1869. ISBN 0-8039-2120-9.

The editors identify several themes governing the contributed chapters in this work: the analysis of verbal and nonverbal behavior, the study of how communication evolves over time in an individual or group, the interface of communication with social behavior, control and persuasion, and the role of individual differences. Fifteen chapters are divided among four general areas: issues and methodology, the fundamental elements of interpersonal communication, individual differences and influences on communication, and communication in specific contexts (e.g., the family, the work setting). The contributions truly serve the function of a handbook, as they include extensive literature reviews and syntheses of theories and research. There are detailed author and subject indexes.

Dictionaries and Encyclopedias

408. **International Encyclopedia of Communications**. New York, Oxford University Press, 1989. 4v. index. $350.00/set. LC 88-18132. ISBN 0-19-504994-2.

This is an excellent, comprehensive reference on human communication systems, modes, and behavior. The topical guide in volume 4 organizes the 550-plus articles under 30 broad categories and gives an indication of the breadth of coverage, which stretches over such topics as the means and function of communication in both animals and humans, historical perspectives, art and literature, government and public policy, language and linguistics, mass media, and communication theories. There are also selected biographical entries. Articles usually represent broad concepts, such as advertising or perception, and run from a page to over 20 pages in length. Illustrations and photographs are plentiful. Cross-references to related articles are provided, and brief bibliographies are appended to most entries. In addition to the topical index, volume 4 also has a detailed general index.

The articles are comprehensive and authoritative, the layout is easy to read and use, and the organization makes information accessible. Overall, the set provides especially good coverage of the psychology of both verbal and nonverbal behavior and psycholinguistics.

409. Roman, Klara G. **Encyclopedia of the Written Word: A Lexicon for Graphology and Other Aspects of Writing**. New York, Frederick Ungar, 1968. 550p. index. price not reported. LC 68-12124.

Although viewed by many psychologists as a pseudoscience, graphology has its adherents and occasionally has a resurgence in popularity among those in personality and personnel assessment. Graphology is defined as the study of handwriting in general and the interpretation of handwriting as an expression of personality, a form of gesture, or a diagnostic tool for determining communicative and linguistic style. Roman tries to cover it all in this unusual reference work.

Most of the entries are alphabetical and vary in length from a few sentences to several pages. There is an interesting hodgepodge of coverage, including writing systems, characteristics of writing patterns of normal and disordered individuals, many illustrations of alphabets, and writing and communication styles and their personality correlates. Seven essays cover the definition, use, and application of graphology and graphoanalysis, including an excellent survey on the history and status of graphology. There are a bibliography and a subject index.

DEVELOPMENTAL PSYCHOLOGY

General Services

Handbooks

410. Wolman, Benjamin B., ed. **Handbook of Developmental Psychology**. Englewood Cliffs, N.J., Prentice-Hall, 1982. 960p. index. $119.00. LC 81-13830. ISBN 0-13-372599-5.

Contributed by 75 authors, the 50 essays comprising this handbook cover the entirety of human development. Its broad coverage also makes the information less accessible than handbooks that deal with more discrete developmental groups, such as *Handbook of Child Psychology* (see entry 425). The first section contains chapters on research methodologies and theories of development. The remaining sections divide essays by age group (infancy, childhood, adolescence, adulthood, and older adults). Discussion of physical growth and development is discussed relative to perceptual and cognitive development throughout life, development or decline of learning and memory, psychophysiology, and sexual behavior.

Some topics in such areas as family and marital relations, environmental influences, social and interpersonal interaction, and attitude formation and personality development are represented in more than one essay, thereby making connections across the life span. These may be accessed from the table of contents under the age group arrangement or the subject index. There is also an author index.

Dictionaries and Encyclopedias

411. **Dictionary of Developmental and Educational Psychology**. Rom Harre and Roger Lamb, eds. Cambridge, Mass., MIT Press, 1986. 271p. index. $13.95pa. LC 86-10400. ISBN 0-262-58007-2.

Articles in this work are based on material published in Harre and Lamb's 1983 *Encyclopedic Dictionary of Psychology* (see entry 170). Entries were selected from the larger work and in some cases were updated. The book's main focus is on theories of development (e.g., Piagetian, Freudian), controversies and issues in development (e.g., Jensen and IQ), educational settings for normal and exceptional individuals, and biographical entries for both living and deceased psychologists and theorists. Many reference lists were updated from the original volume—some 1986 citations are included—and there are liberal cross-references, but there are few illustrations and charts. Although the index is detailed, it is not always as complete as it could be.

Prenatal Development, Childhood, and Adolescence

Guides

412. Haag, Enid E. **Research Guide for Studies in Infancy and Childhood**. Westport, Conn., Greenwood Press, 1988. 430p. index. (Reference Sources in the Social Sciences and Humanities, no.8). $55.00. LC 88-5690. ISBN 0-313-24763-3.

Used with *Childhood Information Resources* (see entry 416), this is a comprehensive and comprehensible guide to the research literature and reference tools for students, researchers, professionals, and all others who need access to the literature on the developmental stages from birth to age 13. The first section introduces general reference materials and research strategies; discusses the application of new technologies (e.g., bibliographic databases); and lists annual reviews, bibliographies, handbooks, encyclopedias, and other reference works on childhood. The second section, on special subject area bibliographies, divides a variety of publication formats under nine broad areas: the family, child care, communication, cognition, the development of behavior, social and cultural development, physical development, abnormal development, and creativity. Each category is further subdivided, for a total of 65 narrower topics, making access by broad subject areas easy. Under these, over 1,400 English-language items are cited, arranged by type of publication: bibliographies, literature reviews, handbooks, dictionaries, research reports, and other references. Most represent book literature, including citations to individual chapters, with selected coverage of conference proceedings and special issues of research journals. Citations reflect current literature, generally the 1970s through 1987. Annotations vary in length from a sentence to a paragraph, and most are descriptive and evaluative. Author, title, and subject indexes end the work.

413. Scheffler, Hannah Nuba, et al. **Resources for Early Childhood: An Annotated Bibliography and Guide for Educators, Librarians, Health Care Professionals, and Parents**. New York, Garland, 1983. 584p. index. (Reference Books on Family Issues, v.1; Garland Reference Library of Social Science, v.118). $63.00; $10.00pa. LC 81-48421. ISBN 0-8240-9390-9; 0-8240-8769-0pa.

Each of the 16 chapters in this volume is preceded by an essay that provides an introduction and a historical perspective of the topic. Citations to trade and professional books and government publications follow, each critically and evaluatively annotated. The audience dictates a broad scope, and this is matched by the comprehensive coverage of parenting guides, professional and association publications for preschool educators and other professionals, and all who seek English-language books on the topic that have been published after 1960.

Chapters encompass prenatal and child development through age five, the family and parenting, health and nutrition, play and self-expression, education and child care, children with special needs, and media influences. Many of the 15 subject chapters contain more than one topical essay. A final chapter provides a selective list of serial publications, research centers, and organizations. Access to the material is provided through author, title, and subject indexes.

414. Scheffler, Hannah Nuba, Deborah Lovitky Sheiman, and Kathleen Pullan Watkins. **Infancy: A Guide to Research and Resources**. New York, Garland, 1986. 182p. index. (Garland Reference Library of Social Science, v.324). $37.00. LC 86-9970. ISBN 0-8240-8699-6.

Covering human development from the prenatal period through age two, this guide is intended for parents, students, and professionals who work with infants or their families. Each of the 10 chapters is preceded by an essay that defines and reviews a topic in mental or physical development, family relations and socialization, play and education, or exceptional infants. The chapters on social-emotional development, cognitive development, play, and family interaction are noteworthy for students of developmental psychology. A bibliography of approximately 50 items, evaluatively annotated, follows each essay. Most references are aimed at the parent or early childhood educator, with a mix of popular and survey works. The last section lists over 100 relevant newsletters and journals from a wide variety of disciplines and professions, as well as magazines and other popular periodicals. There are author and subject indexes.

415. Sheiman, Deborah Lovitky, and Maureen Slonim. **Resources for Middle Childhood.** New York, Garland, 1988. 138p. index. (Reference Books on Family Issues, v.12; Garland Reference Library of the Social Sciences, v.433). $27.00. LC 88-18046. ISBN 0-8240-7777-6.

The focus of this guide is the growth, development, and needs of children between ages 6 and 12. Eight chapters represent physical, psychosocial, and cognitive development; family interaction; the role of play; relationships with peers; education; and societal impact on child-rearing and development. Each section is begun by an essay that discusses important research issues and trends in the literature. A critically annotated bibliography of approximately 50 books and government publications follows. The emphasis is on books published after 1975 that are appropriate for parents, students, and educators. Author and title indexes are supplied.

416. Woodbury, Marda. **Childhood Information Resources.** Arlington, Va., Information Resources Press, 1985. 593p. index. $45.00. LC 84-080534. ISBN 0-87815-051-X.

Woodbury takes an interdisciplinary approach to the dispersed reference literature on childhood. Part 1 discusses initial approaches to information: preparing a research strategy, using thesauri and subject lists, limiting a topic, and using the variety of information formats effectively. Part 2, on printed references works, cites over 500 sources with evaluative annotations, divided into nine sections by type of reference tools: dictionaries and encyclopedias; literature guides and library catalogs; histories; research annuals, and book reviews; bibliographies; guides to media; indexing and abstracting tools; periodicals and newsletters; and directories. Part 3 lists and describes almost 200 nonprint sources, including bibliographic databases, organizations, research institutes, and associations dedicated to the welfare of, or research on, children. Part 4 lists reference sources on tests, statistics, children's literature, and parent education. An appendix contains a classified and annotated list of multidisciplinary handbooks and collected works, primarily for the professional. Closing the book is a combined author, title, and subject index.

Beginning each section are a detailed description and uses to which the sources listed can be put. Illustrations are limited to examples from important reference tools. The comprehensive nature of this guide, its interdisciplinary coverage, and the number of sources cited make it an excellent research tool.

Bibliographies

417. Abel, Ernest L., comp. **Behavioral Teratology: A Bibliography to the Study of Birth Defects of the Mind.** Westport, Conn., Greenwood Press, 1985. 206p. index. $40.95. LC 85-21946. ISBN 0-313-25066-9.

This selective and representative bibliography responds to increasing interest in prenatal exposure of drugs, environmental toxins, and like substances on behavior after birth. Both animal and human studies are represented. Publishing trends in this area dictate that most citations are post-1970, with coverage to 1985. There are selected citations from earlier works, especially of the literature on irradiation, inhalants, and other substances in which there was early research interest.

The 1,993 unannotated citations to books and chapters, research journals, and government documents are derived from the literature of biomedicine, pharmacology and toxicology, neurobiology and physiology, and pediatrics and child development. Entries are listed under 28 agents (e.g., antidepressants, lithium, heavy metals, smoking, ultrasound), with general sections for reviews and basic literature on behavioral teratology. The subject index is scanty and best used to locate studies dealing with specific effects on development.

418. Abel, Ernest L., comp. **Fetal Alcohol Exposure and Effects: A Comprehensive Bibliography**. Westport, Conn., Greenwood Press, 1985. 309p. index. $46.95. LC 85-9864. ISBN 0-313-24632-7.

Abel concentrates on citations to research on the effects of alcohol on pregnancy and fetal and child development. The 3,088 entries represent human and animal research as published in books and journals, with a smattering of audiovisual material and government publications. Material in many foreign languages is listed. Most citations are post-1970, with a cutoff date of 1984, although some references go back as far as the late nineteenth century. Because primary arrangement is by author, the rather scanty subject index provides the only topical access.

Contributions from the health sciences and pharmacology literatures outnumber those from psychology. Abel does, however, provide excellent coverage of the addiction literature from a variety of perspectives. Because of its comprehensive time and language coverage and the substantive nature of the material cited, this is an excellent bibliography on fetal alcohol syndrome and related issues in child development.

419. Brackbill, Yvonne, ed. **Research in Infant Behavior: A Cross-Indexed Bibliography**. Baltimore, Md., Williams & Wilkins, 1964. 281p. index. price not reported. LC 64-25575.

Obviously, this work will be of solely historical interest. However, much of the material cited from the literatures of psychology and medicine predates standard indexing tools, making it difficult to locate elsewhere. Included are citations to books, reports, and articles representing empirical research literature on child behavior and development through age four. Articles of a theoretical nature or that are concerned with abnormal development are excluded.

The 1,733 unannotated references are followed by the author index and seven subject indexes that cover concept groups: perception, motor behavior, learning, communication, cognition, social behavior, and personality. Each subject index contains subheadings, with entry numbers duplicated among the indexes, as appropriate.

420. Hirsch, Elisabeth S. **Problems of Early Childhood: An Annotated Bibliography and Guide**. New York, Garland, 1983. 253p. index. (Garland Reference Library of Social Science, v.129). LC 82-49031. ISBN 0-8240-9216-3.

As Hirsch summarizes in her introduction, the 1,000 references in this book concern the "problems of childhood result[ing] from being a child." Citations are organized under 10 subject categories: separation, illness, death and grief, effects of divorce, the single-parent family, effect of the working mother, siblings, discipline, relationships with peers and others, and emotional life.

Inclusion is selective, and annotations are brief and descriptive. Each section is begun by a concise essay that describes the topic at hand and the distribution of its literature. Most chapters divide citations by format: books and pamphlets for parents and teachers, articles, and children's books. There is coverage of professional and research book and journal literature, ERIC documents and government publications, and popular periodicals (very limited). Literature from the 1970s predominates, with work from earlier years included as appropriate to the topic. There are subject and author indexes. Although entire bibliographies are devoted to some of the issues that Hirsch covers, this is an excellent, well-constructed source for students, parents, and professionals.

421. Laubenfels, Jean. **The Gifted Student: An Annotated Bibliography**. Westport, Conn., Greenwood Press, 1977. 220p. index. (Contemporary Problems of Childhood, no.1). $35.00. LC 77-82696. ISBN 0-8371-9760-0.

Although the title implies interest in gifted children only in the context of education, Laubenfels covers considerably more by including the literatures of medicine, psychology, and counseling. The 1,329 citations are arranged under nine topical areas and numerous subheadings, plus sections for bibliographies and current material. Categories include the causes and characteristics of giftedness, testing and identification, educational programming and curriculum, such problems as social adjustment, longitudinal research, and research in the related areas of creativity and cross-cultural psychology.

Laubenfels's main focus is on research literature published between 1961 and early 1977, although selected earlier work and popular material are also cited. Formats include books, periodical articles, government publications, research reports, and dissertations; all but the last are annotated. Author and keyword subject indexes are provided, and appendixes list organizations concerned with the gifted, diagnostic instruments, audiovisual materials for professional and student use, and bibliographic search tools.

422. Myers, Hector R., Phyllis G. Rana, and Marcia Harris, comps. **Black Child Development in America, 1927-1977: An Annotated Bibliography**. Westport, Conn., Greenwood Press, 1979. 470p. index. $40.95. LC 78-20028. ISBN 0-313-20719-4.

Scholarly and professional periodicals (including journals and annual reviews) are indexed for the book's coverage of Black children from birth to adolescence. Although the preface implies that only periodicals (but not popular magazines) are included, some ERIC documents, government documents, and books are also cited. The abstracts are descriptive, and content aims at inclusiveness rather than selectivity.

A total of 1,274 citations are organized by author under the following areas of development: language, physical, cognitive, personality, and social. The literature covered is almost exclusively from the social science disciplines. There are author and subject indexes.

423. Schulman, Janice B., & Robert C. Prall. **Normal Child Development: An Annotated Bibliography of Articles and Books Published 1950-1969**. New York, Grune & Stratton, 1971. 326p. index. LC 71-178971. ISBN 0-8089-0742-5.

In this book, childhood is defined as ages 3 through 18. The 733 citations and descriptive abstracts represent book and journal literature, especially empirically based research studies and longitudinal studies. Those based on research conducted in experimental settings are, for the most part, excluded. The volume of publishing in this area and during 1950-1969 has required selectivity on the part of Schulman and Prall. Material chosen emphasizes English-language research of most interest to both professionals and students.

References are classified under 18 categories representing social and familial relationships, physical development and health, leisure and vocational activities, achievement, personality, and attitudes. A partial index provides access by the variables of age, socioeconomic status, and family composition. Along with an author index, there is a list of published results from important, national research projects concerning children and adolescents.

Indexes and Abstracts

424. **Child Development Abstracts and Bibliography**. Vol. 2- , No. 1- . Chicago, University of Chicago Press, 1928- . triannual. $52.00/yr. ISSN 0009-3939.

Published on behalf of the Society for Research in Child Development, this service provides excellent, focused access to the research literature of research journals and books. (The first volume in 1927 was published under the title *Selected Child Development Abstracts*.) Over 200 source journals represent sociology and social work, education and psychology, pediatrics, and social issues involving youth. Citations are organized under several broad categories: biomedicine and health, psychological processes, social psychology and personality, education, issues in psychiatry and clinical psychology, and historical and methodological issues. Lengthy, evaluative abstracts of books are included in a separate section; each issue generally contains about 20 such abstracts. The author and subject indexes in each issue cumulate in the third issue. The subject index is easy to use because it allows one to look under subject, then by subheading or population.

Handbooks

425. Mussen, Paul H., ed. **Handbook of Child Psychology**. 4th ed. New York, John Wiley, 1983. 4v. index. $299.95/set. LC 83-6517(v.1); 83-5073(v.2); 83-3468(v.3); 83-6552(v.4). ISBN 0-471-09057-3(v.1); 0-471-09055-7(v.2); 0-471-09064-6(v.3); 0-471-09065-4(v.4).

The most important handbook in developmental psychology, this set enjoys an illustrious pedigree that began with Leonard Carmichael's *Manual of Child Psychology* in 1946. This edition retains the best of the old material (e.g., Piaget's essay on his own theory from the 1970 edition of Carmichael) while incorporating advances in neurological assessment, at-risk development, and sex typing. Among the impressive list of contributors are Jerome Kagan, Robert Sternberg, and Eleanor Maccoby.

Each volume is intended to stand alone, with chapters focusing on specific aspects of child development and psychology. Volume 1, *History, Theory, and Methods*, contains chapters on the perceptions of childhood and development in a historical context, prevalent theories and their development, and research models and methods in the field. Topics in perception, ethology, neurological development, memory, and related areas comprise volume 2, *Infancy and Developmental Psychobiology*. Communication and reasoning, social cognition, intelligence, morality, and creativity are included in *Cognitive Development*, the third volume. Finally, volume 4 covers topics and issues in personality, interpersonal relationships, socialization, self-esteem, and abnormal development and psychopathology. Each volume has its own author and subject indexes. This set represents an outstanding contribution to the discipline.

426. Osofsky, Joy Doniger, ed. **Handbook of Infant Development**. 2d ed. New York, John Wiley, 1987. 1391p. index. (Wiley Series on Personality Processes). $105.00. LC 86-28906. ISBN 0-471-88565-7.

Twenty-seven chapters divided under five broad categories span the breadth of research on human development during the first two years of life. The first section focuses on physiological, behavioral, cognitive, and perceptual aspects of development. Next come six chapters on social and familial interaction and influences, and four essays in part 3 review methodological approaches for assessment and research. Idenfication of at-risk infants—those most likely to develop affective or developmental disorders later in life—and intervention strategies are discussed in the five chapters of part 4. Finally, six essays present recent research on such topics as attachment, individual differences, and infant mental health. Some essays will be of interest only to mental health professionals, graduate students, and academics. There is an author index, and the subject index will assist when locating a topic discussed from a variety of perspectives.

427. Van Hasselt, Vincent B., and Michel Hersen. **Handbook of Adolescent Psychology**. Elmsford, N.Y., Pergamon Press, 1987. 508p. index. (Pergamon General Psychology Series, v.142). $80.00. LC 86-91511. ISBN 0-08-031923-8.

In this handbook, 25 chapters have been contributed by over 40 professionals. The chapters are divided into five broad categories. An introductory chapter reviews the relatively brief history of the scientific study of adolescence as a stage of human development. The second section reviews adolescence as viewed by five theoretical perspectives: psychodynamic, learning, biological, developmental, and phenomenological. The seven chapters of part 3 cover such topics as sexuality, moral growth, family relationships, and social adjustment. Part 4 reviews seven psychological disorders that commonly originate in adolescence (e.g., substance abuse, depression, eating disorders). The last five chapters covers selected topics in adolescence, such as the disabled adolescent, pregnancy and marriage, and vocational planning. There are author and subject indexes.

This handbook is intended for advanced students and professionals. However, essays provide comprehensive reviews of approaches to research, cite liberally from current published literature, and attempt to present the whole in a comprehensible manner.

Dictionaries and Encyclopedias

428. Lerner, Richard M., Anne C. Petersen, and Jeanne Brooks-Gunn, eds. **Encyclopedia of Adolescence**. New York, Garland, 1991. 2v. index. (Garland Reference Library of the Social Sciences, v.495). $150.00/set. LC 90-14033. ISBN 0-8240-4378-2.

This set is part encyclopedia, part handbook. Short chapters that average four pages each describe issues in all aspects of adolescent social, physical, and psychological growth. Education, topics in mental and physical health, economic and employment issues, interpersonal and familial relationships, social relations, attitudes and effect, and a variety of theoretical approaches and historical issues all receive thoughtful coverage within over 200 concise essays. The number of references appended to each article range from under 10 to over 30. The editors rely heavily on publications and statistics from the 1980s, reflecting the recent spurt of research interest on development issues unique to adolescence.

The alphabetical arrangement of essays makes specific information somewhat difficult to find, even with extensive cross-references and the (sparse) subject index. But despite these failings, this is a solid reference to a developmental area that has in the past been afforded relatively little attention.

Adulthood, Aging, and the Elderly

Guides

429. Balkema, John B., ed. **Aging: A Guide to Resources**. Syracuse, N.Y., Gaylord Professional, 1983. 232p. index. price not reported. LC 83-9010. ISBN 0-915794-48-9.

Balkema addresses the research needs and tools of social gerontology in this brief but excellent guide. Nine chapters list over 600 works under broad topics: general works, community services, economics and employment, housing, nursing homes and long-term care, health, mental health, recreation, and education. These chapters are further divided by more specific topics, type of reference tool, format, or source function.

By far the largest category of material is reference works, including guides, handbooks and manuals, indexes, statistical sources, directories, and bibliographies. Although monographic and serial reference tools are the most numerous, literature reviews and bibliographies appearing in journals and survey texts are selectively included. Each item is briefly but evaluatively annotated. There are a subject index and an index by individual and corporate name.

430. Zito, Dorothea R., and George V. Zito. **A Guide to Research in Gerontology: Strategies and Resources**. Westport, Conn., Greenwood Press, 1988. 130p. index. $39.95. LC 88-17773. ISBN 0-313-25904-6.

This is a guide to research strategy and current literature in a field that is inherently interdisciplinary. Introductory chapters demonstrate this highly dispersed body of knowledge by covering law, medicine, psychology, sociology, and economics. Search strategies and the value of types of reference sources are discussed. Most sources are listed under their format or intended use, such as printed reference guides (e.g., handbooks, encyclopedias), indexing and abstracting services, the range of community resources, public and private agencies, and online databases. An introductory essay to each section details the potential of each type of source and how to use it effectively. Most entries are annotated, and the published material is primarily from the 1980s. Individual databases are listed and described in an appendix. Other appendixes provide a selective list of books and professional journals in gerontology and geriatrics.

Bibliographies

431. Edwards, Willie M., and Frances Flynn, comps. **Gerontology: A Core List of Significant Works**. Ann Arbor, Mich., Institute of Gerontology, University of Michigan, 1978. 160p. index. (Resources in Aging Series). price not reported. LC 78-624228.

432. Edwards, Willie M., and Frances Flynn, eds. **Gerontology: A Cross-National Core List of Significant Works**. Ann Arbor, Mich., Institute of Gerontology, University of Michigan, 1982. 365p. index. price not reported. LC 89-622127.

Although these volumes have significant overlap with *Gerontology: An Annotated Bibliography* (see entry 433), they provide better coverage of the topics of social gerontology: economics and demography, psychological and sociological aspects of aging, and education and employment. Coverage of medical and health issues is less complete.

Sections in the earlier volume include lists of 63 indexing tools and journal titles and 90 bibliographies and literature reviews on all aspects of aging. The bibliography is composed of approximately 1,000 unannotated citations to English-language books, government publications, and research reports. In a few cases, literature reviews in journals and special journal issues are cited. Most works are arranged under 20 broad topical categories, with an additional section for general materials. This is the only subject access, although there is an index by author and editor.

The updated and revised 1982 publication of over 2,000 citations is "cross-national" but not international. Emphasis is on Canada, the United States, and the United Kingdom, with highly selective coverage of other countries. A new feature is a section of historical essays on gerontology in the three English-speaking countries. The lists of indexing and reference tools, journals, handbooks, and the like remain and are delineated by country of publication. The selection criteria, scope, and organization used for the update's bibliography are similar to that in the previous edition, with the exception that there are more subject categories and citations are arranged by country. There are a short glossary of terms and author and title indexes.

433. Rooke, M. Leigh, and C. Ray Wingrove. **Gerontology: An Annotated Bibliography**. Washington, D.C., University Press of America, 1978. 262p. index. price not reported. LC 78-303051. ISBN 0-8191-0232-6.

Coverage in this volume is limited to English-language books, research reports, and government documents published between 1966 and 1977. Therefore, it serves as a retrospective source of material produced before the 1980s deluge of literature on aging and the elderly. Approximately 1,500 items are cited and descriptively annotated. Most appear within 33 topical categories, and an additional section is devoted to survey works. Issues in health maintenance, geriatrics, and public policy receive better coverage than psychological and sociological topics. However, sexuality, mental health, retirement, elderly minorities, thanatology, and family relations are covered. Most material is appropriate for practitioners in nursing and counseling, students, and others needing substantive retrospective source material, although some public advocacy, fiction, and self-help titles are also cited. A separate, annotated list of 32 serial publications in the field specifically related to aging and the elderly is appended, and there is an index by author and editor.

Indexes and Abstracts

434. **Abstracts in Social Gerontology: Current Literature on Aging.** Vol. 33- , No. 1- . Newbury Park, Calif., Sage, 1990- . quarterly. $98.00/yr.(institutions). ISSN 1047-4862.

This title is published in cooperation with the National Council on the Aging. Issues each contain about 250 citations to journal articles, books, and government and association publications, all accompanied by lengthy descriptive abstracts. Coverage is aimed at students, researchers, and professionals in a wide variety of fields in the social sciences, health care, and the helping professions. Citations are arranged under about 20 subject areas, most further subdivided for easy browsing. Another 200 unannotated citations in each issue are topically arranged under a separate section, "Related Citations." There are author and subject indexes.

The previous titles *Selected Acquisitions* and *Current Literature on Aging* (1963-1989) were published by the National Council on the Aging and were especially strong in geriatrics, short- and long-term care, adaptive design, and social policy and services. These areas are still covered by the new title, which apparently has better coverage of physiological and neuropsychological aspects of aging, mental illness, aging as a developmental stage, and interpersonal relations.

435. **Index to Periodical Literature on Aging.** Vol. 2- , No. 1- . Detroit, Lorraine, 1984- . quarterly. $150.00/yr.(institutions). ISSN 0882-3405.

About 100 English-language source journals indexed in this title reflect the multidisciplinary approaches to gerontology. Core gerontological journals are supplemented by selected social science titles in demographics, sociology, area studies, education, and public administration. However, works from medicine, nursing, psychology, and psychiatry dominate, especially those on geriatrics, cognition and learning in the elderly, and caregiving. Some animal studies are included, primarily those on the physical consequences of aging. Because the intended audience is researchers, students, and practitioners of helping professions, there is little coverage of popular periodicals.

Each issue is made up of four sections: a subject list of approximately 1,000 citations, a subject arrangement of citations to about 150 book reviews, and two separate author indexes to journal articles and book reviews. This title was previously published as *Areco's Quarterly Index to Periodical Literature on Aging.*

Handbooks and Yearbooks

436. Birren, James E., and K. Warner Schaie. **Handbook of the Psychology of Aging.** 3d ed. San Diego, Calif., Academic Press, 1990. 552p. index. $65.00. LC 89-15061. ISBN 0-12-101280-8.

Although the first edition of this work was published in 1977, the accelerating volume of research in areas associated with human aging has made this handbook a classic. With its companion titles *Handbook of Mental Health and Aging* (see entry 437), *Handbook of the Biology of Aging* (Academic Press, 1990), and *Handbook of Aging and the Social Sciences* (Academic Press, 1990), it provides an authoritative, comprehensive approach to issues associated with the aging process.

Some 29 chapters by noted authorities are organized under four broad topical categories. The first section, on theory and measurement, reviews the concepts, variables, and history of aging research. Part 2 reviews genetic, gender, biological, and environmental factors in the aging processes and their implication. Chapters under the third part, "Behavioral Processes in Aging," discuss physiological, cognitive, and mental health effects of the aging process, and part 4 reviews applications (e.g., psychological and assessment of the aging individual, human factors and environmental design, ethical issues in research). There are subject and name indexes.

437. Birren, James E., R. Bruce Sloane, and Gene D. Cohen, eds. **Handbook of Mental Health and Aging**. 2d ed. San Diego, Calif., Academic Press, 1992. 996p. index. $85.00. LC 91-41083. ISBN 0-12-101277-8.

Certainly the scientific and social interest in the needs of an aging population justifies this comprehensive handbook. In 33 chapters it accomplishes an authoritative review of issues of interest to mental health professionals, researchers, and advanced students. As noted in the preface, "the subject matter [of mental health of the older population] appears as broad as the content of life itself." Many chapters cover the social and physical aspects of the aging process, such as cognitive functioning (e.g., memory, intellectual functioning). Chapters on psychopathology include those on mood disorders and suicide, personality and anxiety disorders, sleep disorders, substance abuse, schizophrenia, and dementias. Eleven chapters focus on treatment and intervention (environmental, medical, and social), psychological assessment, ethical issues, and public policy topics. The breadth and organization of material is supplemented by the lengthy reference lists appended to chapters, containing references as current as 1991.

Dictionaries and Encyclopedias

438. **Encyclopedia of Aging**. George L. Maddox, ed.-in-chief. New York, Springer, 1987. 890p. index. $96.00. LC 86-27965. ISBN 0-8261-4840-9.

This is an outstanding one-volume source of information on the process of aging, with an emphasis on gerontology and some survey coverage of geriatrics. The approach is multidisciplinary, with articles on the biological and physiological effects of aging, legal and public welfare issues, the mental and physical health of the elderly, economic issues, and psychological development and well-being. The articles range in length from one page to several pages. They are clearly written and avoid technical language, making this work appropriate for educated laypeople, students, and researchers searching for information outside their areas of expertise. Abundant cross-references and a detailed subject index provide access to the material. All cited references in articles are cumulated in the 130-page bibliography. Well-selected graphs, statistical tables, and illustrations enhance the text.

439. Harris, Diana K. **Dictionary of Gerontology**. Westport, Conn., Greenwood Press, 1988. 201p. index. $37.95. LC 87-25142. ISBN 0- 313-25287-4.

Although gerontological and geriatric literature derives its vocabulary from a variety of disciplines, terms common to these disciplines often have special definitions. This dictionary provides brief definitions for approximately 900 terms, most appended by at least one reference from the research literature in which further information can be found. As the book lacks a subject index, *see* references and cross-references within entries are provided throughout. However, there is a name index to authors of cited references and individuals mentioned in the definitions.

Terms generally fall into the following categories: medicine and geriatrics; social movements, from the 1930s "Ham and Eggs Movement" to the Gray Panthers of the 1970s; work issues, such as retirement; socialization, psychological adjustment, and related topics in social gerontology; legal, economic, and civil rights of the elderly; the family and the aging process; and the demographics of aging. A few figures and other illustrations mostly display demographic data and various models of aging.

Although the definitions are brief (generally fewer than 200 words long), this is a good source for what can be imprecise terminology. The references are well selected and represent seminal literature.

Death and Dying

Bibliographies

440. Benson, Hazel B., comp. **The Dying Child: An Annotated Bibliography**. Westport, Conn., Greenwood Press, 1988. 270p. index. (Contemporary Problems of Childhood, no.6). $39.95. LC 88-11008. ISBN 0-313-24708-0.

Benson brings organization to the voluminous English-language literature on dying children published between 1960 and 1987 as books, articles in professional and popular periodicals, government documents, published proceedings, and dissertations. All but the last are accompanied by excellent descriptive annotations. References are listed under six broad topics (survey literature, children, adolescents, family aspects, caregivers, and somatic care), which are further divided under 40 subject areas. Citations are drawn from the literatures of pediatrics, social work, clinical psychology and child development, law, philosophy and ethics, and education.

Appendixes include annotated references to children's books, references to audiovisual materials, support groups for victims and their families, hospice and wish-granting organizations, and a basic list of print and online bibliographic sources. Author and keyword subject indexes close out the book.

441. Fulton, Robert, comp. **Death, Grief, and Bereavement: A Bibliography, 1845-1975**. New York, Arno, 1977. 253p. (Literature of Death and Dying). $27.50. LC 76-19572. ISBN 0-405-09570-8.

In this work over 3,800 unannotated references to books, book chapters, journal articles, and published proceedings are derived from a variety of disciplines, with anthropology, sociology, psychology, and medicine being the best represented. Most are in English, with selected foreign materials listed as well. Popular publications and magazines, literary and theological works, and much of the literature on suicide are excluded. Fulton provides particularly strong coverage of death education, bereavement and coping, the impact of culture on attitudes toward death and funerary practices, terminal illness, the definition of death, and impact of the family. The subject index is very detailed.

442. Miller, Albert Jay, and Michael James Acri. **Death: A Bibliographical Guide**. Metuchen, N.J., Scarecrow, 1977. 420p. index. price not reported. LC 77-1205. ISBN 0-8108-1025-5.

Most of the 3,848 citations in this volume are derived from popular, academic, and professional periodicals, books, and pamphlets. The book is similar to *Dying, Death, and Grief* (see entry 445) in coverage, in that an entire section is devoted to audiovisual materials and a directory of sources for them. Most citations are accompanied by an annotation and represent material published in English from the 1940s to 1974. A smattering of foreign-language publications and works published before 1900 make this work complementary to *Death, Grief, and Bereavement* (see entry 441). Use of the subject index is essential, as citations are organized under the broad topics of humanities, education, medicine, religion, science, and the social sciences. There is also an author index.

443. Poteet, G. Howard. **Death and Dying: A Bibliography (1950-1974)**. Troy, N.Y., Whitston, 1976. 192p. index. price not reported. LC 76-24093. ISBN 0-87875-105-X.

444. Poteet, G. Howard, and Joseph C. Santora. **Death and Dying: A Bibliography (1974-1978)**. Troy, N.Y., Whitston, 1989. 520p. index. $38.50. LC 88-50654. ISBN 0-87875-351-6.

Approximately 6,500 citations to English-language periodical articles and over 450 book titles are covered in these two volumes. Poteet and Santora draw their sources from a broad range of professions and disciplines, such as mental and physical health, rehabilitation and social work, gerontology, and interdisciplinary titles in the social sciences and medicine. The earlier volume covers some popular periodicals, whereas focus in the later one is on academic and professional journals. Scope of coverage also differs between the volumes. The older one emphasizes the psychological aspects of death (e.g., attitudes, bereavement, terminal care of the dying). The newer one expands coverage to the related areas of euthanasia, suicide, prevention, therapeutic approaches, ethical and moral issues, and legal implications.

In each volume, books are listed by author. A separate section categorizes periodical articles by a very detailed subject arrangement, thus compensating for the absence of a subject index. However, there are author indexes.

445. Simpson, Michael A. **Dying, Death, and Grief: A Critical Bibliography**. Pittsburgh, Pa., University of Pittsburgh Press, 1987. 259p. index. (Contemporary Community Health Series). $29.95. LC 87-6011. ISBN 0-82229-3561-9.

446. Simpson, Michael A. **Dying, Death, and Grief: A Critically Annotated Bibliography and Source Book of Thanatology and Terminal Care**. New York, Plenum, 1979. 288p. index. price not reported. LC 78-27273. ISBN 0-306-40147-9.

Together, these volumes provide comprehensive coverage of English-language books on thanatology and related fields produced through 1987. Books and association monographs published through 1978 are included in the earlier volume and encompass all areas of death and dying, bereavement, euthanasia, suicide, terminal care and counseling, and medical ethics. Simpson also lists over 300 audio- and videocassettes, films, and other instructional media. All citations are organized by format, and annotations describe and critique the work. Symbols for each work indicate in-print status and ranking according to a qualitative rating system. The section on books has its own author and subject indexes.

Separate categories include a list of thanatology journals and newsletters, selected foreign-language books, a highly selective list of journal article references, and a "stop press" list of recent materials. Most of these citations lack annotations, and only the journal reference section has citations arranged by subject.

The newer publication covers only books published through 1987, omitting other formats. Citations are accompanied by the same evaluative annotations and rating system as the earlier volume, a section for very recent materials, and two unannotated lists of books on murder and nuclear holocaust. There are subject and author indexes to all but the last topical sections.

Encyclopedias

447. Kastenbaum, Robert, and Beatrice Kastenbaum, eds. **Encyclopedia of Death**. Phoenix, Ariz., Oryx Press, 1989. 295p. index. $74.50. LC 89-9401. ISBN 0-89774-263-X.

Coverage of the humanities, social sciences, and biomedicine makes this a comprehensive, one-volume source of information on practically all areas of death and dying. Over 100 articles range from a page to several pages in length. They are well written and free of technical language and usually contain reference lists to current and seminal literature. Liberal cross-references among articles, a subject index, and a topical guide to essays under 14 broad areas make the contents easily accessible. There are a few illustrations, including statistical tables and graphs.

Controversial issues such as euthanasia, artificial life support, and communication with the afterlife are given balanced treatment, with divergent opinions fairly represented. Coverage is particularly strong in the areas of cross-cultural attitudes toward death, bereavement counseling and hospice care, death throughout the life span and impact on survivors, and the legal issues of death and dying.

PSYCHOLOGY OF MARRIAGE AND THE FAMILY

General Sources

Guides

448. Peck, Theodore P. **The Troubled Family: Sources of Information**. Jefferson, N.C., McFarland, 1982. 258p. index. price not reported. LC 80-29397. ISBN 0-89950-028-5.

This comprehensive guide will be useful for the student or professional in counseling, social work, or any psychotherapeutic setting in which dysfunctional families are treated. Part 1 lists federal and state offices and agencies that offer programming or assistance, either directly or indirectly, to at-risk families. Part 2 describes similar private organizations, and part 3 covers research institutes, international organizations, clearinghouses, and directory publications. Many of the over 500 resources are descriptively annotated.

Part 4 consists of a topically arranged and descriptively annotated bibliography of over 1,500 citations to government publications, theses, research reports, professional journals, and books on troubled families and their environment published from 1973 to 1981. A section (mostly annotated) of reference sources, journals, nonprint tools, and information clearinghouses completes the guide. There is a combined author, corporate, and subject index.

Bibliographies

449. Allen, Walter R., ed.-in-chief. **Black American Families, 1965-1985: A Classified, Selectively Annotated Bibliography**. Westport, Conn., Greenwood Press, 1986. 480p. index. (Bibliographies and Indexes in Afro-American and African Studies, no.16). $46.95. LC 86-14959. ISBN 0-313-25613-6.

This bibliography provides interdisciplinary coverage of the research literature on Black American families as found in books and book chapters, academic and professional journals, government publications, university-sponsored research reports, and doctoral dissertations and masters' theses. The 1,153 references to English-language sources were published from 1965 to 1985. The majority are annotated, and all citations are accompanied by a list of assigned subject headings. Subject access is provided by a keyword index and a classified index that lists authors, titles, and their citation numbers in the bibliography under a complex but thorough hierarchical subject arrangement of 120 headings. An index by secondary authors and editors supplements the basic author arrangement.

450. Barnes, Grace M., and Diane K. Augustino, comps. **Alcohol and the Family: A Comprehensive Bibliography**. Westport, Conn., Greenwood Press, 1987. 461p. index. (Bibliographies and Indexes in Sociology, no.9). $59.95. LC 86-27112. ISBN 0-313-24782-X.

Multinational and multilingual in scope, with a wide variety of formats represented among the 6,452 citations, this bibliography to the literature is comprehensive. Among the types of items included are books and journals, conference papers, pamphlets, research reports, government publications, dissertations, and substantial newspaper articles from medicine, psychology and psychiatry, the human service professions, and law.

Primary arrangement is by author (no cross-references for coauthors) and for anonymous works, title or translated title; a subject index is provided. Most of the material is post-1970, reflecting publishing patterns, although there are citations from the very early 1900s. The brief introduction is helpful for defining the scope of the bibliography and provides a historical and interdisciplinary context for the study of interrelated elements of alcoholism and the family structure.

451. Gruber, Ellen J. **Stepfamilies: A Guide to the Sources and Resources**. New York, Garland, 1986. 122p. index. (Reference Books on Family Issues, v.4; Garland Reference Library of Social Science, v.317). $30.00. LC 85-23111. ISBN 0-8240-8688-0.

In this volume, 342 English-language works published from 1980 to 1984 are listed under categories that represent approach and audience: professional journal articles and books, dissertations, unpublished reports and conference papers, and reference works aimed at the helping professional; popular books and periodical articles meant for parents who are part of stepfamilies; and books designed for children in the new "blended families." Additional sections list selected audiovisual products, associations and organizations offering support for stepfamilies or conducting research on their formation and impact, and a list of self-help newsletters.

There are subject and author indexes, although the former is not sufficiently detailed. Throughout, coverage is on the impact of the newly constructed family on parenting and child-raising, with little or no material on the dilemmas of divorce and remarriage.

452. Hausslein, Evelyn B. **Children and Divorce: An Annotated Bibliography and Guide**. New York, Garland, 1983. 130p. index. (Garland Reference Library of Social Science, v.119). price not reported. LC 81-048420. ISBN 0-8240-9391-7.

The purpose of this compilation is to provide an interdisciplinary approach to the literature of divorce and its effects on children. Consequently, citations to the book and journal literature represent the professions of education, sociology, psychology, psychiatry, and social work, with most published between 1975 and 1980.

This professional literature comprises about two-thirds of the 301 citations to print sources and is the core of the bibliography, which is followed by an index to intended professional audience. There are a separate list of popular books and magazine articles to which parents and others might be referred and a list of books on divorce aimed at children and young adults. All are descriptively annotated. A separate section consists of a selected, unannotated list of audiovisual materials. Finally, there is a brief list of national professional and self-help organizations dealing with custody mediation, family counseling, and other concerns of divorced families. Subject and author indexes are provided.

453. Sadler, Judith DeBoard. **Families in Transition: An Annotated Bibliography**. Hamden, Conn., Archon/Shoe String Press, 1988. 251p. index. $30.00. LC 87-37347. ISBN 0-208-02180-9.

The 1970s and 1980s saw an increase in the number of nontraditional families. As a consequence, there is growing interest among researchers and practitioners about the impact on development and family life of single-parent and stepfamilies, adoptive and foster-care situations, unmarried couples, commuter families, children of divorce, and latchkey children. Sadler has compiled an extensive annotated list of nearly 1,000 materials in a variety of formats, including books intended for children, audiovisual materials, journals and popular periodicals, and books meant for professionals and general readers. Nearly two-thirds were published in the 1980s.

Items are listed under 13 broad subject categories, plus sections for audiovisual materials and children's books. There are separate chapters for very recent, unannotated citations and self-help, professional, and research organizations. There are indexes by subjects, authors, and book and article titles. This volume combines currentness and comprehensiveness, making it a substantial contribution to the literature.

454. Schlesinger, Benjamin. **The One-Parent Family: Perspectives and Annotated Bibliography**. 4th ed. Toronto, University of Toronto Press, 1978. 224p. index. price not reported. LC 78-13155. ISBN 0-8020-2335-5.

455. Schlesinger, Benjamin. **The One-Parent Family in the 1980s: Perspectives and Annotated Bibliography, 1978-1984**. 5th ed. Toronto, University of Toronto Press, 1985. 284p. index. $20.95. ISBN 0-8020-6565-1.

These editions are complementary. The bibliography in the earlier one contains 750 citations and descriptive annotations divided by a range of publication dates (e.g., 1930-1969, 1970-1974, 1975-1978). Each category is further subdivided under several broad subject areas. The 1985 edition brings coverage up to mid-1984, with 490 citations divided under 25 categories. A variety of materials is included in both volumes; most represent research and professional books and journal articles, with some coverage of popular books, books intended for the single parent, association publications, research reports, and miscellaneous publications of limited circulation. Each volume has an author index.

The 4th edition has an appendix of books for children and adolescents, with evaluative annotations. It also contains six brief essays reviewing issues concerned with one-parent families (e.g., fatherless families, widowhood, single-parent adoptions), appended by a selected bibliography. The Canadian, British, and United States experiences are emphasized. Essays in the later edition cover more narrow topics and are less useful.

456. Watkins, Kathleen Pullan. **Parent-Child Attachment: A Guide to Research**. New York, Garland, 1987. 190p. index. (Reference Books on Family Issues, v.11; Garland Reference Library of Social Science, v.388) $29.00. LC 86-33548. ISBN 0-8240-8465-9.

Attachment between parent and child as a component of social and emotional development is discussed in a series of 11 review essays and accompanying bibliographies. Each chapter, approximately six or seven pages long, discusses a particular topic, covering the issues, viewpoints, and theories as expressed in the research literature. The annotated bibliographies are strong in current published research from conference proceedings, books, journal articles, and government reports. As such, the reviews and accompanying bibliographies are selective, not comprehensive.

Most of the classic works published before 1970 are included in the chapter discussing theories of attachment. Topic-specific chapters cover such areas as infant bonding, the role of attachment behavior in human development, father-child relationships, attachment behavior in maladaptive or abusive families, the attachment relationships of special children, single-parent and adoptive families, and chronically ill children. There are author and subject indexes.

Indexes and Abstracts

457. Aldous, Joan, and Reuben Hill, comps. **International Bibliography of Research in Marriage and the Family, 1900-1964**. Minneapolis, Minn., University of Minnesota Press, 1967. 508p. index. $129.00. LC 67-63014.

458. Aldous, Joan, and Nancy Dahl, comps. **International Bibliography of Research in Marriage and the Family. Volume II, 1965-1972**. Minneapolis, Minn., University of Minnesota Press, 1974. 1530p. index. $39.50. LC 67-63014. ISBN 0-8166-0726-5.

459. **Inventory of Marriage and Family Literature**. Vol. 3- . Minneapolis, Minn., National Council on Family Relations, 1973/1974- . annual. $199.95/yr. ISSN 0094-7814.

Inventory of Marriage and Family Literature (*IMFL*) provides access to and nonevaluative summaries of articles from approximately 600 source journals in psychology, social work, anthropology, sociology, counseling and therapy, vocational behavior, health, and many interdisciplinary areas. Citations are organized under broad subject categories and subcategories, resulting in effective topical access. Among these broad areas are historical and methodological issues, impact of public policy and work on the family, courtship and family dynamics, sexual behavior and reproduction, counseling and family-life education, and families with special needs. There are author and keyword-in-title indexes.

Over the years, *IMFL*'s frequency, publisher, and format have varied, but its coverage, content, and importance have remained consistent. It is a primary source of literature in family studies and therapy. Its two-volume predecessor, *International Bibliography of Research in Marriage and the Family*, extends coverage to 1900.

460. **Sage Family Studies Abstracts**. Vol. 1- , No. 1- . Newbury Park, Calif., Sage, 1979- . quarterly. $198.00/yr.(institutions). ISSN 0164-0283.

Although *Sage Family Studies Abstracts* is not as comprehensive as *Inventory of Marriage and Family Literature* (see entry 459), it has some strong points. It indexes and abstracts from far fewer journals, but it does include book titles. It covers the core literature in many of the same areas, including child development and family studies, sociology and social work, gerontology, psychology and counseling, communications, and political science. There is particularly strong coverage of cross-cultural and ethnic issues, although the material indexed is in English.

The two services have a similar organization. Sage arranges material under 15 broad categories and numerous subcategories, such as gender roles and sexual attitudes, marriage and reproduction, parenting, divorce and mediation, therapy, economics of family life, social trends, and research. The issue author and subject indexes cumulate annually.

Handbooks

461. Sussman, Marvin B., and Suzanne K. Steinmetz, eds. **Handbook of Marriage and the Family**. New York, Plenum, 1987. 915p. index. $95.00. LC 86-25135. ISBN 0-306-41967-X.

The strength of this handbook lies in its coverage of topics that attracted wide research interest in the 1970s and 1980s: changing definitions of the family unit and nontraditional families; singlehood, single-parent families, and childlessness; stress, family violence, and divorce; gender roles and ethnic families; and the family and working life. The 43 contributors have composed excellent chapters that incorporate discussion of important issues, statistical data, and surveys of the research literature. Most of the 30 chapters discuss therapy and family education, social policy and law, the aging family, sexuality and childbearing, inter- and intrafamilial relationships, and theoretical and methodological issues. A subject index provides access to the material. Although this work is intended for the researcher and professional, students will find chapters useful for their comprehensive, authoritative, and cogent discussions of theory and issues.

Dictionaries and Encyclopedias

462. DiCanio, Margaret. **The Encyclopedia of Marriage, Divorce and the Family**. New York, Facts on File, 1989. 607p. $40.00. LC 89-11838. ISBN 0-8160-1695-X.

Articles in this work are written for students, laypeople, and professionals who need a summary of a theory or concept, a definition of a legal issue, or brief directory information. Therefore, they are relatively jargon-free, citing relevant legislation or publications, and DiCanio provides a lengthy cumulated bibliography to popular and research publications. The essays range from a column to several pages and cover all aspects of family life, including courtship and marriage, sexuality and reproduction, child-rearing, sex education and counseling, and sex roles. There is especially good coverage of recent topics, such as the impact of abortion on the family, extended and blended families, adoption, dysfunctional families, violence, minority families, and family finances. In addition to many cross-references, there is a subject index.

The appendixes contain a wealth of directory and consumer information. Included are practical guides to divorce proceedings, sample prenuptial and cohabitation agreements, a list of support and advocacy organizations, advice on selecting family counseling services, and directories of state offices that handle child-care licensing and child-support enforcement.

Violence in the Family

Bibliographies

463. de Young, Mary. **Child Molestation: An Annotated Bibliography**. Jefferson, N.C., McFarland, 1987. 176p. index. $29.95pa. LC 86-27418. ISBN 0-89950-243-1.

De Young defines child molestation as "exposure of a prepubescent child to sexual stimulation inappropriate for the child's age, psychological development, and psychosexual maturity" (p. 1), but she excludes literature on incest. Intended for legal, medical, and mental health professionals, her bibliography draws heavily from medicine and nursing, law, and the breadth of the social sciences. Most of the 557 citations are to English-language journal articles and are organized under 11 topical categories, including statistical and historical works, personality and clinical characteristics of molesters, effects on children, treatment of both perpetrators and victims, prevention, the role of pornography, and legal considerations. Literature reviews and books are listed in separate sections. The descriptive annotations vary in length from a phrase to a lengthy paragraph. There are author, title, and subject indexes.

464. de Young, Mary. **Incest: An Annotated Bibliography**. Jefferson, N.C., McFarland, 1985. 161p. index. $29.95. LC 84-43226. ISBN 0-89950-142-7.

The subject and publication format scope of this title is more limited than *Incest: The Last Taboo* (see entry 468). De Young cites published English-language books and professional journal articles, with descriptive annotations. Citations survey the types of incestuous relations (e.g., paternal, maternal), intervention and treatment approaches with victims, statistical studies, and books and literature reviews. Each chapter is preceded by an overview of the literature and current trends in research. Author and subject indexes make it easy to find information.

Although coverage begins in the 1930s, most material is from the period 1970 to 1984. The volume of published material in this period dictates selective inclusion. The numbering sequence makes the number of citations appear to be over 400. However, many references are duplicated among chapters, for a total of about 250 unique entries.

465. Engeldinger, Eugene A. **Spouse Abuse: An Annotated Bibliography of Violence Between Mates.** Metuchen, N.J., Scarecrow, 1986. 317p. index. $27.50. LC 85-14546. ISBN 0-8108-1838-8.

This is a list of 1,783 citations to English-language materials, including popular and scholarly books and articles, conference papers, doctoral dissertations and masters' theses, reference works, pamphlets, and government publications. Most of the material was published after 1975 through 1983, reflecting the general publishing trend in this area. Particularly noteworthy is the inclusion of federal legislative publications, especially hearings and committee reports on the problems associated with domestic violence and its effects on children.

Because of the author arrangement, the only subject access is provided by the subject index, which has references to publications mentioned in the annotations, court cases, and other hard-to-find access points. There is also an index by author, both corporate and personal.

466. Johnson, Tanya F., James G. O'Brien, and Margaret F. Hudson, comps. **Elder Neglect and Abuse: An Annotated Bibliography**. Westport, Conn., Greenwood Press, 1985. 223p. index. (Bibliographies and Indexes in Gerontology, no.1). $40.95. LC 84-27982. ISBN 0-313-24589-4.

Although mistreatment of the elderly occurs in a variety of settings, both institutional and social, it most frequently takes place within a family. Therefore, elder abuse in the family is the primary focus of this bibliography, which has 144 references. Books, articles from professional and popular periodicals, conference proceedings and unpublished presented papers, research report series, pamphlets, and a variety of other printed formats published since 1975 are presented. The "annotations" are really outlines that detail the objectives, methods, findings and conclusions of the item. A rather complicated classification chart indexes entries by the first author's professional affiliation and the overall content of the item. This chart provides the only subject access, although an author index supplements the primary author arrangement of the bibliography.

An additional, unannotated list of about 200 citations lists items about elder abuse in a broader spectrum of settings and includes a separate section of state and federal publications. Another section contains lists of mental health, medical, and other organizations of interest to professionals seeking information on adult protective services. An appendix includes a model for future legislation for adult protective services.

467. Kalisch, Beatrice J. **Child Abuse and Neglect: An Annotated Bibliography**. Westport, Conn., Greenwood Press, 1978. 535p. index. (Contemporary Problems of Childhood, no.2). $45.00. LC 78-3123. ISBN 0-313-20376-8.

This essential volume lists the substantive retrospective literature from a variety of perspectives, such as health care, education, law, social work, psychology, child development, and sociology. Coverage focuses on English-language works: books and chapters, professional and popular articles, government publications, conference proceedings, pamphlets, and doctoral dissertations. Publications date from the late 1800s to 1977, with most published after 1960.

Over 2,000 citations and descriptive annotations are categorized under the seven broad areas of introductory and overview material; the prediction, detection, and prevention of abuse; causative factors; manifestation; therapy and treatment issues; sexual abuse; and legal issues. Each is further subdivided within a hierarchical arrangement; for example, the section on manifestations contains subsections on diagnosis, physical signs of abuse, psychological effects of abuse, neglect, and the role of violence and crime. In addition to author and subject indexes, appendixes list the bibliographical tools used to compile the citations, a selected list of professional and advocacy groups, and the text of the Child Abuse Prevention and Treatment Act. A brief introduction summarizes the primary issues in child development research and social policy.

468. Rubin, Rick, and Greg Byerly. **Incest: The Last Taboo: An Annotated Bibliography**. New York, Garland, 1983. 169p. index. (Garland Reference Library of Social Science, v.143). price not reported. LC 82-49181. ISBN 0-8240-9185-X.

Given the quantity of published literature on incest since 1970, Rubin and Byerly offer a highly selective bibliography of 419 citations, most published since 1973, although studies from the 1950s and 1960s are also cited. They focus on the prevalence of incest in and its impact on the contemporary U.S. family, although anthropological and cross-cultural studies are included. With the exception of dissertations, literature was selected, in part, for its anticipated availability in U.S. research libraries.

References are generally listed by author under eight sections: books and dissertations, including ERIC documents; psychological articles; articles on sociological and legal aspects; anthropological articles; medical and scientific articles; articles from popular magazines; articles of contemporary criticism of literary works on incestuous relationships; and audiovisual materials. Annotations are descriptive, and those for books often contain citations to published reviews. Indexes by periodicals cited, authors, and subjects are supplied.The range of published material represented and the selective nature of references make this title useful for students, practitioners, and researchers.

469. Schlesinger, Benjamin, and Rachel Schlesinger, comps. and eds. **Abuse of the Elderly: Issues and Annotated Bibliography**. Toronto, University of Toronto Press, 1988. 188p. index. $15.95. ISBN 0-8020-6694-1.

Most of this volume consists of 10 contributed essays that review the research on the incidence, assessment, and prevention of elder abuse. The bibliography part consists of 267 citations published between 1978 and mid-1987 that are of Canadian and United States origin. The books, journal articles, and reports from governments and associations will be of interest to students and professionals in social welfare, gerontology, geriatrics, psychology, and counseling interested in the abused elderly, their families, and their caregivers.

There is an author index to the entries. Among the appendixes are an annotated mediagraphy and a list of citations to works that would make up a core library.

470. Wells, Dorothy P. **Child Abuse: An Annotated Bibliography**. Metuchen, N.J., Scarecrow, 1980. 450p. index. o.p. LC 79-21641. ISBN 0-8108-1264-9.

Wells has compiled 2,484 citations, most descriptively annotated, that represent work produced between 1962 and 1976. Audiovisual materials, books and chapters, journal articles, pamphlets and government publications, dissertations, ERIC documents, and newsletters are included. There are also lists of 37 information clearinghouses, sources of print and nonprint media, and family advocacy organizations concerned with legal and social issues of child abuse.

References are listed under 21 categories that provide the only subject access. Some categories represent format of publication (e.g., bibliographies, case studies, directories); others are topical (e.g., the role of the school and social service agencies, legal issues and protective services, detection and diagnosis, medical aspects, responsibilities of health care and social service providers, prevention, psychological and sociological aspects). Wells does not cover child neglect or material concerned solely with sexual molestation of children, choosing instead to concentrate on physical and psychological abuse and willful neglect. Audiovisual materials are listed under the section for education materials. A separate section is provided for foreign-language references, although these are also present throughout the bibliography. A list of source periodicals and an author index are provided.

Handbooks

471. Van Hasselt, Vincent B., et al, eds. **Handbook of Family Violence**. New York, Plenum, 1988. 500p. index. $70.00. LC 87-7204. ISBN 0-306-42648-X.

This volume evolved from the increasing research interest in an issue of growing public policy concern in the 1970s and 1980s. Its 19 chapters represent a comprehensive overview of theories and topics associated with the study of family violence. It is the first and best of the research-based survey volumes on this topic.

Part 1 consists of a chapter that discusses the topic in terms of its impact on victims, prevalence, and social and legal aspects. Three chapters in part 2 cover theoretical models applied to the understanding of family violence: psychoanalytical, social learning theory, and sociological. The finest chapters are those addressing the manifestations of family violence and special topics. The eight chapters in part 3, "Forms of Family Violence," discuss spouse battering and marital rape, physical and sexual abuse of children, incest, elder abuse, and homicide. Part 4, "Special Issues," contains chapters on wife abuse prevention and intervention, the influence of physiological disorders and substance abuse on domestic violence, cross-cultural perspectives, and legal and research issues. There are author and subject indexes.

Dictionaries and Encyclopedias

472. Clark, Robin E., and Judith Freeman Clark. **The Encyclopedia of Child Abuse**. New York, Facts on File, 1989. 328p. index. $40.00. LC 88-30880. ISBN 0-8160-1584-8.

This work combines the functions of a dictionary, an encyclopedia, a directory, and a professional sourcebook of information on the legal, psychological, and sociological aspects of child abuse and neglect and family violence. A lengthy survey article on definition, incidence, and consequence of abuse precedes an alphabetical list of terms, concepts, organizations, legal decisions, and individuals important to the study of abuse relationships.

Entries range from a brief definition of a word or term to an essay of several pages on such broad topics as sexual abuse, exhibitionism, and investigation. The text is jargon-free and comprehensible by laypeople and professionals alike. Although many articles cite relevant studies and statistics, longer articles often contain statistical charts, graphs, and a reading list of several items for further information. Rounding out the volume are abundant cross-references, a detailed subject index, and 15 appendixes, among them an annotated list of child welfare organizations; charts providing state-by-state information on legislation and funding; and United Nations, United States, and Canadian statutes and position statements.

PSYCHOSEXUAL BEHAVIOR AND SEX ROLES

General Sources

Guides

473. Frayser, Suzanne G., and Thomas J. Whitby. **Studies in Human Sexuality: A Selected Guide**. Littleton, Colo., Libraries Unlimited, 1987. 442p. index. $47.50. LC 87-25999. ISBN 0-87287-422-2.

Citing over 600 reference books, research studies, collections, surveys, and bibliographies, this is an exhaustive reference guide to the literature of human sexuality. Although over 80 percent of the works cited are post-1970 and cover from 1980 to 1987, some classic works from earlier decades and even centuries are also included. In addition to bibliographical information, the presence of such features as an index, bibliography, or glossary is noted. Abstracts are lengthy and informative. Citations are appended by one or more codes representing the audience for which each is appropriate (professionals, children, young adults, the educated layperson, or a popular audience).

An introductory essay provides an overview of the history of research in human sexuality. Part 1 contains general works, such as reference volumes, collected works and published conference proceedings, historical and theoretical overviews, and statistical surveys. Part 2 lists titles under four topical areas: developmental, sexual, social and cultural aspects, and cross-cultural and area studies. Each category is further subdivided. For example, the section on social and cultural aspects of human sexuality is divided into 19 narrower topics, such as media of artistic expression, advertising, religion and sexual ethics, issues of sexuality in the labor force, and nonverbal communication. Part 3 lists bibliographies under 15 topic areas, and an addendum includes works not classified elsewhere. In addition to the precise topical access, there are author, title, and subject indexes.

Bibliographies

474. Abel, Ernest L., comp. **Drugs and Sex: A Bibliography**. Westport, Conn., Greenwood Press, 1983. 129p. index. $36.95. LC 83-5656. ISBN 0-313-23941-X.

Abel focuses on the effects of psychoactive drugs (those influencing perception or behavior) on sexual behavior, performance, fertility, and dysfunction. References on hormones and neurotransmitters are omitted, as are most popular nonresearch publications. Most of the 1,432 unannotated references are drawn from the biomedical and pharmacological literature, although there is coverage of the psychiatric and substance abuse literatures, as well as selective inclusion of treatment and psychotherapy approaches. Both human and animal studies appear; most are in English, but some foreign-language material in books and journals is listed. Although a few very early works (pre-1900) are cited, most date from 1960 through 1982. Citations are arranged under 15 substances (e.g., alcohol, benzodiazephines, caffeine, nitrates, tobacco), with a section for general reviews. Subject access is available through a subject index.

475. Astin, Helen S., Allison Parelman, and Anne Fisher. **Sex Roles: A Research Bibliography**. Washington, D.C., Government Printing Office, 1975. 362p. index. o.p. (DHEW Publication No. ADM 75-166). (SuDoc HE 20.8113:Se 9).

This is a list of 456 references to scholarly articles, book chapters, government publications, and conference papers published between 1960 and 1972. Items reflect empirical research, represent a theoretical contribution to the literature, or define specific research concerns. The authors have aimed for broad, representative coverage of theories and approaches to research, focusing on English-language publications. Most feminist commentary or items that emphasize the role of women in society are excluded. Citations are listed by primary author and are accompanied by several keywords and a lengthy, descriptive abstract.

References are categorized under sex differences, the development of sex roles and differences, sex roles in social or professional settings, cross-cultural overviews, and reviews and theoretical papers. Some of these broad categories are further subdivided, and providing even more access are a detailed subject index and an author index. Coverage of literature in the social sciences, especially psychology and sociology, is particularly good. Although other bibliographies in this area are more comprehensive, this one provides retrospective, selective access to the research literature before sex roles became a popular research area.

476. **Catalog of Periodical Literature in the Social and Behavioral Sciences Section, Library of the Institute for Sex Research, Indiana University**. By Institute for Sex Research, Indiana University. Boston, G. K. Hall, 1976. 4v. $435.00/set. ISBN 0-8161-0041-1.

477. **Catalog of the Social and Behavioral Sciences Monograph Section of the Library of the Institute for Sex Research, Indiana University**. By Institute for Sex Research, Indiana University. Boston, G. K. Hall., 1975. 4v. $435.00/set. LC 75-310797. ISBN 0- 8161-1141-3.

The Institute for Sex Research Library, established by Alfred C. Kinsey in 1947, houses a unique collection of research materials devoted to human sexuality. A wide variety of formats (e.g., books, journals, unpublished manuscripts and papers, slides and photographs, films, art objects) cover social and behavioral aspects and erotica. These volumes represent the card catalog of printed holdings, primarily produced from the nineteenth and twentieth centuries, that represent research materials from around the world in a wide variety of languages.

The monograph set reproduces the dictionary catalog entries for approximately 30,000 books acquired through September 1973, including some author entries for book chapters. To call the other set a "periodical" dictionary catalog set is a misnomer. It brings monograph coverage up to November 1975; provides an index to articles in the Library's journal holdings and chapters within books; and catalogs research reports and conference papers of limited distribution, government publications, pamphlets, and unpublished testing instruments and surveys. Unlike the monograph set, the periodical volumes use *Sexual Nomenclature: A Thesaurus* (G. K. Hall, 1976) as its controlled vocabulary. There are liberal subject and author cross-references in both sets, including some to the Library's holdings of nonprint media and literature not otherwise represented in either set.

The disciplines encompassed by the collections include law and history; psychiatry, psychology, and medicine; anthropology, sociology, and religion; and biology, pharmacology, and public health. The emphasis throughout is on human sexuality, although there is limited coverage of nonhuman research. This is an excellent bibliographic source of research on all aspects of sexuality: education; cross-cultural, legal, and social attitudes toward sexual behavior, mores, representation, and reproduction; abnormal and normal sexual practices; hetero- and homosexuality; and sex differences.

478. Mason, Mervyn L. **Human Sexuality: A Bibliography and Critical Evaluation of Recent Texts**. Westport, Conn., Greenwood Press, 1983. 207p. index. $36.95. LC 83-12688. ISBN 0-313-23932-0.

Made up of 180 citations to books published in English since 1970, this is a selective list based on materials' availability and their value to students and professionals. Books of a strictly popular nature are omitted. Citations are listed under nine categories: female sexuality, historical studies, male sexuality, ethics and philosophical perspectives, physiology and sex, sex education, research on sexuality, therapy and counseling, and alternative lifestyles. The contents of each book are described in a lengthy summary, then critically evaluated for strengths and weaknesses. There are author, title, and subject indexes.

479. O'Farrell, Timothy J., Carolyn A. Weyand, and Diane Logan. **Alcohol and Sexuality: An Annotated Bibliography on Alcohol Use, Alcoholism, and Human Sexual Behavior**. Phoenix, Ariz., Oryx Press, 1983. 131p. index. $60.50. LC 82-73732. ISBN 0-89774-040-8.

This work is designed to introduce researchers and practitioners to research literature on the relationship between human sexual behavior and alcohol use and abuse. Some 542 citations cover material produced between 1900 and 1982. Books, journal articles, technical reports, conference papers, and dissertations are included. Most are in English and are accompanied by lengthy descriptive abstracts. Many foreign-language studies are also abstracted.

Citations are divided into four categories—the effects of alcohol on sexual behavior and physiology, sexual dysfunction among alcohol abusers and its treatment, social and cultural issues and problems, and literature reviews and commentary articles—each begun by a brief introduction to the scope of the research literature. The broad topics are subdivided in an easily accessible hierarchical arrangement, which compensates for the absence of a subject index (although there is an author index). Literature is drawn from a variety of areas, including biology, medicine and related health sciences, gender roles and sexual behavior, substance abuse, criminology, social work, and social and clinical psychology and psychiatry. Appendixes include brief lists of agencies concerned with alcoholism and sexual behavior and of representative sexuality and alcohol journals.

480. Safilios-Rothchild, Constantina. **Sex Role Socialization/Sex Discrimination: A Bibliography**. Washington, D.C., National Institute of Education, U.S. Department of Health, Education, and Welfare, 1979. 120p. price not reported. (SuDoc HE 19.213:Se 9).

This is a comprehensive list of journal articles, books and book chapters, dissertations, research reports, and papers of limited circulation produced between 1960 and 1974. Little popular material is included. Some foreign-language material is cited, although English predominates. With approximately 700 citations stretching over a broad range of disciplines in the humanities and social sciences, the literatures of psychology, sociology, and education predominate. Personality characteristics, interpersonal communication, life-span development, self- and social-perception of gender roles, and sex-role attitudes are particularly well covered topics, especially in their cross-cultural aspects. However, the lack of indexes makes the contents difficult to access.

481. **Sex Research: Bibliographies from the Institute for Sex Research**. By Institute for Sex Research, Indiana University. Joan Scherer Brewer and Rod W. Wright, comps. Phoenix, Ariz., Oryx Press, 1979. 212p. index. $65.00. LC 78-31942. ISBN 0-912700-48-3.

This is a compilation of bibliographies previously produced by the institute for the use of students and scholars. Popular materials are excluded, but the selective bibliographies contain a variety of information sources, such as books and chapters, journal articles, conference papers, dissertations, nonprint material, government and international agency publications, directory information for research centers and clearinghouses, and periodical titles. Over 4,200 selected sources are listed; most are English-language publications.

The 11 bibliographies cover sex behavior over the life-span, variant behavior (e.g., bisexuality, transvestitism), the physiology of sexual response, sex attitudes and changing gender roles, marriage, and sex education and counseling. Most bibliographies further divide materials by narrower topics and source format. An exhaustive subject index and a title index are provided.

482. Sha'ked, Ami. **Human Sexuality in Physical and Mental Illnesses and Disabilities: An Annotated Bibliography**. Bloomington, Ind., Indiana University Press, 1978. 303p. $78.50. LC 78-17813. ISBN 0-253-10100-X.

The scope of this work encompasses the literatures of sex education; counseling; and the sexual behavior and adjustment of the physically handicapped, the developmentally delayed, and the mentally ill. The material was published from 1940 to 1977, and much of it is drawn from medical and nursing literatures, in addition to psychology and psychiatry (with an emphasis on sexology and sex counseling) and physical rehabilitation. Most entries reference journal articles, books, government documents, and professional conference papers, and all are accompanied by descriptive annotations that vary widely in length. A separate chapter describes about 20 films that are primarily intended for use in educational and rehabilitation settings

Most of the approximately 1,000 items constituting the bibliography are organized according to type of disability or disorder: internal (e.g., cardiovascular disease, cancer), genitourinary, nervous system disorders (e.g., epilepsy, spinal cord injury), muscular and joint disabilities, sensory deficits, substance abuse, mental disorders, and miscellaneous medical conditions. Most further divide the literature under type of disability. Separate sections cover general literature, sex and the elderly, and the sex-education needs of disabled individuals.

483. Wharton, George F., III. **Sexuality and Aging: An Annotated Bibliography**. Metuchen, N.J., Scarecrow Press, 1981. 251p. index. $22.50. LC 81-5097. ISBN 0-8108-1427-7.

This work contains over 1,000 references to published literature in nursing and medicine, sociology and social work, psychology and psychiatry, and the related areas of marriage and family studies. These items are arranged under 15 categories, from the social and psychological factors of sexual life and dysfunction, homosexuality, and counseling and somatic approaches to therapy to marriage and family aspects. Citations are listed under each section by author, with descriptive, informative annotations. There are author and title indexes.

Handbooks

484. **Handbook of Human Sexuality**. Benjamin B. Wolman and John Money, eds. Englewood Cliffs, N.J., Prentice-Hall, 1980. 365p. index. $92.00. LC 79-16907. ISBN 0-13-378422-3.

The 19 chapters in this work are divided into three sections. The first covers sexuality across the life-span, from prenatal and genetic influences to infancy, childhood and adolescence, marriage, and aging. Section 2 deals with social, cultural, and legal issues, such as sex roles, sex discrimination, and pornography. The last section (six chapters) encompass sexual disorders and treatment, concentrating on holistic and behavioral treatment, psychoanalysis, and integrated and multimodal approaches. A subject index rounds out the volume.

This work's contents are more accessible to students and laypeople than are those in the multivolume *Handbook of Sexology* (see entry 485). However, it has scant coverage of comparative sexual behavior, physiological influences, ethics, and the effect of somatic disorders on sexual behavior.

485. **Handbook of Sexology**. John Money and Herman Musaph, eds. Amsterdam, Netherlands, Elsevier/North Holland Biomedical Press, 1977. 1402p. index. o.p. LC 76-42449. ISBN 90-219-2104-9.

486. **Handbook of Sexology**. John Money and Herman Musaph, eds. New York, Elsevier Science Publishing, 1978. 5v. o.p. LC varies. ISBN varies.

487. **Handbook of Sexology. Volume VI: The Pharmacology and Endocrinology of Sexual Function**. J. M. A. Sitsen, ed. New York, Elsevier Science Publishing, 1988. 572p. $194.75. ISBN 0-444-90460-3.

488. **Handbook of Sexology. Volume VII: Child and Adolescent Sexology**. M. E. Perry, ed. New York, Elsevier Science Publishing, 1990. 440p. $200.00. ISBN 0-444-81262-8.

The study of sexual behavior receives comprehensive coverage in this set of handbooks, which emphasize human sexual behavior. The 1977 edition contains 108 chapters arranged under 17 sections. Chapters discuss the role of hormones and the nervous system, medical disorders, and fertility. There is also coverage of social, legal, and psychological issues, such as sexuality throughout the life-span, psychosexual disorders and their treatment, perspectives on sexual ethics and mores, marriage, and parenthood. There are an author index and a scant subject index.

In the five-volume set, a reprint of the 1977 book, each volume focuses on a cogent group of issues, with chapters accordingly arranged; for example, volume 1 covers history and ideology, and volume 2 deals with genetics, hormones, and behavior. As a handbook, this work relies less on extensive reviews of pertinent literature and more on reviewing issues.

Volume 6 is more focused. Its content updates the basic volume's contributions on drugs and hormones and their effect on sexual function, although the book does cover other issues, such as social behavior, comparative aspects of sexuality, and the role of the environment. Volume 7 updates coverage of puberty and adolescent sexual behavior and expands discussion of child sexology.

Men's Studies

Guides

489. August, Eugene R. **Men's Studies: A Selected and Annotated Bibliographic Guide**. Littleton, Colo., Libraries Unlimited, 1985. 215p. index. $30.00. LC 84-28894. ISBN 0-87287-481-8.

August cites and annotates 591 English-language books in the previously ill-defined, interdisciplinary area of men's studies. As defined by August, men's studies books must go beyond the minority of men so prevalent in historical or political spheres; they need to look at the experiences of the vast majority of men to be included, how their gender roles and social roles have evolved and governed their participation in the family and other social institutions.

References are listed under 21 broad categories, with some further subdivisions into narrower areas. Most were published after 1975, indicating the currentness of the academic interest. There is no subject index, but there is an index by author and title. Although there is some coverage of men as portrayed in literature and religion, most titles concern social science issues, and coverage of masculinity and gender roles, marriage and family life, sexuality, and events throughout the life-span is particularly good.

Bibliographies

490. Grady, Kathleen E., Robert Brannon, and Joseph H. Pleck. **The Male Sex Role: A Selected and Annotated Bibliography**. Rockville, Md., National Institute of Mental Health, U.S. Department of Health, Education, and Welfare, 1979. 196p. index. o.p. (DHEW Publication ADM 79-790). (SuDoc HE 20.8113:Se 9/2).

Noting the relative paucity of research literature on the socialization of behavior patterns of men, this bibliography consolidates the extant studies, reflecting "a growing interest in definitions of masculinity, the male sex role, and the male experience" (p. iv). The emphasis is on works of use to researchers, especially empirical studies or works with influential theoretical implications. Over 250 studies are cited, with evaluative summaries that are often several paragraphs long. Books, chapters in books, articles from professional and scholarly journals, and a few dissertations are included, most from the 1970s, with some works that stretch back to the 1930s.

References are listed under 14 subject categories further subdivided to create a total of 49 categories. They cover attitudes about masculinity, socialization, issues in marriage and the family, mental and physical health, physiological factors of behavior, the world of work, and cross-cultural and historical investigations. Cross-references are provided at the end of each section for those citations appropriate to more than one category. An author index is supplied. Although far from exhaustive or even comprehensive, this work does identify some of the most important and influential studies on male sex roles.

Women's Studies

Guides

491. Searing, Susan E. **Introduction to Library Research in Women's Studies**. Boulder, Colo., Westview Press, 1985. 257p. index. (Westview Guides to Library Research). $24.00. LC 85-3162. ISBN 0-86531-267-2.

Although not comprehensive, this guide will be useful for students, beginning researchers, and those new to this interdisciplinary field. In part 1, "Using the Library," Searing defines and interprets the scope of women's studies as an area of research, describes the processes of selecting and investigating a topic in the field, and explains how to use some general library tools for locating sources (e.g., library catalogs, bibliographies, indexes). Part 2, "Tools of Research," lists guides and bibliographies to the literatures of women studies and related disciplines in the arts, social sciences, and sciences; indexing and abstracting sources (divided by disciplines); biographical and organizational directories; online sources and periodicals; published library catalogs and archival lists; major microform collections and directories; and multidisciplinary reference sources. Most cited sources are also annotated. Each section attempts to describe the search process and the use of library resources, as opposed to the simple presentation of a list of reference tools. The three appendixes provide outlines of library classification systems, and a fourth cites literature reviews on selected topics from *Signs*, a major women's studies journal. Additionally, there are indexes for authors, titles, and subjects.

492. Loeb, Catherine R., Susan E. Searing, and Esther F. Stineman. **Women's Studies: A Recommended Core Bibliography, 1980-1985.** Littleton, Colo., Libraries Unlimited, 1987. 538p. index. $55.00. LC 86-27856. ISBN 0-87287-472-9.

493. Stineman, Esther. **Women's Studies: A Recommended Core Bibliography.** Littleton, Colo., Libraries Unlimited, 1979. 670p. index. price not reported. LC 78-13679. ISBN 0-87287-196-7.

Stineman's early work cites over 1,700 English-language books, including English translations of foreign works, and 15 periodical titles, all largely from the post-1970 period. Annotations are evaluative and descriptive. When appropriate, in-print books include purchasing information. Citations are organized under 26 categories and encompass the breadth of scholarly inquiry into the experience and contributions of women, covering the social sciences, fine arts and literature, medicine and health, law, and history. The section on psychology focuses on the psychology of women and sex roles, mental health, the portrayal of women in prominent psychological theories, and life-span development. The section on medicine and health covers female sexuality. Other sections list reference works, audiovisual materials, biographical works, bibliographies, and other reference formats. There are subject, author, and title indexes.

The later volume extends coverage of the 1979 publication, providing more material on minority women, health issues, violence against women, and women in the workplace. In general, the criteria of selection is the same, focusing on substantive rather than popular titles. The annotations are more extensive than before; essentially bibliographical essays of about 200 words, they cite related and contrasting works. The large number of references (over 1,200 books and 57 periodical titles in women's studies) attests to the growth of such publishing in the early 1980s. References are arranged under categories similar to the earlier volume, with subject, author, and title indexes and an appendix of publishers' addresses.

Bibliographies

494. Ballou, Patricia K. **Women: A Bibliography of Bibliographies.** 2d ed. Boston, G. K. Hall, 1986. 268p. index. (G. K. Hall Women's Studies Publication). $30.00. LC 86-18475. ISBN 0-8161-8729-0.

Ballou lists 906 bibliographies and literature reviews published from 1970 to June 1985, covering books, published catalogs, microformat documents, pamphlets, annual reviews, and journal articles. Both annotated and unannotated bibliographies are listed, regardless of the language of the included citations. Ballou concentrates on bibliographies containing over 50 references and (for books) items that are in print, and she provides descriptive and evaluative annotations for everything. Additionally, she limits potential obsolescence by citing indexing tools, databases, and continuing bibliographies published in journals.

Citations are arranged under four broad categories: general and interdisciplinary bibliographies, bibliographies limited to a particular publication format or type (e.g., government documents, databases, journal titles, biographies), bibliographies on women in specific geographic regions, and a topical list. The last section provides the most in-depth access by broad subject area, such as literature and history, the arts, law, economics and education, anthropology, sociology, and health. Most areas are further subdivided, providing a hierarchical subject arrangement of more than 100 topics. Sections of special interest include achievement, communication, mathematics learning, sexuality, sex differences, women and therapy, substance abuse, crime and violence, developmental stages, marriage and family, and sex roles. There are subject, name, and title indexes.

495. Borenstein, Audrey. **Older Women in 20th-Century America: A Selected Annotated Bibliography**. New York, Garland, 1982. 351p. index. (Women's Studies Facts and Issues, v.3; Garland Reference Library of Social Science, v.122). price not reported. LC 82-6082. ISBN 0-8240-9396-8.

Borenstein emphasizes a cross-disciplinary approach to literature, from mid-life (generally age 40) to old age. Although she does cover some literature and fiction, she emphasizes the social sciences, especially the literatures of gerontology, creativity, cross-cultural and anthropological approaches to female aging, social and public policy issues, and social and interpersonal relations of individuals. The section on psychology stresses mental health, sex roles, and developmental research.

Many of the 16 sections under which citations are listed include general literature on aging and life-span development. Published works (books, journal articles, and government documents) and dissertations are represented. Reflecting publishing output, most were produced after 1970, although many earlier works (e.g., works by Jung) are included. As there is no subject index, there are cross-references between sections to related material. However, there is a name index, along with a list of additional bibliographies on gender and aging.

496. Coyle, Jean M., comp. **Women and Aging: A Selected, Annotated Bibliography**. Westport, Conn., Greenwood Press, 1989. 135p. index. (Bibliographies and Indexes in Gerontology, no.9). $35.95. LC 88-28975. ISBN 0-313-26021-4.

Thanks to the recentness of the gerontological literature, most of the material cited here was published between 1980 and early 1988. The majority of the works cover elderly women, with some discussing middle-aged women. English-language books, journal articles, films, government documents, and dissertations are featured. The annotations are brief and descriptive. Citations are arranged under 12 topical categories that deal with interpersonal and social relationships, health and sexuality, economics and employment, housing, the social and public policy implications of aging populations, and general materials. There is especially good coverage of relationships with family and adult children, widowhood, and women of racial and ethnic minorities.

Most of the 622 items are easily accessible under 13 topic areas and thereunder by publication format. Subject and author indexes provide access to the material. Few popular items are included; Coyle intends this work for students, researchers, and social and health-care workers who need access to current, substantial research.

497. Dilling, Carole, and Barbara L. Claster, Eds. **Female Psychology: A Partially Annotated Bibliography**. New York, New York City Coalition for Women's Mental Health, 1985. 328p. index. $25.00. LC 86-116795. ISBN 0-9616028-0-5.

Originally intended as a resource list to increase awareness of women's concerns among therapists, this is a comprehensive bibliography of approximately 2,000 English-language references to journal articles, books, conference papers, and unpublished manuscripts. Most of the unannotated citations are topically arranged under categories for history; gender differences; the changing roles of women; mental health concerns; psychotherapy and women; and female psychology from sociological, physiological, and political perspectives. Divisions under subtopics are the only subject access; there is an author index.

Given the original intent of this bibliography, the best coverage is afforded to literature on gender differences, mental health, and psychotherapy. Because most works represent literature produced from 1970 to 1985, the book is best used as a source of current material.

498. Kemmer, Elizabeth Jane. **Rape and Rape-Related Issues: An Annotated Bibliography**. New York, Garland, 1977. 174p. index. (Garland Reference Library of Social Science, v.39). price not reported. LC 76-52701. ISBN 0-8240-9873-0.

A list of 348 citations to literature published in English from 1965 to 1976, this work includes material from about 170 periodicals (professional, academic, and popular) and books. A variety of disciplines are represented: psychology, sociology, medicine and health, law and public policy, and feminist studies. The subject index provides the only topical access, as citations are listed by author. Although not exhaustive, this work does provide coverage of the literature from the 1960s and early 1970s and citations to a readily accessible body of literature.

499. Wilson, Carolyn F. **Violence Against Women: An Annotated Bibliography**. Boston, G. K. Hall, 1981. 111p. index. (Reference Publication in Women's Studies). price not reported. LC 81-6232. ISBN 0-8161-8497-6.

This book's 213 citations to books and journal articles (and selected other sources in popular magazines and government publications) are organized under five chapters: introductory and overview material, battered women, rape and sexual harassment, sexual abuse of children, and pornography. (A sixth chapter consists of a brief essay on government responses to public issues at the time of publication.) The five chapters further classify citations by publication format, approach, and narrower subject areas. Each of these chapters is preceded by a brief introduction. There are subject and author/title indexes.

Material was chosen to be representative and therefore is highly selective, with most having been published in the 1970s. The audience for the book is primarily students of women's studies and related areas. However, the lengthy abstracts are at once evaluative, comparative, and descriptive, so it is a good introductory work to a productive publishing period in this area.

Indexes and Abstracts

500. **Women's Studies Abstracts**. Vol. 1- , No. 1- . Rush, N.Y., Rush Publishing, 1972- . quarterly. $84.00/yr.(institutions). ISSN 0049-7835.

Approximately 300 journals and feminist magazines are indexed and selectively annotated in this title. Academic journals have been selected from the disciplines of law, sociology, psychology, public policy, and a variety of subareas; more popular feminist publications are also included. Entries are arranged under about 200 broad categories, with separate book and media review sections. Quarterly issues contain a very detailed subject index. Cumulative author and subject indexes appear in winter issues, as well as a cumulated list of source journals and a directory of women's studies journal titles and their publishers.

Homosexuality

Bibliographies

501. Bullough, Vern L., et al. **An Annotated Bibliography of Homosexuality**. New York, Garland, 1976. 2v. index. price not reported. LC 75-24106. ISBN 0-8240-9959-1.

Almost 13,000 books and book chapters, pamphlets, journal articles, conference papers, and proceedings are listed in this title. Works published in a variety of languages are included, resulting in comprehensive, international coverage of homosexuality. Contrary to what the title implies, only a small minority of the citations are annotated, and these with a phrase rather than a sentence.

Approximately 2,000 entries in the first volume cite literature on the psychological and psychiatric aspects of homosexuality, with works from other behavioral sciences, education, law, medicine, ethics, and related disciplines. The aim is to cover research (as opposed to popular) literature, so that publication dates extend from the late nineteenth century to 1975. Some of this literature is fugitive, and foreign-language material will be hard to obtain. Volume 2 contains works on literature, autobiography and biography, the homophile movement, and transvestitism and transsexualism. There are indexes only by author and pseudonym; most citations can be found only through the brief table of contents, which organizes them under broad academic disciplines or types of materials.

502. Dynes, Wayne R. **Homosexuality: A Research Guide**. New York, Garland, 1987. 853p. index. (Garland Reference Library of Social Science, v.313) $49.00. LC 85-45109. ISBN 0-8240-8692-9.

This is perhaps the most comprehensive one-volume bibliography and guide to the literature on homosexuality literature to date. An annotated bibliography of over 4,800 references, it includes international literature from journals, books, pamphlets, and other published sources. Although much material comes from the post-1960 era, when publishing on the subject dramatically increased, some items go as far back as the 1700s.

The scope is extremely broad, encompassing almost every aspect of human activity as it relates to the homosexual experience, such as history, area studies, the arts and sciences, travel and leisure, religion and philosophy, the social sciences, public affairs and policy, law, medicine, and psychology and sociology. A separate section includes psychological investigations in attitudes, psychopathology, sex roles, psychological assessment, consciousness, and adjustment and social relationships. Subject and personal name indexes finish the volume.

503. Maggiore, Dolores J. **Lesbianism: An Annotated Bibliography and Guide to the Literature, 1976-1986**. Metuchen, N.J., Scarecrow, 1988. 150p. index. $18.50. LC 87-20613. ISBN 0-8108-2048-X.

Although this work is intended as an introduction to lesbian literature for social workers, its audience includes students and researchers in sociology, psychology, law, and women's studies. Articles, books and book chapters, and dissertations are included for their empirical approach, theoretical contributions, or implications for judicial or legislative actions. Works that denigrate the lesbian experience have been excluded.

Over 350 references are descriptively annotated and organized under the following topics: the individual, including lifestyle and self-identity; lesbians who are members of minority groups; lesbian families; political, legal, and civil rights issues; and mental and physical health. These categories are subdivided into narrower areas such as aging, parenting, alcoholism, counseling, and the "differently-abled." A sixth section, on resources, lists selected bookstores and subject-specific archives, additional books, and newsletters and directories. As appropriate, each section includes a list of information clearinghouses and other organizations dealing with that particular issue. The first introductory essay describes each subject section, including the issues addressed by its body of literature. The second delineates issues for future investigation and action. Access to the material is through author and title indexes.

504. Parker, William. **Homosexuality: A Selective Bibliography of Over 3,000 Items**. Metuchen, N.J., Scarecrow, 1971. 323p. index. price not reported. LC 71-163430. ISBN 0-8108-0425-5.

505. Parker, William. **Homosexuality Bibliography: Supplement, 1970-1975**. Metuchen, N.J., Scarecrow, 1977. 337p. index. $29.50. LC 77-1114. ISBN 0-8108-1050-6.

506. Parker, William. **Homosexuality Bibliography: Second Supplement, 1976-1982**. Metuchen, N.J., Scarecrow, 1985. 395p. index. $35.00. LC 84-20299. ISBN 0-8108-1753-5.

Together, these volumes constitute a comprehensive source to significant English-language literature on homosexuality, with much of it having been published since 1950. There is highly selective coverage of popular literature. Most of the material is derived from professional and research literature in law, sociology, psychology, medicine, anthropology, theology, and a host of interdisciplinary areas. Each volume contains over 3,000 unannotated references organized under source or publication format (e.g., books, dissertations, magazine and newspaper articles, articles from medical and scientific journals, gay and homophile literature, citations to court cases, nonprint media). Each also contains a section entitled "American Laws Applicable to Consensual Adult Homosexual Acts," containing the criminal code and penalties for each state. Author indexes and detailed subject indexes make the large volume of material relatively easy to access.

507. Weinberg, Martin S., and Alan P. Bell, eds. **Homosexuality: An Annotated Bibliography**. New York, Harper & Row, 1972. 550p. index. LC 70-160653. ISBN 0-06-014541-2.

The 1,265 references in this book reflect English-language research literature published from 1940 to 1965 in scholarly and professional journals and books. There is also some coverage of limited circulation and unpublished research reports. Annotations are descriptive and evaluative, and the preface acknowledges the uneven quality of the research represented. The literatures of psychology, sociology, and anthropology are the most heavily represented, with selected coverage of law, social work, and medicine. The time period covered results in the presence of certain theoretical assumptions reflected in the literature cited, such as that homosexuality is a clinical and treatable psychological disorder.

Citations are listed under broad categories for physiological, psychological, and sociological and anthropological aspects and issues, with most further categorized under male or female subjects. In general, there is broad coverage of such topics as stereotyping of and attitudes towards homosexuals, as well as assessment and treatment of homosexuality as a disorder, treatment of other disorders with homosexual clients, social and familial relationships, and gender role and identity. There are subject and author indexes.

Encyclopedias

508. **Encyclopedia of Homosexuality**. Wayne R. Dynes et al., eds. New York, Garland, 1990. 2v. index. $150.00/set. LC 89-28128. ISBN 0-8240-6544-1.

This unique reference contains comprehensive coverage of the gay and lesbian experience, from entries on the Scythians and Pindar to AIDS and telephone sex. Approximately 800 articles cover almost all aspects of male and female homosexual and bisexual behavior, including its representation in the media and arts, law and social thought, history, and society and ethics. As appropriate, concepts are discussed in a historical, cross-cultural context. There are biographical entries for deceased individuals. Articles range from a few paragraphs to several pages in length and are usually appended by bibliographic references. The "Bibliography" article discusses problems associated with research on gay topics and cites many bibliographies and other reference works. In addition to articles on psychological theories on homosexuality (e.g., Freudian concepts) there are articles on self-esteem and self-perception, socialization, psychotherapy, and attitudes toward homosexuality by the mental health professions. Besides a detailed subject index, there are numerous cross-references within articles.

SOCIAL, INTERPERSONAL, AND ENVIRONMENTAL INTERACTION

Guides

509. Gottsegen, Gloria Behar. **Group Behavior: A Guide to Information Sources**. Detroit, Gale, 1979. 219p. index. (Psychology Information Guide Series, v.2; Gale Information Guide Library). $68.00. LC 79-63744. ISBN 0-8103-1439-8.

Although this title covers applied group behavior in work and therapeutic settings, its emphasis is on behavior as a social phenomenon (e.g., group formation, interaction, behavior, conflict). Books are cited and descriptively annotated; most were published after 1960.

Citations are organized partly by format, partly by content. Most fall into the latter category, listing references under general works; problem solving; interpersonal interaction; power and influence; and a variety of applied settings in education, social work, and the like. There are separate lists for reference works, periodical titles, and organizations, as well as author, title, and subject indexes.

Bibliographies

510. Abel, Ernest, comp. **Homicide: A Bibliography**. Westport, Conn., Greenwood Press, 1987. 169p. index. (Bibliographies and Indexes in Sociology, no.11). $45.00. LC 87-7553. ISBN 0-313-25901-1.

Due to widespread interest across many disciplines in the causes and effects of homicide, Abel covers relevant English-language research literature from demographics and urban studies, law, criminal justice, anthropology, and sociology. He provides especially good coverage of violence and victimology, intergroup and interpersonal aggression, and psychopathology. Consequently, numerous citations to the books and journal literature are from medicine, clinical and social psychology, and forensic psychology and psychiatry. The 1,919 unannotated citations are organized by author; a scant subject index affords some access to the material. The cutoff date is 1985; most items were published in the 1970s and 1980s, with selected coverage of earlier work.

511. Ahearn, Frederick L., and Raquel E. Cohen, comps. and eds. **Disasters and Mental Health: An Annotated Bibliography**. Rockville, Md., National Institute of Mental Health, 1984. 145p. index. o.p. (DHHS Publication No. ADM 84-1311). (SuDoc HE 20.8113:D 63).

The scope of this bibliography includes the impact of natural and man-made disasters and their psychosocial effects, intervention strategies, and the role of mental health caregivers in treatment and prevention. Reflecting publication trends, most of the works cited were published in the last 20 years. The 297 citations to journal articles, books, and government publications are accompanied by lengthy descriptive annotations. Subject access is provided by the arrangement of entries under nine broad topics representing theories of disaster behavior, the effects of disasters on and responses of individuals and groups, relief services for victims and disaster workers, and prevention programs.

512. Barkas, Jan L. **Friendship: A Selected, Annotated Bibliography**. New York, Garland, 1985. 134p. index. (Garland Bibliographies in Sociology, v.4; Garland Reference Library of Social Science, v.244). $36.00. LC 84-48381. ISBN 0-8240-8937-5.

This title's primary focus is on friendship as a part of the human socialization process. It includes works of fiction and philosophical essays, but the role of friendship in life-span development and the aging process, friendship's value in fulfilling psychological needs, and sex roles and their differences in friendship behavior are also addressed. Most of the 693 entries are annotated and are organized under format or type of resource, such as books, dissertations, and research reports; articles from books, journals, and popular publications; unpublished materials and nonprint media; and organizations. Most materials are from 1960 to the early 1980s, with a smattering of earlier works.

513. Canary, Daniel J., and David R. Seibold. **Attitudes and Behavior: An Annotated Bibliography**. Westport, Conn., Praeger/Greenwood Press, 1984. 221p. index. $35.00. LC 84-3389. ISBN 0-03-060293-9.

The authors cite approximately 600 references to research literature, primarily from journal articles but also that in books. The period 1969-1982 is the focus of the title, with selected earlier works included. Coverage is of literature on both attitudes and behavior, such as consumer behavior, prejudice and discrimination, job-related behaviors, and persuasion. The list of source journals draws from psychology, sociology, medicine, communications, management, and evaluation research. An introductory essay discusses the development and direction of research on attitudes. The annotations follow a consistent format, with predefined codes and a phrase indicating the type of study or experiment, the moderating factors (if any) on behavior, and the impact of attitude on behavior. The final section, "Specialized References," serves as a subject index, with authors' names listed under 13 subject categories (e.g., altruism, deviance, health care behaviors), many further subdivided into a hierarchical arrangement.

514. Coelho, George V., and Richard I. Irving, eds. **Coping and Adaptation: An Annotated Bibliography and Study Guide**. Rockville, Md., National Institute of Mental Health, U.S. Department of Health and Human Services, 1981. 480p. index. o.p. (DHHS Publication No. ADM 81-863). (SuDoc HE 20.8113:C 79).

The focus of this work is on human adaptation to "responses to catastrophic events, to life-threatening episodes of injury and illness, and to the more or less stressful crises of developmental transitions" (p. iii), primarily from a mental health perspective. Books, academic and professional journals, doctoral dissertations, and published conference proceedings are represented. Most are English-language, with a smattering of research in other European languages. Entry numbers are listed under 10 very broad subject categories. The bibliography is arranged by author, and a supplemental author index is supplied. Most items were published in the 1960s and early 1970s. Citations contain lengthy, descriptive annotations. Subject access is provided by a study guide that precedes the bibliography.

515. Crabtree, J. Michael, and Kenneth E. Moyer. **Bibliography of Aggressive Behavior: A Reader's Guide to the Research Literature.** New York, Alan R. Liss, 1977. 416p. index. $54.00. LC 77-12900. ISBN 0-8451-0200-1.

516. Moyer, Kenneth E., and Michael Crabtree. **Bibliography of Aggressive Behavior: A Reader's Guide to the Research Literature, Volume II**. New York, Alan R. Liss., 1981. 459p. index. $51.00. LC 77-12900. ISBN 0-8451-0212-5.

Together these unannotated bibliographies cite almost 8,000 published sources on the causes, manifestations, and incidences of aggression in humans and animals. Coverage of the first volume centers on publications from the previous 20 years, although some older studies are included; the later volume covers only 1975-1979. Only published journal articles and books, primarily English-language materials, are cited.

The 1977 publication organizes references in separate sections for humans and animals. Under each are listed general materials and review sources, physiological bases, learning, environmental interactions, behavioral and social influences, physical disorders, types of conflict and their manifestations, individual differences, and other subjects appropriate to the population. A further hierarchical subject arrangement (e.g., the effects of temperature, sex-related aggression, the influence of mass media), results in a very detailed subject arrangement. For cross-indexing, each citation is assigned one or more code word abbreviations from a list of about 200 as defined and interpreted in the appendix. This is the basis for the code word index, which supplements the subject arrangement by providing access by species, publication format, concept, or other narrow subject areas. In contrast, the later volume lists its materials by first author and provides subject and author indexes.

517. de Grazia, Alfred, Carl E. Martinson, and John B. Simeone, eds. **Public Opinion, Mass Behavior and Political Psychology**. Princeton, N.J., Princeton Research Publishing, 1969. 1225p. index. (Political Science, Government, & Public Policy Issues, v.6). price not reported. LC 68-57822. ISBN 0-87635-006-6.

This massive tome "deals with individual and group social psychology, of attitudes, predispositions, prejudices, perceptions, and participation in social action" (p. vii). Most of the 3,400-plus descriptively annotated citations to journal articles and books are to research-oriented publications in English. The citations, listed alphabetically by author, actually comprise a relatively small part of the volume. The remainder consists of the subject index, which contains approximately 36,000 entries that reflect headings listed in the topical and methodological index and the dictionary of descriptors in this volume. Consulting these guides (which precede the references) is therefore essential to locating specific topics. Entries in the index supply an entry citation and author, title, primary, and secondary descriptors assigned to the work. Despite the work's complex topical arrangement, distracting computer-generated typeface, and age, it is especially useful for its coverage of leadership, conformity and conflict, political and mass behavior, attitudes, and public opinion.

518. Eitinger, Leo, and Robert Krell. **The Psychological and Medical Effects of Concentration Camps and Related Persecutions on Survivors of the Holocaust: A Research Bibliography**. Vancouver, B.C., University of British Columbia Press, 1985. 168p. index. price not reported. LC 86-120224. ISBN 0-7748-0220-0.

The published research literature in psychology, psychiatry, medicine, and social work that appeared from 1945 through 1984 is the main focus of this book. Although most material is in English, literature in German, French, Dutch, Polish, and other languages is included with translated titles. Formats cited are journal articles, books, dissertations, and unpublished manuscripts held by major holocaust research centers. In addition to first-person accounts and reports based on direct observation, materials deal with the rehabilitation of survivors, the delayed effects of physical deprivation and psychological trauma, children as survivors, and the offspring of survivors. Noteworthy is the coverage of psychopathology and psychological rehabilitation, especially given the clinical difficulties of working with a patient population resistant to classical therapies. The approximately 1,400 citations are accessible through the subject index.

519. Jerath, Bal K., Paul E. Larson, and Jesse F. Lewis. **Homicide: A Bibliography of Over 4,500 Items**. Augusta, Ga., Pine Tree, 1982. 600p. index. $62.00. LC 82-82195. ISBN 0-943974-00-3.

520. Jerath, Bal K. **Homicide: A Bibliography. Supplement 1984**. Augusta, Ga., Pine Tree, 1984. 43p. index. $8.95pa. LC 84-202150. ISBN 0-943974-01-1.

These volumes provide comprehensive international access to nonfiction book and periodical literature for both laypeople and professionals. The authors cast a broad net, encompassing the humanities (e.g., religion, philosophy), the sciences (e.g., forensics, biomedicine), law and political science (e.g., political assassination, legal aspects of homicide), and psychological and sociological investigations on causes. Taken together, the volumes cover publications from the late nineteenth century to 1983, expanding the coverage of Ernest Abel's *Homicide: A Bibliography* (see entry 510). They also list some foreign-language (mostly European) publications.

Both volumes organize citations under 12 chapters that encompass general and statistical literature, characteristics of perpetrators and victims, causes of homicide, legal and forensic aspects, and prevention and law enforcement. Throughout, there is very good coverage of psychological issues, including psychological and mental health profiles of perpetrators; the social, environmental, and psychiatric evolution of interpersonal violence; forensic psychology and the prediction of violent behavior; and the psychiatric management of offenders and violent individuals.

Given the book's broad scope and sizable number of citations, finding material could be challenging. Numerous subheadings in categories and the subject and author indexes make the contents accessible, although the use of abbreviated journal titles without a list of abbreviations may cause users difficulty.

521. Kinloch, Graham C. **Race and Ethnic Relations: An Annotated Bibliography.** New York, Garland, 1984. 250p. index. (Garland Bibliographies in Sociology, v.3; Garland Reference Library of Social Science, v.226). $40.00. LC 83-49297. ISBN 0-8240-8971-5.

Several sections of this bibliography deal with social attitudes, perceptions, stereotypes of ethnic groups, social group conflict, minority group conformity and identity, and other aspects of group behavior and interaction. Some 1,068 descriptively annotated citations are included, primarily from the 1970s and 1980s but with some earlier works. There are author and subject indexes, although subject access is best provided by the detailed table of contents and the arrangement of the citations.

522. Kruse, Lenelis, and Reiner Arlt. **Environment and Behavior: An International and Multidisciplinary Bibliography. 1970-1981.** Munich, New York, K. G. Saur, 1984. 2v. index. $75.00/set. LC 84-204184. ISBN 3-598- 10494-4.

523. Kruse, Lenelis, and Volker Schwartz. **Environment and Behavior, Part II: An International and Multidisciplinary Bibliography, 1982-1987.** Munich, New York, K. G. Saur, 1988. 2v. index. $198.00/set. ISBN 3-598-10783-8.

In these works, literature on the relationship of individual and group behavior and the environment is drawn from a broad range of disciplines: psychology, geography and demography, architecture, environmental studies, anthropology, and sociology. English- and German-language materials are included. There is welcome coverage of some areas difficult to research elsewhere, such as the architectural design of home and work, proxemics, urban planning and development, and the impact of auditory and visual noise. The earlier set contains approximately 6,000 citations produced from 1970 through 1981. The supplement contains another 4,000 items, most published from 1982 to 1987.

The format and organization of both sets are identical. Each volume has a list of citations by primary author to books and their chapters, published proceedings, dissertations, and journal articles. Citations are also coded for the type of study, the population studied, and the presence of an abstract in volume 2. A rotated keyword subject index finishes the first volume. Volume 2 contains abstracts for about half of the citations in the first volume.

524. Morrison, Denton E., and Kenneth E. Hornback. **Collective Behavior: A Bibliography.** New York, Garland, 1976. 534p. index. (Garland Reference Library of Social Science, v.15). price not reported. LC 75-24098. ISBN 0-8240-9975-3.

Although collective phenomena are mostly of interest to sociologists, Morrison and Hornback provide considerable coverage of collective behavior in a social psychological context: intergroup conflict and aggression, group attitudes and perceptions, social and individual alienation, leadership and obedience, and group attitudes and identity and their effects on collective behavior. Most of the literature cited covers English-language books, journals, theses and dissertations, published proceedings, and research and technical reports produced after 1960; a good selection of earlier material also appears.

In a detailed introduction, Morrison and Hornback discuss the universe of literature on collective behavior and how it is represented in the bibliography. The 5,014 citations are listed by author. A subject index precedes the entries, listing entry numbers and titles under 65 broad categories. A second index arranges entry numbers under persons, places, specific occurrences, and groups.

525. Moss, Carolyn. **Bibliographical Guide to Self-Disclosure Literature, 1956-1976**. Troy, N.Y., Whitston Publishing, 1977. 219p. index. $15.00. LC 77-89643. ISBN 0-87875-132-7.

In this volume approximately 1,500 citations to books, journal articles, dissertations, and unpublished research reports and conference papers on the process, manifestation, and implications of self-disclosure are cited. The contents will be of most interest to researchers and students in social and developmental psychology, personality, and clinical psychology. Citations are organized according to a complicated topical arrangement, including reviews and methodological literature, characteristics of the disclosure and recipient, interpersonal and environmental aspects, the modification of disclosure behavior, and special populations. Most categories are hierarchically subdivided by age groups, personality characteristics, nature of the interpersonal relationship, and so on as appropriate to the topic. There are a relatively scant subject index and an author index.

526. Reden, C. W. van, A. G. Grondel, and R. F. Geyer. **Bibliography Alienation**. 3d ed. Amsterdam, Netherlands., SISWO, 1980. 455p. index. (SISWO Publication, v.208). price not reported.

Over 7,000 references to the scientific literature in a variety of languages and approaches are listed in this work. Citations were drawn from searches of major print and online bibliographic sources in sociology, anthropology, education, psychology, philosophy, biomedicine, literature, and history. References are divided into two sections: those published before 1978, and those that appeared from 1978 to 1979. Within each, citations are organized by publication format, including articles, books and chapters, dissertations, unpublished research reports and conference papers, research in progress, bibliographies, and audiovisual material. Selected non-English-language materials are represented by translated titles.

An elaborate series of subject indexes includes separate keyword indexes for the broad topics of alienation, anomie, and social isolation, with subheadings under each topic. A fourth keyword index provides single-word subject entries. Other indexes afford access by coauthors, authors of book chapters, and authors of books reviewed.

527. Ruben, Douglas H. **Progress in Assertiveness, 1973-1983: An Analytical Bibliography**. Metuchen, N.J., Scarecrow, 1985. 328p. index. $30.00. LC 85-1853. ISBN 0-8108-1793-4.

As Ruben admits in his introduction, professional and popular interest in assertiveness as a means of social communication predates the years covered here. However, this was an especially active publishing period, as indicated by the wealth of academic, clinical, and popular publications listed. Items are categorized by format; journal articles are by far the most numerous, with 892 citations that are accompanied by descriptive annotations. Other sections list unannotated citations to doctoral dissertations, books, and films, bringing the total number of items to 1,672. The literatures of clinical psychology, psychiatry, and rehabilitation and social work are the best represented, with some coverage of the health science, management, and education literatures. There are an index by journal title and a subject index to all items in all formats. Although many of the books are intended for laypeople, most references will interest counselors and students of social psychology studying interpersonal and group interaction.

528. Wohlwill, Joachim, F., and Gerald D. Weisman. **The Physical Environment and Behavior: An Annotated Bibliography and Guide to the Literature**. New York, Plenum, 1981. 474p. index. $75.00. LC 81-4840. ISBN 0-306-40739-6.

Wohlwhill and Weisman succeed in surveying the literature of environmental psychology—the role of environmental factors in behavior—as it is dispersed across psychology, sociology, engineering, architecture, and area studies. Works included are restricted to published books and journal articles, with only selective appearances of dissertations, government publications, and research reports of limited circulation. The emphasis is on items that report empirical research, theoretical contributions, and reviews. Coverage is primarily from the 1960s and 1970s.

The 1,491 citations are organized under three broad areas: materials of a general nature; applied areas and special issues in urban housing, environmental problems, interior environments, transportation, and leisure and natural settings; and literature from related disciplines, such as anthropology, geography, political science, and economics. These broad areas are further subdivided, providing subject access under 48 headings (there is no subject index), and many sections are preceded by a description of the scope of materials included therein. Most citations are descriptively annotated, and references to edited books often contain a list of their individual essays or chapters. Cross-references between sections are provided, and some book chapters are cited and individually annotated. An author index rounds out the book.

Handbooks

529. Goldberger, Leo, and Shlomo Breznitz, eds. **Handbook of Stress: Theoretical and Clinical Aspects**. New York, Free Press/Macmillan, 1982. 804p. index. $49.95; $25.95pa. LC 82-8448. ISBN 0-02-912030-6; 0-02-911950-2pa.

The popular and research interest in stress is broad, covering social, environmental, and biological causes; the implications of stress for interpersonal relations and health; therapy and treatment; and stress's prevalence among normal and pathological populations. Even with such sprawl, this volume gives balanced coverage to major issues in stress research from a variety of perspectives. After a pair of brief introductions to the state of research, the remaining 44 chapters cover stress as it occurs in basic psychological and biological processes, stress in a variety of social environments, the results of life-span change and development, common causes and effects of stress, stress under extreme conditions (e.g., war, disaster), and treatment and management issues. A subject index provides access to the material.

530. Hare, A. Paul. **Handbook of Small Group Research**. 2d ed. New York, Free Press/Macmillan, 1976. 781p. index. $34.95. LC 75-28569. ISBN 0-02-913841-8.

Almost half of this book is composed of a retrospective bibliography to over 6,000 books and journal articles on small group research. The first section, "Group Process and Structure," discusses issues in intragroup interaction and decision processes, the roles of participants, and group development. The second section elucidates such variables as tasks, leadership, group size, and social and personality characteristics. Individual and group performance characteristics are covered in the third section. Appendixes include lab experiments for class demonstrations or student use, a brief historical overview of publishing trends in the field, and a short discussion of the variety of research methods employed in conducting research on small group behavior.

One advantage of this volume over many other handbooks is that Hare is the sole author and not the editor of a multiauthored work. Therefore, the essays have more internal continuity and less overlap among the chapters.

531. Knutson, Jeanne N., ed. **Handbook of Political Psychology**. San Francisco, Jossey-Bass; repr., Ann Arbor, Mich., UMI Books on Demand, 1973. 542p. index. (Jossey-Bass Behavioral Science Series). $139.80pa. LC 72-5893. ISBN 0-685-16211-7.

This remains a basic—indeed, classic—reference in political psychology, a field of study that employs psychological theory and research methodology to understand political behavior and attitudes. Reflecting the field's interdisciplinary roots, the 15 contributors represent perspectives from political science, sociology, and psychology. An introductory chapter discusses a variety of theoretical underpinnings of the study of political behavior, traced generally to work beginning in the nineteenth century. Three chapters focus on the roles of personality, attitudes, and belief systems approaches—psychological constructs most frequently applied to political psychology. Additional chapters cover political socialization, the authoritarian personality, political alienation, leadership, aggression and violence, and international politics. Five more chapters deal with research methodologies and problems, including psychobiography, survey research, controlled experimental research, simulation, and projective testing techniques. A concluding chapter explains the future of political psychology and its continuing interdisciplinary nature, current problems and limitations, and challenges. There are author and subject indexes. Despite its age, this volume is a solid contribution to the literature. Several chapters in *Handbook of Social Psychology* (see entry 532) help alleviate its lack of currentness.

532. Lindzey, Gardner, and Elliot Aronson, Eds. **Handbook of Social Psychology**. 3d ed. New York, Random House; distr., Hillsdale, N.J., Lawrence Erlbaum, 1985. 2v. $150.00/set. LC 84-18509. ISBN 0-89859-720-X.

This has been the standard handbook in social psychology since it was first published in 1954. As did its predecessor, Carl Murchinson's 1935 *Handbook of Social Psychology*, it has a well-deserved reputation for comprehensive and authoritative coverage of both theoretical concepts and applied areas. It is intended for both researchers and students.

The 13 chapters in volume 1, "Theory and Methods," discuss those areas that have significant impact on social psychology: learning theory, cognitive psychology, decision theory, role theory, and organization theory. Chapters on methodology cover the experimental method, quantitative methods, attitude measurement, observation, surveys, and program evaluation.

The topics and content of chapters in volume 2, "Special Fields and Applications," show the most significant changes over previous editions. Among the topics addressed are aggression, attribution, socialization, sex roles, leadership and political action, social deviance and intergroup interaction, and language and mass communication. Tables and charts present research results of highly significant studies, and the literature reviews and evaluative discussion of concepts and research are first-rate. A minor inconvenience is that the subject and author indexes are exclusive to each volume.

Dictionaries and Encyclopedias

533. Harre, Rom, and Roger Lamb, eds. **Dictionary of Personality and Social Psychology**. Cambridge, Mass., MIT Press, 1986. 402p. index. $12.50pa. LC 86-15190. ISBN 0-262-58078-0.

This is another spinoff volume of the 1983 *Encyclopedic Dictionary of Psychology* (see entry 170). The focus of this work is on personality, self-psychology, and social psychology. Articles on disordered social behavior, such as aggression, are included,but personality disorders are not, presumably because they fall into the realm of clinical psychology

Some articles are virtually identical to those in the original volume or to some of the other updated spinoff volumes (notably *Dictionary of Developmental and Educational Psychology* [see entry 411]). However, other articles show substantial differences, most frequently in their reading lists.

PERSONALITY

Bibliographies

534. Sleet, David A. **Interdisciplinary Research Index on Play: A Guide to the Literature.** Toledo, Ohio, University of Toledo, 1971. 92p. price not reported.

Sleet cites approximately 900 published articles and books on the theory and research of play in humans across the life-span. Given the relatively imprecise definition of *play*, which can be considered either a social, learning, or developmental activity, the body of literature draws from a spectrum of disciplines. Citations are organized under broad categories reflecting psychology, psychiatry and psychotherapy, sociology and cultural anthropology, philosophy and religion, child development, education and learning, and physical education and recreation. Animal studies are cited as they contribute to the understanding of human behavior and personality. Items solely on play therapy or play as recreation are, for the most part, excluded. Most items date from the 1930s through mid-1970, with some earlier coverage; the book has a predominate English-language focus. The lack of an index is a handicap in identifying specific concepts or authors.

535. Welch, I. David, George A. Tate, and Donald C. Madeiros. **Self-Actualization: An Annotated Bibliography of Theory and Research**. New York, Garland, 1987. 262p. index. (Garland Reference Library of Social Science, v.352). $42.00. LC 86-31996. ISBN 0-8240-8568-X.

Self-actualization, or the development of an individual's fullest potential, is the focus of this work's 1,100-plus references to English-language journal articles, books, and dissertations. The earliest works cited are from the 1930s, with coverage through mid-century major research up to the mid-1980s.

Citations to journal and thesis literature are arranged under 20 broad categories, with each section preceded by a brief survey essay on the scope of research. Only citations to journal literature are annotated. There is a separate listing for books, and there are author and subject indexes.

Handbooks

536. Pervin, Lawrence A., ed. **Handbook of Personality: Theory and Research**. New York, Guilford Press, 1990. 738p. index. $75.00. LC 90-37936. ISBN 0-89862-430-4.

Some 27 essays by 38 distinguished individuals in personality research (e.g., Raymond Cattell, Hans Eysenck, Robert Plomin) constitute this handbook. It provides excellent, up-to-date articles on all aspects of personality theory, with current and extensive reference lists and a writing style that makes the contents comprehensible to students as well as researchers.

Part 1 consists of an introductory chapter that reviews the development of modern personality theory from the 1930s through the 1980s. Seven chapters dedicated to a variety of theoretical approaches to understanding personality compose part 2. Chapters in part 3, "Interface with Other Fields," cover the influence of intersecting areas in the discipline on personality research: biological and genetic effects, social psychology, psychopathology, psychotherapy and behavior change, and cultural influences. Part 4 includes selected topics in intrapersonal, interpersonal, and environmental influences, such as the unconscious, sex and gender, change across the life-span, the roles of emotion and adaptation, the political environment, the relationship between personality and health, and personality assessment. A subject index closes the book.

PHYSICAL AND PSYCHOLOGICAL DISORDERS

General Sources

Bibliographies

537. Bauman, Mary K., comp. **Blindness, Visual Impairment, Deaf-Blindness: Annotated Listing of the Literature, 1953-75.** Philadelphia, Temple University Press, 1976. 537p. index. $39.95. LC 76-14724. ISBN 0-87722-067-0.

538. Lende, Helga. **Books About the Blind: A Bibliographical Guide to Literature Relating to the Blind**. rev. ed. New York, American Foundation for the Blind, 1953. 357p. index. price not reported.

These bibliographies provide approximately 8,000 references retrospective to the early 1800s. International coverage is provided for professional journals, books and chapters, government and association publications, conference proceedings, dissertations, and technical reports. The annual bibliography *Blindness, Visual Impairment, Deaf-Blindness* (Nevil Interagency Referral Service, 1976-) updates these volumes.

Citations in each volume are listed under conceptually broad categories, supplemented by author and subject indexes. Throughout, the cultural and social aspects of blindness, such as education and rehabilitation, adaptive living, and perceptual and communicative problems and their solutions, take precedence. In particular, there is extensive coverage of literature on the psychology of blindness, including sensory perception and deprivation, imagery and dreams, memory, mental health concerns, personality studies, attitudes toward blindness, and psychological assessment.

539. Leland, Henry, and Marilyn W. Deutsch. **Abnormal Behavior: A Guide to Information Sources**. Detroit, Gale, 1980. 261p. index. (Psychology Information Guide Series, v.5; Gale Information Guide Library). price not reported. LC 80-65. ISBN 0-8103-1416-9.

The number of citations (1,238) in this work, compared to the breadth of the topic and volume of publishing, means that it is highly selective, providing a core of readily available literature to the professional and layperson. Only book and journal literature from the preceding 10 years is included, primarily from the fields of medicine, psychology, and psychiatry, and all works are English-language. Most are annotated, albeit by just a sentence or two.

Six chapters organize citations by type of disorder: developmental disabilities, organic disorders, psychoses and affective disorders, neuroses (mostly depression, phobias, and compulsive behaviors), personality disorders, and behavior disorders. These chapters are further subdivided by specific disorder. The remaining two chapters include reference tools and works of general interest, such as histories, legal and ethical issues, and treatment approaches. There are author, title, and subject indexes. An appendix lists about 70 core journal titles.

540. Sacks, Michael H., William H. Sledge, and Phyllis Rubinton, comps. **Core Readings in Psychiatry: An Annotated Guide to the Literature**. Westport, Conn., Praeger/Greenwood Press, 1984. $35.00. LC 83-21287. ISBN 0-03-062542-4.

This work is intended as a guide for psychiatric students, but the breadth and selectivity of the books and journal articles cited make it useful for students of clinical psychology as well. Throughout, citations represent the most significant books and journals in medicine, psychology, psychiatry, and related mental health areas. Social science disciplines are not as well covered.

Some 62 subject specific sections, each preceded by a brief introduction to the scope of the literature, are listed under six parts, including basic sciences (e.g., biological, psychological, social), psychopathology, psychiatric assessment, treatment approaches, human development, and special topics in such areas as professional education and ethics. Annotations are descriptive, and literature currentness varies as appropriate to the topics. Chapters on neuroscience, genetics, and crisis intervention draw heavily from the 1970s and 1980s. Sections on psychoanalytic therapy, historical perspectives, and psychoanalysis cite older, seminal works from early in the century. There are an author index and a very detailed subject index.

541. Skodol, Andrew E., and Robert L. Spitzer, eds. **An Annotated Bibliography of DSM-III.** Washington, D.C., American Psychiatric Press, 1987. 649p. index. $38.50. ISBN 0-88048-257-5.

This is not a bibliography for more information on specific mental disorders or diagnoses as used in the *DSM-III* (see entry 543). Instead, it is intended for researchers, academics, and students in psychiatry and clinical psychology who are interested in the development, intellectual underpinnings, and use of the nosology of mental disorders, and is therefore valuable regardless of which DSM edition is currently in use.

The first section consist of six essays on the development, use, and impact of the DSM-III. The eight review articles in section 2 analyze the literature of the diagnostic areas, such as childhood, physical symptoms, substance use, psychosis and schizophrenia, effect and adjustment, anxiety and disassociative disorders, and disorders of personality. A selective list of 300 professional and research articles is contained in section 3, including detailed descriptive summaries of research on the validity of *DSM-III* categories, comparisons with other diagnostic systems, and other issues dealing with the use and impact of the classification. A final section of 2,010 unannotated citations to the international literature, primarily from 1980 to mid-1986, lists journal articles, research reports, and books and chapters. There is a subject index to the references.

Handbooks and Yearbooks

542. Adams, Henry E., and Patricia B. Sutker. **Comprehensive Handbook of Psychopathology**. New York, Plenum, 1984. 1091p. index. $95.00. LC 83-19193. ISBN 0-306-41222-5.

In this book, 34 chapters by 58 contributors are organized under six broad research areas. Part 1, "Issues in Psychopathology," covers the classification and diagnosis of disorders, factors influencing the manifestation of abnormal behavior (e.g., biological, genetic, cultural), and treatment options. Chapters in part 2 discuss diagnosis and treatment options for nonpsychotic behavior patterns, such as phobias and anxiety disorders, motor dysfunctions, and somatoform disorders. Psychotic and personality disorders such as schizophrenias, those associated with violence and aggression, and schizoid disorders are covered in part 3. Addictions and behaviors manifested as physiological symptoms (e.g., sleep and eating disorders, sexual dysfunctions and deviations) are covered in part 4, whereas behaviors associated with somatic illness or physical trauma are covered in part 5. The final four chapters discuss childhood disorders.

Chapters provide excellent coverage of psychopathological disorders and their origins, assessment, and treatment. They attempt to take a broad, inclusive, and historical approach that is largely without bias toward any method of diagnosis or treatment plan. Extensive reference lists are appended to each chapter, and a subject index finishes the book.

543. **Diagnostic and Statistical Manual of Mental Disorders**. 3d rev. ed. Washington, D.C., American Psychiatric Association, 1987. 567p. index. $39.95; $29.95pa. LC 87-1458. ISBN 0-89042-018-1; 0-89042-019-Xpa.

Originally published in 1952, with revisions in 1968 and 1980, the *DSM* is recognized as the standard reference for the classification and nomenclature of mental disorders and the behavioral manifestations of psychological or biological dysfunction. Syndromes, disorders, and the like are listed under one of 19 disorder types, such as delusional, mood, adjustment, personality, sexual, sleep, and somatoform. Each entry supplies guidelines for the disorder's diagnosis: general description and age of onset, symptomology and predisposing factors, prevalence in the population, and how it is differentiated from other disorders or syndromes.

A variety of appendixes provide supplemental material, including decision trees for differential diagnoses, a glossary, and comparisons of the *DSM-III-R* with previous editions and other classification systems. Indexes by symptoms and by diagnoses and diagnostic terms are provided.

544. Kaplan, Harold I., and Benjamin J. Sadock. **Synopsis of Psychiatry: Behavioral Sciences, Clinical Psychiatry**. Baltimore, Md., Williams & Wilkins, 1988. 725p. index. $38.95pa. ISBN 0-683-04518-0.

This is a condensed version of Kaplan and Sadock's 5th edition of *Comprehensive Textbook of Psychiatry* (Williams & Wilkins, 1989), a two-volume work intended for the practicing clinical psychiatrist or psychologist. About half of the 47 chapters in the *Synopsis* elucidate and expand on disorders in the *DSM-III-R* classifications, generally avoiding highly technical jargon. Several chapters discuss and differentiate among the many psychotherapeutic approaches, such as psychopharmacology, psychosurgery, hypnosis, and the range of "talking therapies." Other chapters focus on psychiatric needs of specific populations, including children, adolescents, individuals with AIDS, and the elderly.

The remaining chapters discuss psychiatric practice (e.g., the physician-patient relationship, clinical examination, forensic psychiatry) and the origins and influences on psychiatry as it has evolved and developed. The latter area is of most interest to psychology students, because chapters discuss the role of physiology in human behavior, testing, theories of personality and psychopathology (from Sigmund Freud to Abraham Maslow to Raymond Cattell), and the human life cycle and its role in mental health and illness. The appendix provides 30 clinical case vignettes with discussion and diagnosis. There is a very detailed subject index.

545. **Mental Health, United States, 1990**. By National Institute of Mental Health. Ronald W. Manderscheid and Mary Anne Sonnenschein, eds. Rockville, Md., National Institute of Mental Health, U.S. Department of Health and Human Services, 1990. 260p. (DHHS Publication No. ADM 90-1708). $14.00. (SuDoc HE 20.8137:990).

This 4th edition of *Mental Health* contains a great deal of statistical information on mental health services in the United States. Over 100 figures and tables illustrate the provision of mental health care and the characteristics of care providers and those served. Data and brief narrative summaries are divided into six chapters: setting or facility, the characteristics of those receiving services, patients served by state mental hospitals, the characteristics of mental health care providers, data on funding and expenditures, and the characteristics of patients in long-term care facilities. Charts and tables break down much of the data in such ways as by state, by type of facility, by sociological or demographic characteristics, or by type of mental disorder. The narrative summaries are extremely useful. The chapter "Human Resources in Mental Health" has information on all professions that provide mental health services, data that are difficult to find elsewhere. Although many tables only include data through 1986, some are as recent as 1988.

Dictionaries and Encyclopedias

546. Campbell, Robert Jean. **Psychiatric Dictionary**. 6th ed. New York, Oxford University Press, 1989. 811p. $45.00. LC 88-12579. ISBN 0-19-505293-5.

This is an excellent, comprehensive source of terms used in clinical psychiatry and psychology. Up-to-date definitions of all concepts dealing with mental disorders, their symptoms, and treatment; biographical and eponymous entries; and abundant cross-references make this a very useful source. Most entries include pronunciation guides, the origin of the term, and a literal translation if the term originated in a foreign language. A surprising number of definitions will be of interest to a wide range of users who are not clinical psychologists or psychiatrists.

Definitions are brief, from a phrase to several paragraphs. Diagrams, charts, and other illustrations and figures are almost nonexistent. Quotations from and citations to research literature occasionally are included as part of the definitions, but references are not commonly appended to articles.

547. Doctor, Ronald M., and Ada P. Kahn. **The Encyclopedia of Phobias, Fears, and Anxieties.** New York, Facts on File, 1989. 487p. index. $40.00. LC 88-31057. ISBN 0-8160-1798-0.

Entries in this one-volume resource on fears include the clinical names of phobias and their causes, treatments in a variety of therapeutic approaches, concepts basic to the cause and treatment of fear, physiological aspects of fear, and individuals whose ideas or research are important to the understanding of phobia.

Coverage varies greatly among entries, depending on the literature and popular interest in a concept. For example, most phobias are defined in about 10 words, but the definition, incidence, and treatment of agoraphobia covers 14 pages, while fear of radon receives a page. Longer articles on therapy, theoretical orientations on the etiology of fears, and issues such as testing have a few citations on the concept or issue, primarily to journal articles or other reference works; there is also a 30-page bibliography. Besides abundant cross-references between entries, there is a subject index. Although this work might serve as a reference to phobic terminology for mental health professionals, it will be of most interest to laypeople and students.

548. **Encyclopedia of Clinical Assessment.** Robert Henley Woody, ed. San Francisco, Jossey-Bass; repr., Ann Arbor, Mich., UMI Books on Demand, 1980. 2v. index. (Jossey-Bass Social and Behavioral Science Series). $160.00pa./v. LC 80-0463. ISBN 0-87589-446-1 (set).

The biggest handicap of this set is that it reflects now outdated *DSM* (see entry 543) definitions. However, for the nonclinician, 91 lengthy essays offer critical, evaluative discussion of important aspects of and topics in clinical psychology. Chapters focus on specific mental or behavior disorders or classes of disorders (e.g., substance abuse, organic brain syndromes, epilepsy, depression), physical or mental states (e.g., amnesia, daydreaming, pain), social or environmental factors (e.g., marital adjustment, self-disclosure, risk-taking, stigma, rehabilitation need), and individual or cognitive abilities (e.g., personal needs, altruism, mnemonic organization).

Articles are organized under 11 broad categories, with an alphabetical list of essays provided in the front of the first volume and a cumulated subject index in volume 2. Reference lists for each article are lengthy and supplemented by a cumulated author index. Articles follow a well-organized, uniform format, with introductory and background information, critical comment on important issues in research and practice, discussion of comparative theories on the issue, and variables that occur in clinical assessment.

549. Howells, John G., and M. Livia Osborn. **A Reference Companion to the History of Abnormal Psychology**. Westport, Conn., Greenwood Press, 1984. 2v. index. $125.00/set. LC 80-27163. ISBN 0-313-22183-9.

Abnormal psychology is defined broadly to include not only pathological but also "unusual" behavior and phenomena of human experience. Therefore, scattered among the over 4,200 entries are definitions of UFOs, telepathy, and other psychic phenomena. Most entries, however, provide descriptions of people, theories and concepts, philosophies, organizations, places, and institutions important to the history of pathological behavior and treatment. Biographies of those whose contributions had an impact on attitudes toward and treatment of the mentally ill are particularly numerous. Coverage is fairly international, with material as diverse as Far Eastern literary works, ancient philosophers, and modern thinkers in psychiatry. Particularly interesting are descriptions of practices used as "cures" for mental illness.

Definitions range from a sentence to about a page in length, with numerous cross-references. Almost all have one key reference as a source of further information. There is a combined name and subject index, and an appendix lists the entries under approximately 40 broad categories.

550. Krauss, Stephen, ed. **Encyclopaedic Handbook of Medical Psychology**. London, Boston, Butterworths, 1976. 585p. index. price not reported. LC 75-33106. ISBN 0-407-00044-5.

More an encyclopedia than a handbook, this volume consists of articles on the contributions of psychology to illness prevention, diagnosis, and treatment. Essays vary from one to five pages in length and are appended by reference lists that also vary widely from just a few to over 50 citations. Because some topics are covered by very broad articles (e.g., psychopathology, counseling) and others represent narrow ones (e.g., body rights, graphology, pathography), use of the subject index is important. The strength of the essays is their emphasis on the historical context of the subject, and the contributors are distinguished. However, the considerable research in health psychology since 1980 is, of course, not represented.

Emotional Disorders and Suicide

Guides

551. Lester, David, Betty H. Sell, and Kenneth D. Sell. **Suicide: A Guide to Information Sources**. Detroit, Gale, 1980. 294p. index. (Social Issues and Social Problems Information Guide Series, v.3). $68.00. LC 80-71. ISBN 0-8103-1415-0.

The 12 chapters of part 1 in this book constitute the research guide proper, as they introduce reference materials by their functions and explain their uses for locating information on the incidence and prevention of suicidal behavior. Users are shown book catalogs, basic reference works, print and nonprint periodical indexes, legal and statistical sources, unpublished material, nonprint media, organizations, and conferences. Most sources are accompanied by evaluative annotations that often suggest appropriate subject headings or access points to use.

The remaining four parts list annotated references to books and journal articles on theories of suicidal behavior, social and environmental influences, mental health issues, developmental and familial correlates, and prediction and prevention. Most works date from the 1960s and 1970s, although earlier works are cited as appropriate. There are name, title, and subject indexes in support of the numerous cross-references among topical sections.

Bibliographies

552. Farberow, Norman L. **Bibliography on Suicide and Suicide Prevention, 1897-1957, 1958-1970**. Rockville, Md., National Institute of Mental Health, 1972. 1v. (various paging). index. (DHEW Publication No. HSM 72-9080). price not reported.

This is essentially two publications bound in one volume. The first lists over 2,100 books, book chapters, and articles published between 1897 and 1957. References are drawn from the medical, psychological, and sociological literature, although work that is solely of a medical or physiological nature has been omitted. Coverage is international and multilingual, with foreign-language titles provided both in the original and in translation. The second section contains over 2,500 works published between 1958 and 1970 and that meet the same criteria. Each section has its own pagination and subject and author indexes.

553. Kruckman, Laurence, and Chris Asmann-Finch. **Postpartum Depression: A Research Guide and International Bibliography**. New York, Garland, 1986. 162p. index. (Garland Reference Library of Social Science, v.335). price not reported. LC 85-31136. ISBN 0-8240-9121-3.

In this work, the literature cited on the etiology, treatment, and psychosocial effects of "postpartum blues" is derived from a variety of disciplines: medicine and the health sciences, anthropology, psychology and psychiatry, sociology, and social work. There is particularly good cross-cultural and ethnographic coverage. The emphasis is on current books, book chapters, and journal articles published in English from 1960 to 1985. However, earlier works and those in other languages are selectively represented among the 663 citations. About 10 percent of the citations have lengthy, descriptive abstracts.

The bibliography is preceded by an introduction to research and published literature on postpartum depression that covers definitions and occurrence, theories on etiology (including environmental and individual variables on its development), and anthropological perspectives. There are a subject index and an index by geographical area and culture.

554. McIntosh, John L., comp. **Research on Suicide: A Bibliography**. Westport, Conn., Greenwood Press, 1985. 323p. index. (Bibliographies and Indexes in Psychology, no.2). $40.95. LC 84-15706. ISBN 0-313-23992-4.

Because of the comprehensive nature of previous bibliographies, the over 2,300 citations in this work are limited to English-language publications published from 1970 to 1983. Books and journal articles are the most numerous types cited, with some association publications of limited circulation, government publications, and material from the popular literature also included. Predictably, McIntosh draws heavily on the literature of psychology and psychiatry, sociology and social work, law, and the health care fields.

Citations are arranged under 10 topical chapters that represent survey and reference works, nonprint information sources, theories and historical perspectives on suicide, demographic and social factors, prediction and intervention, ethics, and the roles of the helping professions. Each is preceded by a brief essay of introduction to the literature. Chapters are further subdivided for a total of almost 80 categories. About one-quarter of the citations contain a brief evaluative annotation or reference to an abstract in a standard indexing source. In addition to a subject index, an author index is supplied.

555. Osgood, Nancy J., and John L. McIntosh, comps. **Suicide and the Elderly: An Annotated Bibliography and Review**. Westport, Conn., Greenwood Press, 1986. 193p. index. (Bibliographies and Indexes in Gerontology, no.3). $35.00. LC 86-14935. ISBN 0-313-24786-2.

The compilers begin this bibliography with a thorough literature review of the incidence, factors, and assessment of suicide among the elderly. Next is a list of 400 citations, most published after 1970, organized under the following categories: bibliographic sources, overview and other nonempirical works, case studies, ethics, empirical studies, and non-English works. For the most part, readily available, published work is listed, including conference proceedings, journal articles, books, and government publications. The spectrum of disciplines includes psychology and psychiatry, medicine, and the burgeoning interdisciplinary area of death studies. Annotations are descriptive throughout.

Citations in the section of foreign-language material have translated titles, and many are annotated or cite English abstracts from standard abstracting tools. An interesting "Demographic Appendix" cites sources of statistical data on suicide in general. This section also includes selected tables and figures from some of the sources, supplying data on the incidence of suicide among distinct ages groups and the elderly in particular. The subject and author indexes provide access to all references, whether as part of the literature review, the bibliography proper, or the lists of statistical sources.

556. Picquet, D. Cheryn, and Reba A. Best, comps. **Post-Traumatic Stress Disorder, Rape Trauma, Delayed Stress and Related Conditions: A Bibliography, with a Directory of Veterans Outreach Programs**. Jefferson, N.C., McFarland, 1986. 204p. index. $29.95. LC 85-43585. ISBN 0-89950-213-X.

This bibliography goes beyond the most prevalent published literature, which deals with post-Vietnam stress and its etiology, manifestations, effects, and treatment. Cited literature produced before the recent conceptualization of this disorder includes post-World War I "war neurosis," effects on survivors of both manmade and natural disasters (e.g., the Holocaust, atomic bomb attacks, blizzards, and tornadoes). More recent identifications of this syndrome include long-term stress responses to toxic spills and nuclear plant accidents, its manifestation after rape and spousal abuse, victims of crime, and survivors of all manner of personal and social disasters.

The 1,895 citations reflect English-language books and articles from widely distributed newspapers, magazines, and journal articles from medicine and the health sciences, psychology and psychiatry, social work, law and public affairs (including some government publications), and sociology. Published items through early 1986 are included. Citations are separated into sections of books and articles, with indexes to coauthors and subjects. A Veterans Administration outreach program directory lists almost 200 programs by state or territory that offer support and treatment services to PTSD veterans.

557. Poteet, G. Howard, and Joseph C. Santora. **Death and Dying: A Bibliography, 1950-1974. Supplement, Volume I: Suicide**. Troy, N.Y., Whitston Publishing, 1978. 166p. index. $12.50. LC 76-51034. ISBN 0- 87875-108-4.

This volume supplements Poteet's *Death and Dying* bibliographies (see entries 443 and 444). The focus is on psychological aspects of suicide; forensics and technical causes of suicide are excluded. There is particularly good coverage of attitudes and incidence toward self-destructive behavior in other cultures and countries and the motivating factors behind suicide. Less coverage is afforded to counseling and therapeutic intervention than in *Research on Suicide* (see entry 554) and *Suicide and the Elderly* (see entry 555).

Much of the literature cited is from popular periodicals and professional journals. It is organized under approximately 200 subject categories, which almost compensates for the lack of a subject index. (An author index appears, however.) A separate section lists about 100 book titles, for a total of almost 2,000 references.

Dictionaries and Encyclopedias

558. Evans, Glen, and Norman L. Farberow. **The Encyclopedia of Suicide**. New York, Facts on File, 1988. 434p. index. (Social Problems Series). $40.00. LC 88-11173. ISBN 0-8160-1397-7.

This volume is part encyclopedia, part almanac, part directory. As an alphabetical encyclopedia, it covers concepts, organizations, researchers on suicidology, and biographies of writers and suicides in entries that range from several sentences to several pages. Statistics, addresses of organizations, and discussions of relevant research make each article almost self-contained, although cross-references are provided as needed. Use of the subject index is necessary, as headings for articles are not always consistent. Some articles are appended by a list of additional readings, although a bibliography follows the appendixes.

An introductory essay by Farberow surveys historical attitudes toward suicide and the study of suicidology. Two of the appendixes provide tables and graphs for statistics on youth suicides and suicides in general. A third appendix lists organizations, periodicals, and prevention and intervention services, predominantly in the United States.

Mental Retardation, Developmental Disabilities, and Learning Disabilities

Bibliographies

559. Evans, Martha M., **Dyslexia: An Annotated Bibliography**. Westport, Conn., Greenwood Press, 1982. 644p. index. (Contemporary Problems of Childhood, no.5). $50.95. LC 81-20319. ISBN 0-313-21344-5.

Coverage in this work is limited to developmental dyslexia, or the genetic inability to read and interpret written language properly. Excluded are materials intended for dyslexics, reading disabilities resulting from other causes, items on aphasia, and most material on acquired dyslexia. Within this narrow definition there are 2,401 citations to books and conference proceedings, government publications and ERIC documents, book chapters, journal articles, and some popular articles. All have nonevaluative abstracts, and some date from as early as the nineteenth century. Sections on causes, diagnoses, and treatments constitute the largest of the 11 classification categories and are further subdivided by subject. Other sections concentrate on the formats of the materials, including collections and general works, surveys, historical works, case studies, bibliographies, and reference and serial publications.

There are author and keyword subject indexes. Appendixes include information on indexing tools for further searching, working definitions of dyslexia excerpted from reference works and the research literature, and a glossary of terms and phrases.

560. Winchell, Carol Ann. **The Hyperkinetic Child: A Bibliography of Medical, Educational, and Behavioral Studies**. Westport, Conn., Greenwood Press, 1975. 182p. index. $35.00. LC 74-28527. ISBN 0-8371-7813-4.

561. Winchell, Carol Ann. **The Hyperkinetic Child: An Annotated Bibliography, 1974-1979**. Westport, Conn., Greenwood Press, 1981. 451p. index. (Contemporary Problems of Childhood, no.4). $36.95. LC 81-6200. ISBN 0-313-21452-2.

The study of hyperkinesis or hyperactivity, a childhood behavior disorder characterized by excessive restlessness and attention deficits, spans many areas of psychology. These areas are well represented in the content and organization of these volumes, which draw on a variety of relevant disciplines, primarily education, pharmacology, biomedicine, and psychology. The best coverage is of the controversial issues regarding etiology and influential factors, testing and diagnosis, and management and treatment. Other sections cite animal studies, longitudinal studies, sociological aspects, ethical and legal issues, and research methodologies.

The organization of both volumes is similar, with citations listed under several broad categories and numerous subheadings. The original volume includes 1,874 items—books, journal articles, dissertations, government reports, and research reports and ERIC documents—produced from 1950 through mid-1974. The supplement includes over 2,000 additional items published through 1979 and annotates them. Some popular literature is cited, but the emphasis is on research studies. Other features offered by the volumes include a glossary, drugs commonly used in treatment, lists of audiovisual materials and service organizations, and author and keyword subject indexes.

Indexes and Abstracts

562. **Developmental Disabilities Abstracts**. Vols. 12-13. Washington, D.C., U.S. Department of Health, Education, and Welfare, Developmental Disabilities Office, 1977-1978. o.p. (SuDoc HE 1.49).

This index filled an important need by indexing books, journal articles, dissertations, and government documents on mental handicap and developmental delay. Its demise, joined shortly after by the cessation of *DSH Abstracts* and its focus on communication impairment, leaves coverage of literature on the identification and rehabilitation of the handicapped to *Exceptional Child Education Resources* (see entry 145) and *Psychological Abstracts* (see entry 129). This service was also published under the titles *Mental Retardation Abstracts* (vols. 1-10, 1964-1973) and *Mental Retardation and Developmental Disabilities Abstracts* (vol. 11, 1974-1976).

Handbooks

563. Cohen, Donald J., and Anne Donnellan, eds. **Handbook of Autism and Pervasive Developmental Disorders**. New York, John Wiley, 1987. 757p. index. $59.95. LC 87-6104. ISBN 0-471-81231-5.

Pervasive developmental disorder covers a wide range of disabilities, generally those that impair intellectual functioning, social interaction, and language and comprehension skills. Fifty-four chapters in this work are divided among four broad sections. The first two, "Characteristics of Autistic Syndromes" and "Intervention," contain discussions about influences on behavior and biological functioning and therapy. The remaining chapters cover social and legal issues of autistic individuals and their treatment and special topic essays that do not fit into any of the other categories: educational and residential placement, the international perspective, aspects of communication limitations, and the causes of autism. There is a brief subject index. Although intended for advanced students, researchers, and professionals in psychology and education, the chapters are readable and not overly technical, although most of the lists of cited references are woefully brief.

564. Matson, Johnny L., and James A. Mulick, eds. **Handbook of Mental Retardation.** 2d ed. Elmsford, N.Y., Pergamon Press, 1991. 672p. index. (Pergamon General Psychology Series, v.121). $95.00. LC 90-7441. ISBN 0-08-035862-4.

The editors state in their preface that they intend a comprehensive rather than an in-depth approach to mental retardation, given the volume of literature and diversity of research on societal, medical, and therapeutic issues. With a few exceptions, the 40 chapters are less functional as literature reviews than as exploratory essays on these issues. Part 1 discusses the philosophy of care (service delivery and public advocacy), and part 2 contains chapters on societal issues (e.g., community living, mainstreaming, legal rights of the retarded). Seven essays deal with diagnosis and classification, and another section covers issues on assessment practices and techniques. Five chapters on prevention and therapeutic approaches expound upon prenatal counseling, early intervention and identification, community health, therapeutic interventions for the mentally retarded and their families, and ways to ease the integration of mentally retarded citizens into society. The last section provides an overview of methodological approaches to research. There are subject and author indexes.

565. Van Hasselt, Vincent B., Phillip S. Strain, and Michel Hersen, eds. **Handbook of Developmental and Physical Disabilities.** Elmsford, N.Y., Pergamon Press, 1988. 553p. index. (Pergamon General Psychology Series, v.148). $90.00. LC 86-30282. ISBN 0-08-031595-X.

A total of 27 chapters discuss developmental and physical disabilities from a variety of approaches, including human life-span, evaluation, and biomedical perspectives. Topics in the general issues section encompass prevention, family issues, sexual adjustment, social and workplace integration, and legal issues. The largest and most useful section consists of 16 chapters, each devoted to a specific disabling condition. These include those that involve physical limitations (e.g., cerebral palsy, chronic pain, musculoskeletal disorders, spinal cord injury), sensory disorders (e.g., hearing and visual impairments), language and communication limitations, learning disorders and attention deficit, those caused by physical distress (e.g., epilepsy, stroke), mental retardation, and the multiply handicapped. These chapters are useful because they do not espouse a specific point of view or philosophical bent. Instead, authors summarize the issues and research literature concerned with etiology, diagnosis, and treatment and rehabilitation. Along with substantial reference lists, there are subject and author indexes.

Dictionaries and Encyclopedias

566. Lindsey, Mary P. **Dictionary of Mental Handicap.** New York, Routledge, Chapman & Hall, 1989. 345p. $49.50. LC 89-190759. ISBN 0-415-02810-8.

Lindsey provides concise descriptions for a wide variety of concepts commonly found in mental retardation research. Entries are not limited to quick definitions of terms, although these are abundant. Lengthier descriptions define assessment tools; legislation; organizations and associations; syndromes associated with retardation; and many other issues in medicine, counseling and rehabilitation, education, and psychology. Definitions contain a minimum of technical jargon and many brief lists of citations to professional literature. Names and addresses are provided for organizations. Despite the British bias in the discussions of issues in law or education, this remains a valuable, useful work for American audiences.

Substance Abuse

Bibliographies

567. Andrews, Theodora. **A Bibliography of Drug Abuse, Including Alcohol and Tobacco.** Littleton, Colo., Libraries Unlimited, 1977. 306p. index. price not reported. LC 77-22606. ISBN 0-87287-149-5.

568. Andrews, Theodora. **A Bibliography of Drug Abuse: Supplement 1977-1980**. Littleton, Colo., Libraries Unlimited, 1981. 312p. index. price not reported. LC 81-8194. ISBN 0-87287-252-1.

These volumes contain almost 1,500 citations to English-language books, booklets, government documents, and United Nations publications. The scope is broad, from medicine to the physical sciences and social sciences and from popular works to research volumes. Most titles were published in the 1960s and later, with selected, important earlier works. The lengthy annotations are both descriptive and evaluative.

Both volumes are started by lists of general references tools organized by format, such as dictionaries, bibliographies, and periodicals. Most titles are listed in a broad topical arrangement, after which there are sections dealing with specific substances: hallucinogens, marijuana, stimulants, alcohol, and tobacco. Providing access is a combined index by author, subject, and title.

Of specific interest to individuals within psychology are sections on substance abuse in the work environment and prevention and rehabilitation.. The section on psychosocial factors concerns lifestyle and the drug subculture. The most pertinent titles on abnormal behavior and psychopathology of abusers, psychopharmacology, and clinical treatment of abuse are included in the sections on medical literature in each volume.

569. Chalfant, H. Paul, and Brent S. Roper, comps. **Social and Behavioral Aspects of Female Alcoholism: An Annotated Bibliography**. Westport, Conn., Greenwood Press, 1980. 145p. index. $35.00. LC 80-1021. ISBN 0-313-20947-2.

This work consists of 488 citations to the professional and academic journal literature in sociology, psychology, social work, medicine, and psychiatry. Among the content areas covered are the families and spouses of female alcoholics, psychological aspects, psychotherapy and treatment concerns, suicide and deviant behavior, and social and cultural factors. An introductory essay defines and clarifies alcohol abuse among women, including a history of research trends, definitions, patterns and epidemiology of abuse by women. Only English-language items are represented, most published after 1970. The sole subject access is provided by the nine broad categories under which citations are listed by author; there is an author index, however.

570. Jordy, Sarah Spock, and Vera Efron. **International Bibliography of Studies on Alcohol.** New Brunswick, N.J., Rutgers Center of Alcohol Studies, 1966-1981. 3v. index. $150.00/set. LC 60-14437. ISBN 0-911290-07-9.

This exhaustive retrospective bibliography has particularly good coverage of physiological effects of alcohol use and abuse, social control and social attitudes, and the nature and treatment of alcoholism. According to prefatory material in volume 1, the first two volumes in this set contain 25,342 references to books and book chapters, journal articles, and research reports of limited circulation on alcoholism and alcohol use published from 1901 though 1950. Volume 3 covers 1951 to 1960. References are arranged by year of publication and then by author in volume 1. Volume 2 consists of subject and author indexes and separate indexes for personal names as subjects, institutions as subjects, and geographic areas. Most citations are derived from the research literatures in addiction, medicine, psychology, psychiatry, and law. Jordy and Efron provide international, multilingual coverage to the research literature, with the majority of entries in English, German, French, or Italian.

571. Kurtz, Norman R., Bradley Googins, and William Howard. **Occupational Alcoholism: An Annotated Bibliography**. Toronto, Addiction Research Foundation, 1984. 218p. index. (Bibliographic Series, no.17). $15.00pa. LC 85-149700. ISBN 0-88868-101-1.

The scope of this work indicates that the human and economic costs of alcoholism are not new issues for employers or health professionals. The 481 references to journal articles, technical reports, books, and government and foundation reports date from the early 1940s to the early 1980s. The literatures of medicine and health science, occupational medicine, and psychology and substance abuse are well represented, whereas management and personnel literature receives lesser coverage.

Citations are arranged under 20 categories, including general works, employee assistance programs, prevention strategies, occupation risk and legal implications, the role of supervisors and unions, and education. There are separate lists of literature reviews and bibliographies. A category index serves as a cross-reference index to references that belong in more than one category; there is also an author index.

572. Menditto, Joseph. **Drugs of Addiction and Non-Addiction, Their Use and Abuse: A Comprehensive Bibliography, 1960-1969**. Troy, N.Y., Whitston Publishing, 1970. 315p. index. $11.50. LC 79-116588. ISBN 0-87875-003-7.

573. **Drug Abuse Bibliography for [year]**. Vol. 1- . Troy, N.Y., Whitston Publishing, 1971- . annual. $68.50/year. LC 79-116599. ISSN 0093- 2515.

Menditto's one-volume 1970 bibliography contains about 6,000 entries for books and book chapters, doctoral dissertations, and periodical literature. Materials are intended for both the general public and research-oriented individuals. Entries are arranged under substances or concepts (e.g., narcotics trade, rehabilitation, crime and legal issues) for a total of 12 categories, plus an author index. The drugs covered are largely limited to barbiturates, amphetamines, hallucinogens, and marijuana.

The annual *Drug Abuse Bibliography* supplements Menditto's work and expands coverage to practically every drug of addiction, including nicotine, alcohol, and solvents. There is also better coverage of social and psychological issues. Selective coverage is provided for over 1,000 periodicals in all areas of medicine and pharmacology, psychology, sociology, and education; interdisciplinary titles are also included. Materials are international, multilingual, and comprehensive; each annual volume includes up to 9,000 citations. The lag between coverage and publication is a handicap; for example, the volume covering 1985 was published in 1989. A list of subject headings provides a basic table of contents under which periodical citations are listed, followed by citations to books and other publications. Each volume has an author index.

574. Miletich, John J., comp. **Work and Alcohol Abuse: An Annotated Bibliography**. Westport, Conn., Greenwood Press, 1987. 263p. index. (Bibliographies and Indexes in Sociology, no.12). $42.95. LC 87-23619. ISBN 0-313-25689-6.

In this book, all citations and their descriptive annotations represent English-language works published between 1972 and 1986. The largest single category is the literature of management, labor and industrial relations, alcohol abuse, and vocational rehabilitation literature. Some literature also represents medicine and nursing, law, and social work. Most of the 1,100-plus citations are to professional and scholarly journals and books, although trade and popular periodicals, dissertations, and research reports of limited circulation are also included.

Citations are arranged under seven categories: general literature and diagnosis of alcohol abuse, the impact on and response of corporate management, unions and safety, public sector employment, occurrence within specific occupational and professional groups, women, and therapeutic approaches. There are indexes to authors, subjects, and company names.

575. Page, Penny Booth. **Alcohol Use and Alcoholism: A Guide to the Literature**. New York, Garland, 1986. 164p. index. (Garland Reference Library of Social Science, v.350). $28.00. LC 83-49073. ISBN 0-8240-9020-9.

This is a list of published English-language books, pamphlets, and government documents that address a variety of audiences: students, parents, teachers, counselors, social workers, and anyone else interested and involved in alcohol use, abuse, and rehabilitation. References that would be primarily of interest to medical and scientific researchers are excluded. Most were published from the mid-1970s through 1985, with selected coverage of earlier material.

The 405 citations are descriptively annotated and listed under 16 categories that encompass reference works and guides, history, prevention and rehabilitation, alcohol use among specific populations, effects on prenatal development, effects on the family and children, abuse and the workplace, and legal and social issues. In addition to books of general interest there are books for children and young adults, biographies, testimonials, and other works intended for clients in therapy or their families. Appendixes list important periodicals and organizations that deal with alcohol use and abuse, and there are author and title indexes.

Handbooks

576. Blum, Kenneth. **Handbook of Abusable Drugs**. New York, Gardner Press, 1984. 721p. index. $85.00. LC 83-5667. ISBN 0-89876-036-4.

Although Blum's audience includes physicians and pharmacologists, those interested in the behavioral aspects of substance abuse will benefit from his "social pharmacology" approach. Throughout, chapters stress the "interrelationships among chemical agents (drugs), consciousness (a person), and social systems (society)" (p. xxiii). Chapters are understandable by advanced students, the reference lists are very helpful, and there are many illustrative tables and charts.

The opening chapters include an introduction, discussions of the social aspects of abuse, basic pharmacological topics in abuse, and the classification of abused drugs. Most remaining chapters discuss specific classes of drugs: narcotics, opioids, "narcotic maintenance drugs" (e.g., methadone), inhalants, depressants, alcohol and tobacco, stimulants, tranquilizers, cannabis, psychedelics, and over-the-counter drugs. Appendixes include a glossary of drug slang and scientific names and the classification of drugs with their behavioral and physiological characteristics. A well-organized and detailed table of contents supplements indexes by authors and drug names.

577. Herrington, Roland E., George R. Jacobson, and David G. Benzer, eds. **Alcohol and Drug Abuse Handbook**. St. Louis, Mo., Warren H. Green, 1987. 490p. index. (Allied Health Professions Monograph). $55.00. LC 87-121122. ISBN 0-87527-274-6.

The editors take an "orthopsychiatric" approach to substance abuse (defined here as including alcohol and prescription drugs). The audience, as well as the contributors, consist of health care professionals and mental health care professionals of diverse backgrounds.

The 18 chapters are divided into three groups. "Symptoms and Consequences" addresses the characteristics, etiology and pharmacology, and problems associated with abuse of various classes of drugs: cannabis, opiates, stimulants, hallucinogens, and sedatives. Next, 10 chapters are dedicated to identification and treatment. For the most part, these contributed chapters, although reflecting a variety of treatment approaches, do not advocate one philosophical bent. Among the issues addressed are drug screening, the general identification and treatment of each class of abused drugs, alcohol abuse treatment methods, medical complications of abuse, family and self-help approaches, and community-based treatment programs.

A third part addresses special problems, primarily those involving special populations (e.g., women, children and adolescents) and the interplay of abuse disorders with other psychiatric problems. The appendixes consist primarily of various screening instruments and forms and diagnostic criteria. There is a subject index.

Dictionaries and Encyclopedias

578. Fay, John J. **The Alcohol/Drug Abuse Dictionary and Encyclopedia**. Springfield, Ill., Charles C. Thomas, 1988. 167p. $17.50. LC 88-4947. ISBN 0-398-05491-6.

Fay defines approximately 800 terms related to substance abuse as used in a variety of disciplines and settings. Terms generally fall into one of the following categories: pharmaceutical and slang terms for substances open to abuse and addiction; legislation, judicial decisions, and government programs for law enforcement, treatment, or regulation; terms used in criminology, biomedicine, the health sciences, and pharmacology, including drug use and production; organizations and associations concerned with rehabilitation from, punishment for using, or regulation of drugs and alcohol; and important publications, including government studies. Definitions range in length from a few words to one or two pages, generally avoiding highly technical language. Fay's emphasis is on the slang terminology of the drug subculture, legal terms, and pharmaceutical and biomedical definitions; he provides relatively scant coverage of terms used in treatment and rehabilitative contexts.

Among the eight appendixes are those that list slang, chemical, and brand names for drugs; a list of state agencies concerned with alcohol and drug control; poison information centers in each state and Canada; research centers, government agencies, and private organizations that deal with treatment, public safety, and research issues; and sources of information on drugs of abuse and their effects. Besides a list of toll-free numbers from which assistance or information services are available, there is a brief bibliography.

579. O'Brien, Robert, and Morris Chafetz. **The Encyclopedia of Alcoholism**. 2d ed. New York, Facts on File, 1991. 346p. index. $45.00. LC 89-23333. ISBN 0-8160-1955-X.

In this book over 600 articles, ranging from a few sentences to several pages, define alcohol as a substance of abuse, the impact and role of customs and social institutions, and the physical and psychological consequences of abuse. Tables, statistics, and lists of further readings appear in the text, although most statistics appear in the appendixes. Another appendix lists national, state, and territorial clearinghouses and organizations on alcohol abuse (but not treatment centers) in the United States, Canada, and selected foreign countries; it also indicates selected English-language periodicals. A bibliography is provided, and in addition to liberal cross-references, there is a subject index.

An introductory essay discusses alcohol as a chemical substance and its history of consumption. Throughout the whole work, the focus is on social and psychological approaches to consumption, abuse, treatment, and recovery. The articles are well written and easy to understand without being simplistic. This feature and the appendixes make this work a one-stop resource.

580. O'Brien, Robert, and Sidney Cohen. **The Encyclopedia of Drug Abuse**. 2d ed. New York, Facts on File, 1991. 500p. index. $45.00. LC 89-71531. ISBN 0-8160-1956-8.

This is an extremely useful dictionary on substances of abuse and their origins, effects, use, and legal status, as well as the treatment of abusers. In addition to illicit drugs, there is also coverage of nicotine, prescription and nonprescription drugs, inhalants, and alcohol. (The last is better covered in *The Encyclopedia of Alcoholism* [see entry 579].)

The length of the entries varies from a sentence or phrase to several pages, and the entries occasionally include brief lists of references to popular or professional literature. Terms include legal and social aspects of drug use and rehabilitation, trade and generic names of drugs, syndromes associated with their use, treatment approaches, psychosocial aspects, groups and individuals, and geographic areas. Among the appendixes are a list of drug slang, statistical and information tables, and a directory of agencies (international, national, and state) concerned with drug enforcement and use research. An introductory essay discusses the history of drug use from prehistory to the present. There are a lengthy bibliography and a subject index.

Directories

581. **Drug, Alcohol, and Other Addictions: A Directory of Treatment Centers and Prevention Programs Nationwide**. Phoenix, Ariz., Oryx Press, 1989. 775p. $65.00pa. LC 89-2867. ISBN 0-89774-416-0pa.

This directory lists and describes approximately 18,000 treatment facilities and prevention programs in the United States and its possessions. Included are programs addressing drug and alcohol addictions, sex and addictions, tobacco dependence, and codependency. Entries are listed under state or possession and thereunder by city. All include basic information on location, telephone number, and contact person. The completeness of entries varies, but most include a description of the disorders treated, therapeutic or treatment orientation, specialization of groups served (e.g., children, adolescents, veterans), setting (e.g., residential versus outpatient), number of clients served, ownership, and sources of funding.

Directory information of this scope and detail is difficult to find. The only other source as comprehensive and detailed is the National Drug and Alcoholism Treatment Utilization Survey (NDATUS), a National Institute of Drug Abuse directory file used as a primary resource to compile this directory. (Additional compilation sources include local, state, and professional publications.) Much of the detailed information contained for each facility was obtained directly from the services.

TREATMENT AND PREVENTION OF PSYCHOLOGICAL DISORDERS

General Sources

Bibliographies

582. Biegel, David E., Ellen McCarie, and Susan Mendelson. **Social Networks and Mental Health: An Annotated Bibliography**. Beverly Hills, Calif., Sage, 1985. 391p. index. price not reported. LC 84-23585. ISBN 0-8039-2420-8.

583. Biegel, David E., et al., comps. **Social Support Networks: A Bibliography, 1983-1987**. Westport, Conn., Greenwood Press, 1989. 334p. index. (Bibliographies and Indexes in Sociology, no.15). $45.00. LC 88-32824. ISBN 0-313-2664-2.

Social Networks and Mental Health contains 1,340 citations to literature published from the 1950s to 1982, and *Social Support Networks* provides 2,693 additional references through 1987. According to the newer volume, the focus is on the "role that significant others play in affecting individuals' life satisfaction, health and mental health status" (p. xii). The scope of the works includes English-language books and journals intended for family and friends of clients and helping professionals in social work, psychology, and medicine.

References are organized in both volumes under five topical categories that address the theoretical underpinnings, the role of social support in physical and mental health, treatment and intervention strategies, and the roles of professionals and significant others. Author and subject indexes provide access to the citations.

584. Buckner, John C., Edison J. Trickett, and Sara J. Corse. **Primary Prevention in Mental Health: An Annotated Bibliography**. Rockville, Md., National Institute of Mental Health, U. S. Department of Health and Human Services, 1985. 425p. index. (DHHS Publication No. ADM 85-1405). o.p. (SuDoc HE 20.8125:P 32/2).

In the context of this bibliography, *primary prevention* is defined as "the prevention of specific disorders and the enhancement of competencies related to mental health in general" (p. vi). Publication dates range from the 1950s to the mid-1980s, and the citations to 1,008 English-language books and journals are accompanied by descriptive abstracts. Although there is no subject index, the detailed contents arrangement provides excellent topical access. The 19 categories cover, for example, theories and issues, the role of mental health professionals, early intervention and parent training, prevention in the dysfunctional family, early intervention strategies, crisis intervention, competence building and social support, community prevention settings, and prevention activities among minorities and the elderly. There are many subheadings under each category, with numerous cross-references among sections. There is also an author index.

585. Freeman, Ruth St. John, and Harrop A. Freeman. **Counseling: A Bibliography (with Annotations)**. New York, Scarecrow, 1964. 986p. price not reported. LC 64-11793.

Counseling is defined broadly to include practically any therapeutic relationship that will help an individual function more effectively. According to this definition, the 8,690 citations are arranged under professional aspects of counseling, religion and pastoral counseling, the medical setting, legal counseling, social work, guidancc and assessment, student counseling, marriage and family therapy, and psychotherapeutic intervention and the behaviors influencing it.

English-language books, journal articles, and doctoral theses produced between 1950 through 1963 are included, with the aim being comprehensiveness rather than selectivity. Most entries (probably more than half) are descriptively annotated. Because there is no subject index, each item is coded for one of 15 concept categories and one of several subdivisions within each category, as defined at the end of the body of entries. This cumbersome subject coding arrangement necessitates scanning entries within the larger nine sections to find a specific topic.

586. Lambert, Michael, and Lorraine Lauper. **Behavior Change Research: A Bibliography.** Jonesboro, Tenn., Pilgrimage, 1980. 500p. price not reported. LC 82-158078. ISBN 0-932930-26-3.

587. Strupp, Hans H., and Allen E. Bergin. **Research in Individual Psychotherapy**. Rockville, Md., National Institute of Mental Health, 1969. 167p. (Public Health Service Publication, no.1944). price not reported. LC 70-604225. (SuDoc FS 2.22/13:P 95/2).

The basic volume by Strupp and Bergin contains over 2,700 references about individual psychotherapy with adult clients and also references of a more general nature about psychotherapy research. Coverage is retrospective to 1967. Emphasis is on English-language journal citations, although research in other formats (e.g., dissertations, books, proceedings) is also represented.

Lambert and Lauper extend coverage to journal articles and books published from 1968 to 1975. Almost 7,000 citations include published reviews, empirical research, and methodological studies. Unlike the 1969 publication, which has an author arrangement, the later book lists references according to 40 subject categories, including the training and role of therapists, dysfunctional situations or abnormal behaviors, treatment settings, and treatment techniques or theoretical orientations. The materials covered are mostly core works within psychology and psychiatry.

588. Mandel, Harvey P. **Short-Term Psychotherapy and Brief Treatment Techniques: An Annotated Bibliography, 1920-1980**. New York, Plenum, 1981. 682p. index. $65.00. LC 81-221. ISBN 0-306-40658-6.

As Mandel discusses in his excellent introduction, the use of brief therapy (generally therapy limited to 10-20 sessions and addressing a specific behavior or group of behaviors) is increasingly prevalent across theoretical orientations of treatment, client populations, and mental health settings. Publication in this area accelerated after 1970 and is found in a variety of professional literatures, such as psychology, social work, psychiatry, medicine, and other health care professions. The contents of this bibliography reflect these publishing trends, citing 1,522 English-language professional and scholarly books and journal articles. Most have descriptive annotations, many reprinted from the original journal source. The references are readily accessible through a detailed subject index and an author index.

589. Simmerlin, Florence A., comp. **Religion and Mental Health: A Bibliography**. Rockville, Md., U.S. Department of Health and Human Services, National Institute of Mental Health, 1980. 251p. index. (SuDoc HE 20.8113:R 27).

Over 1,800 citations and descriptive annotations in this book represent post-1970 material, including scholarly and professional journal articles, books, research reports, dissertations, and a limited number of nonprint sources. Most are English-language contributions. Throughout, the emphasis is on individuals' transpersonal and spiritual beliefs, their relationships with personal functioning and behavior, and their roles in seeking professional mental health assistance. There is especially welcome coverage of non-Western religious traditions, the role of religious belief in mental wellness, and pastoral counseling in a variety of settings.

Material is organized under 38 broad subject categories dealing with such topics as religious attitudes, the role of clergy, the needs of special populations and dysfunctional behaviors, pastoral counseling, and social and legal issues. Besides an author index, there is an exhaustive keyword subject index.

590. Williams, Carolyn L. **An Annotated Bibliography on Refugee Mental Health**. Rockville, Md., National Institute of Mental Health, U.S. Department of Health and Human Services, 1987. 335p. index. (DHHS Publication No. ADM 87-1517). o.p. (SuDoc HE 20.8113: R 25).

This bibliography of approximately 500 citations represents a growing awareness of the mental health and social support needs of refugees. Williams focuses on refugees from Asia and Latin America. The primary concern of the book is research journal literature, research reports, and books, most published since the mid-1970s and derived not only from traditional mental health disciplines but also from demographics, area studies, and anthropology.

Citations and descriptive abstracts are arranged under four broad categories (the cultural context of refugee status, mental health issues, special needs of the elderly and women, and bibliographies), with most further subdivided. The subject index concentrates on concepts. Additionally, there are a refugee and ethnic group index and an author index.

591. Zuckerman, Elyse. **Changing Directions in the Treatment of Women: A Mental Health Bibliography**. Rockville, Md., National Institute of Mental Health, U.S. Department of Health, Education, and Welfare, 1979. 494p. index. (DHEW Publication No. ADM 79-749). o.p. (SuDoc HE 20.8113:W 84/2).

Given the volume of literature on the psychological treatment of women that has appeared since the publication of this book, this bibliography is already out of date. However, the 407 citations to books, journal articles, and popular articles are an indication of the considerable interest in the topic that arose in the 1970s. Coverage is mostly from 1960 through 1977, with earlier citations to the psychoanalytic literature. Throughout, emphasis is given to materials on women as recipients of mental health care that is based on traditional sex bias, stereotyped attitudes, and subservient roles of women in society. Topics under which citations are organized include a discussion of traditional therapies and their critics, the effects of gender and role expectations on the professional-client relationship and treatment outcome, alternatives to traditional therapy, and the treatment of specific problems and populations. Annotations are descriptive and lengthy. Most areas are further subdivided for effective access, and there are subject and author indexes.

Handbooks

592. **American Handbook of Psychiatry**. 2d ed. Silvano Arieti, ed.-in-chief. New York, Basic Books, 1974-1986. 8v. index. cost varies per volume. LC varies. ISBN varies.

Despite the fact that psychiatric practice seems to undergo continuous change, this set remains a substantial, authoritative reference to the identification and treatment of mental disorders. The first six volumes, published in 1974 and 1975, constitute the basic set. Although the work was written for the advanced student, researcher, and professional, the organization of chapters and writing style make much of the text accessible to educated laypersons. Chapters are appended by lengthy reference lists. The first volume discusses the historical and theoretical foundations of psychiatry. Volumes 2 and 3 focus on child, adolescent, and adult psychiatry, and volumes 4 and 5 cover organic disorders, psychosomatic medicine, and treatment approaches. Volume 6, *New Psychiatric Frontiers,* contains chapters on the social context of psychiatry, the role of life-span development in mental health, psychopharmacology, and innovative therapies.

Volume 7, *Advances and New Directions*, was published in 1981 and updates some earlier material on the impact of biological factors on psychiatry and psychiatric practice, childhood and adolescent mental health, new treatment approaches (e.g., art therapy, poetry therapy, therapy for the chronically mentally ill), and issues in professional practice and ethics. Chapters in volume 8, *Biological Psychiatry*, discuss neurological and chemical aspects of both psychiatric disorders and treatment and controversial issues such as psychosurgery and electroconvulsive therapy.

593. Brown, Steven D., and Robert W. Lent, eds. **Handbook of Counseling Psychology**. New York, John Wiley, 1984. 982p. index. $74.95. LC 84-7395. ISBN 0-471-09905-8.

Intended for the professional, academician, and graduate student in counseling psychology, this handbook consists of 23 essays spanning the breadth of this area of professional practice. Essays are divided among six broad categories. The first part discusses historical, ethical, and legal issues in professional practice. Five chapters on vocational and career counseling and assessment comprise the second part. Part 3 focuses on individual counseling, and part 4 discusses counseling's roles in prevention and intervention strategies. Professional training and supervision is covered in part 5. The last part contains essays on emerging areas of concern in professional interest and practice: working with minority populations and women, bibliotherapy, self-help, and health psychology. Each chapter is appended by a lengthy reference list that cites classic and current sources in counseling. A subject index closes the book.

594. Corsini, Raymond J., ed. **Handbook of Innovative Psychotherapies**. New York, John Wiley, 1981. 969p. index. (Wiley Series on Personality Processes). price not reported. LC 80-29062. ISBN 0-471-06229-4.

This is an authoritative handbook to therapeutic approaches considered by many to be on the fringe of psychology but that in fact have traditions and research bases that are not widely known. Corsini notes in his preface that it "contains a disciplined, authoritative, concise, and readable account of 64 major innovative approaches to psychotherapy in current use." He interprets *innovative* to include systems of or approaches to psychotherapy not generally well known to professionals and perhaps known to laypeople only through the popular media. Therefore, more well-known systems such as behavior therapy and psychoanalysis are not represented, although covert conditioning and direct psychoanalysis are. Some chapters discuss expressive therapies, such as the use of art, music, and literature. Others are philosophically based, such as those on feminist approaches to therapy, crisis management, and stress management. Especially interesting are articles on approaches with non-Western origins, such as meditation and Morita therapy.

Although each chapter is written by a proponent of the therapeutic approach that it expounds, every one conforms to an organizational outline covering definition, history and current uses, theory, methodology and applications, case studies, a summary, and references. There are subject and name indexes and a glossary of terms.

595. Gelder, Michael, Dennis Gath, and Richard Mayou. **Oxford Textbook of Psychiatry**. 2d ed. New York, Oxford University Press, 1988. 1079p. index. $95.00; $45.00pa. LC 88-38712. ISBN 0-19-261630-7; 0-19-261629-3pa.

Intended as a guide to psychiatric assessment, diagnosis, and treatment, this book's technical terminology makes it a handbook for advanced students and practitioners. However, the 22 chapters provide comprehensive reviews of the etiology, symptoms, treatment options, and prognosis for the entire range of *DSM-III-R* (see entry 543) disorders. Other chapters discuss professional and service issues such as clinical interviewing, forensic psychiatry, and drug and somatic treatment of mental disorders. Chapter 18 provides a cogent discussion of the varieties of psychotherapeutic approaches, including group, family, behavioral, and cognitive.

Dictionaries and Encyclopedias

596. **The Psychotherapy Handbook**. Richie Herink, ed. New York, New American Library, 1980. 724p. index. $14.95pa. LC 79-29716. ISBN 0-452-00525-6.

Differentiation among the theories, evolution, goals, and techniques of various psychotherapeutic approaches is difficult to find, especially as defined in lay terms. In this work, approximately 300 psychotherapies from a spectrum of philosophical viewpoints are each described in several pages. Written in everyday language, they cover the history, techniques, and applications of each therapeutic approach. Obscure and controversial therapies (e.g., past-life therapy, cooking therapy, Tibetan psychic healing) are afforded the same coverage as are such recognized conventional approaches as psychoanalysis, bibliotherapy, and behavior modification. Contributors were selected for their expertise in using a particular approach, and in some cases are the originators of particular therapies. Every article includes a brief bibliography of relevant works. A cross-reference index is supplied.

597. Walrond-Skinner, Sue **A Dictionary of Psychotherapy**. New York, Routledge, Chapman & Hall, 1986. 379p. index. $59.95. LC 85-28267. ISBN 0-7100-9978-9.

Students and laypeople will find this dictionary to be of considerable assistance, especially for terms and concepts that differ according to the therapeutic context in which they are used. Articles cover the most current issues, trends, and contributions in psychotherapy research. Theories and concepts are discussed in terms of their historical and theoretical origins, and an abundance of cross-references lead users to related topics. Many entries are biographical and emphasize individuals' contributions and historical significance to the development of psychotherapy. Most articles also provide a list of key references.

Marital, Family, and Group Therapy

Bibliographies

598. Corsini, Raymond J., and Lloyd J. Putzey. **Bibliography of Group Psychotherapy 1906-1956 (1906 through 1955)**. Beacon, N.Y., Beacon House, 1957. 75p. index. (Psychodrama and Group Psychotherapy Monographs, no.29).

This work organizes its citations by year of publication, with author and subject indexes. The latter lists citations by over 70 broad categories representing group therapy theory, techniques, and populations. Approximately 1,700 unannotated citations to books and book chapters, journal articles, and theses are listed. Most are English-language contributions, although there is a smattering of German, French, Italian, and other languages from the literatures of psychology and counseling, psychiatry, medicine, and related areas.

Despite its age, this bibliography retains its value as a historical tool. It illustrates the infancy of practice and thought in this area, especially reflecting a variety of theoretical persuasions, applications, and techniques.

599. Grobman, Jerald, comp. **Group Psychotherapy for Students and Teachers: A Selected Bibliography, 1946-1979**. New York, Garland, 1981. 113p. index. (Garland Reference Library of Social Science, v.102). price not reported. LC 81-43339. ISBN 0-8240-9291-0.

This bibliography originated as a list of supplemental readings for psychiatric residents and advanced students in psychology, social work, and nursing to introduce them to various group methods. The content heavily reflects psychoanalytic theory, with literature from other theoretical frameworks (e.g., behavior, gestalt, psychodrama, creative arts therapies) included on a selective basis. Throughout the book, the therapeutic group is the main focus, so that materials solely on group dynamics, interaction, and related issues are not included.

The 758 citations are primarily to journal articles, supplemented by book titles and chapters. They are topically arranged in 44 relatively narrow areas covering basic theory, group work in particular settings and with specific populations, and work with children. Further subdivisions within categories make the subject index almost unnecessary. There is also an author index.

600. Lubin, Bernard, and Alice W. Lubin. **Comprehensive Index of Group Psychotherapy Writings**. Madison, Wis., International Universities Press, 1987. 667p. index. (American Group Psychotherapy Association Monograph Series, 2). $60.00. LC 86-10683. ISBN 0-8236-1045-4.

As the title indicates, this bibliography is not selective. The 13,304 unannotated entries, covering the years 1906 through 1980, were gleaned from *Psychological Abstracts* (see entry 129), *Index Medicus* (see entry 388), *Sociological Abstracts* (see entry 72), *Dissertation Abstracts* (see entries 20 and 140), and *Books in Print*. Most publications appeared after 1945 and especially after 1960. The works are arranged alphabetically by first author. English-language academic and professional journals comprise the majority of citations, although other European languages are also represented. Providing access to the citations is a subject index by very broad terms and by publication formats.

601. Lubin, Bernard, Alice W. Lubin, Marion G. Whiteford, and Rodney V. Whitlock, comps. **Family Therapy: A Bibliography, 1937-1986**. Westport, Conn., Greenwood Press, 1988. 470p. index. (Bibliographies and Indexes in Psychology, no.4). $49.95. LC 88-18682. ISBN 0-313-26172-5.

Going as far back as the earliest professional publication in family therapy (dated 1937), this is a comprehensive bibliography to the substantive literature on family, marital, and couples therapy and counseling. The 6,167 unannotated citations represent books and book chapters, book reviews, scholarly and professional articles, and dissertations. Coverage is predominantly English-language and represents a variety of social science disciplines and the helping professions. A considerable amount of foreign-language material is listed, with titles given in English translation.

There is an author index, and the subject index lists references under 125 concept and format categories. The latter is not as useful as it might be, as many of the categories are too broad and list hundred of references. For breadth and depth of coverage in family therapy, however, this is an outstanding compilation.

602. Zimpfer, David G. **Group Work in the Helping Professions: A Bibliography**. Washington, D.C., Association for Specialists in Group Work, 1976. 452p. index. price not reported. LC 76-363090.

603. Zimpfer, David G. **Group Work in the Helping Professions: A Bibliography**. 2d ed. Muncie, Ind., Accelerated Development, 1984. 612p. index. $19.95. LC 84-71161. ISBN 0-915202-44-1.

These volumes supplement each other. The first includes approximately 6,000 citations from the early twentieth century through mid-1975, with most publications post-1960. The second has about 10,000 citations and extends coverage from 1975 to 1983. Both provide exhaustive coverage to the literature of counseling and guidance, small group processes, group processes in education, rehabilitation settings, social work and psychiatry, and any other setting that employs group work. Comprehensive coverage is provided for a list of core journals directly related to group work and group processes, with additional selective coverage of dissertations cited in *Dissertation Abstracts International* (see entry 20), books, popular literature, and foreign-language material.

The exhaustiveness of the two works precludes annotations. The arrangement of entries in both provides the only subject access: a hierarchical listing under 12 or 13 sections, which are further subdivided under nearly 100 subject categories. Together, the two editions afford an excellent, comprehensive approach to all aspects of group work in the therapeutic and rehabilitative settings.

Handbooks

604. Gurman, Alan S., and David P. Kniskern, eds. **Handbook of Family Therapy**. New York, Brunner/Mazel, 1981. 796p. index. $50.00. LC 80-20357. ISBN 0-87630-242-8.

Unlike the chapters in many handbooks intended for professionals and advanced students, those by the 31 contributors in this book are well integrated and constitute a comprehensive reference to family and marital therapy. Among the topics covered are sex therapy and preventive approaches to family dysfunction. Twenty chapters are divided among seven topical sections, with four of these devoted to specific therapeutic approaches: psychoanalytic, intergenerational, systems theory, and behavioral. Remaining sections discuss the historical development of family and marital therapy, research and methodology in the field, and family enrichment and divorce therapies. Given the broad scope of most of the chapters, the use of the subject index is a must. There is also an author index.

605. Piercy, Fred P., and Douglas H. Sprenkle. **Family Therapy Sourcebook**. New York, Guilford Press, 1986. 396p. index. (Guilford Family Therapy Series). $40.00; $19.95pa. LC 86-19588. ISBN 0-89862-971-6; 0-89862-913-6pa.

This excellent guide to the diverse field of family therapy draws on the many fields within mental health that contribute to its body of knowledge. It is part handbook, part guide. Eight of the fourteen chapters focus on a specific aspect or approach to family therapy (e.g., transgenerational, systemic, behavioral, sex, divorce therapy, premarital counseling, marriage and family enrichment). The remaining chapters cover such specific topics in family therapy as feminist issues, professional supervision and training issues, ethical and legal considerations, and research issues in the field. Each chapter consists of a series of essays that follow a standard format. For example, the chapter on divorce therapy contains an overview of the history of the area, describes different approaches to therapy, defines key concepts and terminology used in the professional communication, outlines key therapeutic techniques employed, and concludes with an evaluative annotated bibliography of books and articles on divorce for therapists and clients. There are subject and name indexes.

Dictionaries and Encyclopedias

606. Pinney, Edward L., and Samuel Slipp. **Glossary of Group and Family Therapy**. New York, Brunner/Mazel, 1982. 149p. price not reported. LC 82-4193. ISBN 0-87630-300-9.

Pinney and Slipp provide brief definitions for students and professionals of terms used in the group and family therapy literature. Approximately 600 entries reflect therapeutic techniques, theoretical orientations, and the client-patient relationship. In addition, articles on individuals highlight their contributions and important publications, and there are entries for important professional and research organizations. The length of articles averages about 50 words.

The volume is divided into separate sections for group and family therapy concepts. Abundant cross-references compensate for this division and for the lack of an index.

Behavior Modification and Therapy

Bibliographies

607. Benson, Hazel B. **Behavior Modification and the Child: An Annotated Bibliography**. Westport, Conn., Greenwood Press, 1979. 398p. index. (Contemporary Problems of Childhood, no.3). $40.95. LC 79-7358. ISBN 0-313-21489-1.

Benson has compiled 2,309 citations to books and chapters, journal articles, dissertations, conference proceedings, and ERIC documents, the majority produced between 1956 and 1978.

Eleven sections divide references by format and content into bibliographies, books of readings, introductory material, techniques applied to specific behaviors, techniques for handicapped children, applications in the educational setting, applications in special settings, behavior modification applied in specific professions, training and education issues, research issues, and an addendum of recent unannotated citations. Most sections subdivide citations by population, age group, disorder or behavior, applications of behavior modification techniques, and the like as appropriate. Most references are descriptively annotated. For journal articles and other documents reprinted in books, cross-references are made to the books in which they are reprinted. References to dissertations are not annotated but refer the user to *Dissertation Abstracts International* (see entry 20).

A complex hierarchical arrangement provides subject access, supplemented by a selective keyword subject index as well as an author index. Appendixes include a glossary, a list of audiovisual materials, and a list of indexing and abstracting tools used to compile the citations.

608. Britt, Morris F. **Bibliography of Behavior Modification, 1924-1975**. Durham, N.C., Morris F. Britt, 1975. 1v. (unpaged). index. price not reported. LC 78-315784.

This volume has a lot of flaws. The major one is that the 6,780 unannotated citations are listed by primary author, with no supplementary author index and only a rudimentary subject index. Hence, it does not meet one of the author's goals of providing a convenient guide to the literature. Britt includes books and chapters, journal articles, dissertations, pamphlets, films, and unpublished papers and research reports of various types. He also interprets *behavior modification* broadly to include a variety of related therapeutic approaches and applications in such controlled and applied settings as psychiatry, education, management, and medicine. Despite its organizational shortcomings, the bibliography provides unique and retrospective coverage to materials not covered elsewhere.

609. Morrow, William R. **Behavior Therapy Bibliography, 1950-1969**. Columbia, Mo., University of Missouri Press, 1971. 165p. index. (University of Missouri Studies, v.54). price not reported. LC 73-633730. ISBN 0-8262-0596-8.

Morrow defines *behavior therapy* as "the use of behavior modification procedures to alter human behaviors . . . that are defined as dysfunctional or deviant" (p. 1), so that all citations concern therapeutic or rehabilitative applications of behavior change methods in human subjects. Published English-language works that represent contributions to empirical research are included.

References are not annotated in the usual sense; instead, each citation in the author listing is coded for certain features found in the item (e.g., research design employed, setting, target behavior, type of procedures employed, description of the subject population). The complexity, detail, and exacting terminology used in this coding make reading the explanatory material essential. There are no indexes as such, but a series of eight "Tables of References" provide access to variables such as the aversive contingency and type of reinforcer employed. Two additional appendixes list unanalyzed books and primary behavior modification journals.

Handbooks and Yearbooks

610. **Review of Behavior Therapy**. Vol. 1- . New York, Guilford Press, 1983- . biennial. $50.00. LC 76-126864. ISSN 0091-6595.

Early volumes of this annual review consisted of reprinted articles preceded by commentary by the editors. Beginning with volume 8, the scheme of publication changed, so that each volume followed a consistent format and coverage of topics. For example, each volume since 1982 has contained review essays on research methodologies in behavior therapy, its application in treatment of anxiety disorders and addictions, cognitive processes in therapy, behavior therapy with children and adolescents, and clinical issues. Although general areas of coverage are replicated from volume to volume, the continuity of authors and the focus on new and evolving research in the field make this a true annual review. Because of this replication, however, the *Review* has moved from an annual to a biennial publication schedule. In fact, recent volumes have appeared at three- to four-year intervals.

611. Bellack, Alan S., Michel Hersen, and Alan E. Kazdin, eds. **International Handbook of Behavior Modification and Therapy**. 2d ed. New York, Plenum, 1990. 885p. index. $95.00. LC 90-6900. ISBN 0-306-43348-6.

This work is intended for researchers, mental health practitioners, and advanced students. Most of its 41 chapters focus on applications of behavior modification techniques applied to specific classes of disorders with either adults or children. Chapters in the first three parts discuss issues in history and theory, assessment and research methodology, and training and practice. Part 4 consists of 15 chapters that cover intervention with adults and deal with anxiety, aggression and criminal behavior, obsessive-compulsive disorders, schizophrenia, marital and interpersonal dysfunction, pain, and behavioral medicine. The 13 chapters in part 5 focus on children and adolescents, with such topics as depression and anxiety, conduct disorders, mentally retarded and abused children, autism, and eating disorders. Some topics (e.g., obesity, substance abuse, depression, medical disorders) are covered in both sections. The amount of overlap among essays is minimal, the literature referenced is abundant and current, and topics are evaluatively discussed. A scanty subject index supplements the detailed table of contents.

SCHOOL PSYCHOLOGY

Handbooks

612. Gutkin, Terry B., and Cecil R. Reynolds, eds. **Handbook of School Psychology**. 2d ed. New York, John Wiley, 1990. 1056p. index. $59.95. LC 89-39299. ISBN 0-471-01181-9.

This volume examines the breadth of school psychology for both students and professionals. The 40 chapters are categorized under six sections. The first two focus on the history of school psychology, current and anticipated directions, and past and present contributions of other subareas of psychology to school psychology theory and practice. The remaining sections concern specific aspects of practice: testing and assessment, instructional and therapeutic intervention in the school environment, staff and programming, and legal and ethical issues of practice. There are author and subject indexes. Two appendixes reprint the ethical codes of practice for the American Psychological Association and the National Association of School Psychologists. Additional appendixes reprint regulations pursuant to major federal legislation.

Bibliographies

613. Fagan, Thomas K., et al. **A Bibliographic Guide to the Literature of Professional School Psychology, 1890-1985**. Stratford, Conn., National Association of School Psychologists, 1986. 339p. $20.00pa. ISBN 0-932955-03-7.

It would be extremely difficult to access much professional literature on school psychology were it not for this comprehensive and well-organized bibliography. Approximately 5,000 unannotated citations were collected from professional literature in journals, books and their chapters, newsletters, conference papers and proceedings, government publications, and reports sponsored by associations and academic departments. English-language journal literature is featured, although there is a smattering of foreign-language material. Most references are organized under four broad subject categories, which include areas of general interest to the development of school psychology;

the roles of the school psychologist, including traditional and alternative roles and settings, child advocacy, and research and evaluation of services; professional issues, such as legal and ethical considerations, training and professional development, student personnel services, and assessment; and historical literature, primarily material published between 1890 and 1945. These categories are further subdivided to provide subject access to the bibliography. The final three sections are format oriented: additional nonjournal publications, special issues of journals, and doctoral dissertations. Each section is preceded by a brief explanation of the literature and how it reflects the development of school psychology.

ERGONOMICS AND HUMAN FACTORS

Indexes and Abstracts

614. **Ergonomics Abstracts**. Vol. 1- , No. 1- . London, Washington, D.C., Taylor & Francis, 1969- . bimonthly. $490.00/yr.(institutions). ISSN 0046-2446.

This is a primary source of international literature on all aspects of ergonomics and human factors, including biomechanics, environmental work design, and the growing area of human-computer interaction. Over 350 source journals are indexed each year, as well as published proceedings and books in a variety of languages. A separate book review section provides about 10 reviews in each issue.

Citations and descriptive abstracts are categorized in a detailed hierarchical arrangement under 12 broad sections (e.g., display and control design, performance-related factors, health and safety), with approximately 600 subheadings. Use of the classification scheme outline preceding the abstract section is essential to locating relevant information in a broad area. There is an index to applications, such as type of industry, instruments or tools, and population studies. Unfortunately, the indexes do not cumulate, making an extensive search a tedious undertaking.

Handbooks

615. Helander, Martin, ed. **Handbook of Human-Computer Interaction**. New York, North Holland/Elsevier Science Publishing, 1988. 1167p. index. $251.50; $83.00pa. LC 88-25981. ISBN 0-444-70536-8; 0-444-88673-7pa.

Intended for advanced students, academics, and professionals, this work aims to incorporate principles of human factors engineering into the design of human-computer interfaces. Fifty-two individual chapters are organized under seven broad sections: models and theories, design of the user interface, implications of individual differences for training and performance, impact of computer technology, interface design and evaluation, artificial intelligence, and the impact of psychological and work organization issues. Some chapters, especially those covering models, theories, and interface design, assume considerable technical expertise on the part of the reader. The work is well illustrated with an abundance of tables and charts. Reference lists are very good and (predictably) current. There are subject and author indexes.

616. Salvendy, Gavriel, ed. **Handbook of Human Factors**. New York, John Wiley, 1987. 1874p. index. $99.50. LC 86-9083. ISBN 0-471-88015-9.

To quote from the preface, "this handbook provides vital information about the effective design and use of systems requiring the interaction among human, machine (computer), and the environment." It is an excellent source on the theoretical, applied, and professional aspects of human factors. A total of 68 chapters by over 100 contributors are organized under 12 broad topics, including the function and fundamentals behind human factors, evaluating needs and undertaking the design of the environment and organization, performance modeling, and the design and applications of human factors in the computing environment. Less coverage is afforded to ergonomics and the physiological aspects of work. Charts, formulas, tables, and illustrations are abundant, and there are author and subject indexes. Some sections, such as those on worker health and safety, personnel selection, training, and job design, will be of special interest to researchers and advanced students in industrial and organizational psychology.

617. Woodson, Wesley E. **Human Factors Design Handbook: Information and Guidelines for the Design of Systems, Facilities, Equipment, and Products for Human Use**. 2d ed. New York, McGraw-Hill, 1991. 846p. index. $96.50. LC 91-28019. ISBN 0-07-071768-0.

Intended as a ready-reference guide for engineers and designers, this work provides a wealth of fascinating information on how human abilities, limitations, and behaviors must be accommodated in tool and environmental design. For example, guidelines for typefaces used in number and letter displays must take into account visual contrast and recognition time; recommended light levels are provided for degrees of alertness required for various types of activities; and there are discussions of psychological responses to color and of personal space expectations and their implications for workplace design.

Data are provided for the design context (e.g., industrial, agricultural, consumer products), environment space and architectural settings, considerations in design of tools and displays, human physiological and psychological considerations (e.g., reaction time, auditory response, fatigue), and human engineering methods. A sizable reference list, statistical tables, and a subject index are supplied. As might be expected, there are large numbers of flowcharts, tables, and line drawings.

INDUSTRIAL AND ORGANIZATIONAL BEHAVIOR

Guides

618. Peck, Theodore P. **Employee Counseling in Industry and Government: A Guide to Information Sources**. Detroit, Gale, 1979. 121p. index. (Management Information Guide, no.37). price not reported. LC 79-16028. ISBN 0-8103-0837-1.

For the purpose of this guide, intervention and counseling are not limited to employee problems such as chemical dependence, stress, and emotional problems. Peck also covers assistance programs for preretirement counseling, career advancement, and issues specific to women in the workforce. Part 1 lists and briefly describes organizations interested in employee counseling: private and professional associations, government agencies, international associations, and research institutes. Part 2 consists of a topically arranged, unannotated bibliography of books, dissertations, government publications, research reports, and articles from trade and professional publications. Part 3 provides cursory information on journals, indexing and abstracting tools, directories, and databases that can assist in updating the literature cited. There is a sparse but serviceable subject index.

Bibliographies

619. **Bibliography on Major Aspects of the Humanization of Work and the Quality of Working Life**. 2d ed. Geneva, International Institute for Labour Studies, 1978. 299p. index. price not reported.

This work consists of approximately 2,000 citations to articles in trade and academic journals, government publications, and books. Coverage is international, and an asterisk precedes material recommended for basic reading. Citations are arranged under very broad subject categories, supplemented by an author index.

620. Poyhonen, Terhi. **Man and Work in Psychology: A Selected and Partially Annotated Bibliography**. Helsinki, Finland, Institute of Occupational Health, 1978. 2v. index. price not reported. LC 80-506712.

Poyhonen divides this bibliography into two distinct sections. The first, "General Psychology for Occupational Psychologists," lists citations from the following areas: theoretical and historical perspectives, cognition, "purposive behaviour" (e.g., attitude), personality, mental and physical health, and research methods. The second section, "Man at Work," lists citations most relevant to the study of organizational behavior, ergonomics, and all aspects of an individual's relationship to the work environment and its reciprocal effects. Each section is subdivided into narrower subareas in a hierarchical arrangement, covering such topics as occupational safety and risk behavior. The result is a very detailed and well-arranged subject access. Each item is cited only once, so checking numerous headings is necessary for complete coverage.

The prefatory material indicates that there are over 11,000 references, with 85 percent representing English-language materials. (Within any given subject section, Finnish materials are cited first, followed by works in all other languages.) Although there are materials from as early as the 1910s, most citations are from the 1960s and 1970s. Journal articles are the most frequently cited, although dissertations, books, chapters, reviews, technical reports, government documents, and a variety of other formats are included. Annotations are rare and consist of a phrase or a few sentences, a citation to a review, key terms, or the source of a reprint.

The section on general psychology is too selective to be very useful. However, the section specific to work life, organizational and occupational behavior, and ergonomics provides extensive access to the international research literature in this area.

621. Riggar, T. F. **Stress Burnout: An Annotated Bibliography**. Carbondale, Ill., Southern Illinois University Press, 1985. 299p. index. $19.95. LC 84-5447. ISBN 0-8093-1186-0.

Approximately 200 references and lengthy, descriptive annotations in this book address the topic of occupational stress. Most represent articles in professional journals published from 1976 through 1982, although there is selective coverage of books, citations to popular periodicals, and material from earlier years. All are in English. Three "tables of contents" in the back of the volume are, in fact, indexes of broad concepts to the body of the bibliography: signs and symptoms, causes and sources of burnout, and coping strategies.

622. Shonyo, Carolyn. **Job Satisfaction**. Springfield, Va., National Technical Information Service, 1976. 2v. price not reported. (NTIS/PS-76/0817 and NTIS/PS-76/0818).

This is a published compilation of a computerized literature search of the NTIS database. Volume 1 contains 229 citations and abstracts produced between 1964 and 1975; volume 2 supplements coverage through October 1976 and contains 153 additional items. One shortcoming of this source is its lack of indexes, and the reports appear to be listed in random order. Another problem is the availability of the federally supported reports represented; such access requires the purchase of these materials from NTIS or proximity to an NTIS microfiche depository collection.

The subject scope includes studies on general and specific areas of job satisfaction, both civilian and military, with an emphasis on the evaluation and improvement of personnel development and management techniques. In addition to basic bibliographic information and a descriptive abstract, the entries include subject headings assigned, report ordering numbers, and federal report and contract numbers.

623. Stogdill, Ralph M. **Leadership Abstracts and Bibliography 1904-1974**. Columbus, Ohio, College of Administrative Science, Ohio State University, 1977. 829p. index. (College of Administrative Science Monograph, no.AA-10). $30.50. LC 77-368888. ISBN 0-87776-310-0.

Stogdill cites and annotates 3,690 references to the research literature on leadership. Self-help and inspirational literature on good leadership skills is omitted; the book concentrates on material that contributes to the experimental and theoretical understanding of leadership attributes and behavior regardless of setting. Reflecting publishing trends during the time period covered, citations heavily represent the journal literature from all relevant areas of psychology, including industrial, organizational behavior, social, personality, and environmental. Also cited are journal literature from business management and economics, political science, sociology, and education; books; published and published conference papers; unpublished research and technical reports; documents produced by government at all levels; and doctoral dissertations. Descriptive annotations vary in length from a brief sentence to about 200 words. References are listed by author, and additional access is provided by an author index, a subject index, and a list of journal title abbreviations.

Due to the time period covered, the considerable literature about leadership research on women and minority groups is sparse. As a retrospective source of information, this book remains an excellent entree to the vast literature by an outstanding researcher.

624. Walsh, Ruth M., and Stanley J. Birkin, comps. and eds. **Job Satisfaction and Motivation: An Annotated Bibliography**. Westport, Conn., Greenwood Press, 1979. 643p. index. $50.95. LC 78-67915. ISBN 0-313-20635-X.

Although the preface indicates that the material cited in the bibliography covers the preceding 10 years, most is literature published between 1970 and 1978, reflecting the volume of works on employee satisfaction and motivation published during this period. Approximately 1,000 citations are descriptively annotated, the annotations varying from a phrase to several paragraphs. Formats include NTIS and other published and unpublished research reports, dissertations and books, government documents, and articles in professional and academic journals. The latter, constituting the largest format type, are derived from the literatures of management, psychology (primarily counseling, social, and applied), sociology, and personnel administration and training. The professional and trade literatures from a wide variety of occupations are also included (e.g., nursing, education, the military).

Author and keyword-in-title indexes precede the citation and abstract section. The latter index is particularly helpful for locating studies on particular professions, settings, or occupations.

Indexes and Abstracts

625. **Human Resources Abstracts**. Vol. 10- , No. 1- . Newbury Park, Calif., Sage, 1975- . quarterly. $188.00/yr.(institutions). ISSN 0099-2453.

This source continues *Poverty and Human Resources Abstracts* (1966-1974). Books and articles from over 200 journals in psychology, sociology, urban and public affairs, law, management, and human services are arranged under 15 broad categories. The scope encompasses the human and social issues of urban rehabilitation and poverty, job development and vocational rehabilitation, social and human resources necessary to meet the demands of urban life, and minority and disadvantaged groups. Included within this broad spectrum are employee training and development, work life and unemployment, and workforce involvement and performance. Quarterly issues contain detailed subject and author indexes, which cumulate in the December issue. The journal source list also appears in this issue.

626. **Personnel Literature**. Vol. 1- , No. 1- . Washington, D.C., U.S. Office of Personnel Management Library, 1941- . monthly. $18.00/yr. ISSN 0031-5753.

Over 200 journal articles, books, government documents, and documents from other agencies are cited in each issue of this title. Items are arranged under 60 or 70 broad concept categories that are not necessarily repeated in each issue but provide good subject access. (This is the only subject access afforded in the monthly issues.) All aspects of personnel relations and employment are included.

Each citation is assigned up to three subject descriptors, most of which are used as headings in the annual cumulated index. These descriptors and their subheadings provide efficient, specific access to the volume's citation numbers (albeit only on an annual basis). There is also an annual personal and corporate author index.

627. **Personnel Management Abstracts**. Vol. 1 - , No. 1- . Chelsea, Mich., Personnel Management Abstracts, 1955- . quarterly. $60.00/yr. ISSN 0031-577X.

Although the list of almost 100 academic and professional source periodicals abstracted in this source draws heavily on management and labor relations fields, the scope of coverage is wide. Work environment, job design and satisfaction, employee motivation and appraisal, organizational communication, and numerous other facets of industrial and organizational behavior are covered. Citations and brief, nonevaluative abstracts are listed by title under approximately 70 subject categories; an author index furnishes supplementary access. There is a separate list of selected management books, each accompanied by a lengthy abstract. Quarterly issues are supplanted by an annual cumulative publication.

628. **Work Related Abstracts**. Warren, Mich., Harmonie Park Press, 1973- . monthly updates (loose-leaf). $350.00/yr. LC 76-646272. ISSN 0273-3234.

This index was formerly published as *Employment Relations Abstracts* (1959-1972). About 250 professional, government, and academic periodicals on management and labor are indexed. Articles are arranged under 20 conceptually broad subject categories and are accompanied by descriptive abstracts. More specific topical access is provided by a detailed subject index, which cumulates each month with the annual index as part of the December update. Industrial and organizational psychologists will be particularly interested in the coverage of the psychology of work, personnel management, vocational choice and training, and organizational communication. The biennial subject heading list, published separately, acts as a thesaurus and cross-reference guide. Despite the service's narrow focus and excellent coverage, publication of each issue runs several months behind.

Handbooks and Yearbooks

629. Bass, Bernard M. **Bass & Stogdill's Handbook of Leadership: Theory, Research and Managerial Applications**. 3rd ed. New York, Free Press/Macmillan, 1990. 1182p. index. $80.00. LC 89-17240. ISBN 0-02-901500-6.

In the latest edition of Ralph Stogdill's 1974 *Handbook of Leadership*, Bass retains those qualities that make this one of the most important reference works on leadership. Part 1 reviews the extensive literature on leadership theory and research. Part 2 discusses the personal attributes of leaders and leader behavior. Parts 3 through 6 cover leadership roles and actions in the context of the organization: the role of power, leader-follower interaction, management styles, and the immediate environmental situations in which leaders exist. Considerably expanded is coverage of the emergence and impact of traditionally underrepresented minorities in leadership positions and of international perspectives. Further sections review leader training strategies and areas of likely future research concentration.

The list of cited references reveals the exhaustiveness of Bass's literature reviews, as it consists of approximately 5,000 references, a large number to unpublished and limited circulation reports. The glossary is new to this edition. Author and subject indexes allow complete access.

630. Dunnette, Marvin D., ed. **Handbook of Industrial and Organizational Psychology.** Chicago, Rand McNally, 1976; repr., New York, John Wiley, 1983. 1740p. index. $95.00. LC 83-42702. ISBN 0-471-88642-4.

631. Dunnette, Marvin D., and Leaetta M. Hough, eds. **Handbook of Industrial and Organizational Psychology.** Vol. 1- . 2d ed. Palo Alto, Calif., Consulting Psychologists Press, 1990- . $89.00(v.1); $99.00(v.2); $99.00(v.3). LC 90-2294. ISBN 0-89106-041-3(v.1); 0-89106-042-1(v.2); 0-89106-043-X(v.3).

The long-awaited revision of Dunnette's original work is as solid a contribution as was the original edition. The new volumes have not supplanted their predecessor, however. Volume 1 contains five chapters on the role of theory in industrial and organizational psychology, including motivation theory, judgment and decision making, learning theory, and individual differences. Six chapters focus on topics in measurement and methodology. Chapters in volume 2 discuss the role of individual attributes and behavior in organizational behavior, employee recruitment and vocational choice, job design and analysis, employee performance and satisfaction, and personality and personality measurement. Volume 3 contains chapters on organizational effects on individual performance, organizational conflict and stress, consumer psychology, and employee compensation. Cross-cultural issues and industrial and organizational psychology practice are included in the 1976 edition, although these sections will probably be revised in the upcoming final volume.

All editions are well edited, with the contents of each chapter integrated with others but not unduly repetitive. The writing is clear, and technical terms are defined in the text, so that the contents should be comprehensible to the undergraduate student. Reference lists accompanying each chapter are extensive, citing both classic and current works. Numerous and clear figures and tables illustrate theories, measurement procedures, and statistical results. There are name and subject indexes in all the volumes.

632. **International Review of Industrial and Organizational Psychology.** Vol. 1- . Cary L. Cooper and Ivan T. Robertson, eds. New York, John Wiley, 1986- . annual. price varies. ISSN 0886-1528.

This is an annual review series in the mold of *Annual Review of Psychology* (see entry 159) and of the same caliber. According to the editorial foreword in the 1986 volume, its "aim is to provide a regular, comprehensive, and scholarly review of research and theory of major topics within industrial and organizational psychology." Each annual volume contains about 10 review articles. Some topics, such as job satisfaction and issues dealing with an aging workforce, appear every few years. Others, such as health promotion in the workplace, quality circles, and I/O research in a given country, reflect current research trends. Volumes include their own subject indexes.

633. Lorsch, Jay W., ed. **Handbook of Organizational Behavior.** Englewood Cliffs, N.J., Prentice-Hall, 1987. 430p. $78.00. LC 86-4866. ISBN 0-13-380650-2.

Twenty-seven contributed essays organized under six broad topics cover the breadth of industrial and organizational psychology. One section concerns the history of the field and a broad overview. A second section acknowledges the influence of other disciplines, such as sociology and political science, as well as other areas of psychology, which receives better coverage here than in

Handbook of Industrial and Organizational Psychology (see entries 630 and 631). Other sections cover the evaluation and assessment of organizations, behavior at each level of an organization, issues in management of work, and behavior in the nonbusiness setting. The lack of indexes makes finding specifics difficult. Although a few chapters were reprinted from other sources or derived from previously prepared reports, they nonetheless form a coherent view of the important topics in industrial and organizational psychology.

634. **Research in Organizational Behavior: An Annual Series of Analytical Essays and Critical Reviews.** Vol. 1- . Greenwich, Conn., JAI Press, 1979- . annual. $63.50/yr. ISSN 0191-3085.

Each volume of this title contains approximately 10 review articles on aspects of organizational behavior. Topics are not limited to innovations and recent research trends (e.g., comparable worth) but also include reviews on theoretical and methodological issues. Contributors are more frequently affiliated with schools of management or business than with psychology.

635. Walsh, W. Bruce, & Samuel H. Osipow, eds. **Handbook of Vocational Psychology.** Hillsdale, N.J., Lawrence Erlbaum, 1983. 2v. index. $59.95/set. LC 83-8856. ISBN 0-89859-285-2(v.1); 0-89859-286-0(v.2).

As the editors indicate in their preface, vocational psychology cuts across a number of psychology's subdisciplines: counseling, industrial and organizational, rehabilitation, the psychology of women and minorities, and psychometrics. The extent of these intersections is reflected in the coverage in this book's chapters. Those that comprise volume 1 cover the history and evolution of the field, current issues, issues in the vocational psychology of women and racial and ethnic minorities, adult vocational behavior, the concepts and research associated with career maturity, and research methods. Volume 2 focuses on methods and outcomes associated with career counseling and vocational rehabilitation, as well as their applications in the workplace. Each volume has a separate subject and author index. Due to its emphasis on theoretical and historical perspectives in the field, this set would be most appropriate for advanced and professional students in vocational psychology, counseling, and rehabilitation rather than practicing professionals in these fields.

CONSUMER BEHAVIOR

Bibliographies

636. **A Bibliography of Theory and Research Techniques in the Field of Human Motivation.** By Advertising Research Foundation. New York, Advertising Research Foundation, 1956. 117p. index. price not reported. LC 57-397.

The value of this bibliography is its contemporaneous (now historical) approach to applying psychological motivation research and techniques to marketing and advertising. References in the first three sections provide an overview of motivation research and its applications in social sciences research. The last two sections, "Application of Techniques in Marketing and Advertising" and "Social Science Research Techniques in Marketing and Advertising," contain over 200 descriptively annotated references. Included are trade and popular periodicals, books, marketing reports, and journals from business, management, and psychology. Most were published in the 1950s before the area of consumer behavior had a cogent research base of its own. There is an author index.

637. Williams, Emelda L., and Donald W. Hendon. **American Advertising: A Reference Guide.** New York, Garland, 1988. 208p. index. (Garland Reference Library of Social Science, v.398) $28.00. LC 87-32148. ISBN 0-8240-8490-X.

This is a highly selective list of 648 items, including articles from trade and academic publications, books and book chapters, and doctoral dissertations. Advertising as a medium and as an art is the work's primary focus; for advertising as a field of scholarly interest, there is less emphasis. Citations are arranged under four broad areas (an overview of advertising, advertising as a business and use of media, creative aspects, and special types of advertising), with subcategories under each. As there is only an author index, the subject arrangement (under 24 categories) and cross-references are the only access points. Although there is coverage of classic works, the majority were published during the previous 20 years.

The psychological and social aspects of advertising are covered under the advertising overview section, specifically the categories on theoretical issues, economic and social issues, and motivation and psychological research as it affects advertising practice. Topics included are consumer involvement and response, the effect of advertising on children, consumer attitudes, subliminal methods, and gender and stereotyping.

Indexes and Abstracts

638. **Market Research Abstracts.** Vol. 1- . London, Market Research Society, 1963- . biannual. $154.00/yr. ISSN 0025-3596.

In addition to covering the core journal literature in psychology, statistics, and marketing, this index is helpful for locating papers in published proceedings that are otherwise difficult to find. Entries are arranged under nine conceptually broad areas, including statistics and forecasting, communications and advertising, applied market research, and product development. Abstracts are lengthy and detailed. Of particular interest to psychologists is the coverage of consumer behavior research and market survey literature: attitudes, decision making, and personal and social variables in marketing and promotion. The citations are supplemented by a detailed subject index (including product and company names) and author and source indexes.

Handbooks

639. Robertson, Thomas S., and Harold H. Kassarjian. **Handbook of Consumer Behavior.** Englewood Cliffs, N.J., Prentice-Hall, 1991. 614p. index. $74.00. LC 90-40459. ISBN 0-13-372749-1.

Despite the amount of popular and student interest in consumer behavior topics, there has been a paucity of good reference tools that are independent of marketing research and advertising. The appearance of this handbook, therefore, meets a need in the literature. It provides researchers and advanced students with a current, comprehensive approach to psychological theory applied to consumer behavior research. Although this title is written at an advanced level, the comprehensive reference lists and theoretical focus distinguish it from marketing research handbooks.

Most chapters are divided between two parts. The seven chapters included in part 1, "Micro Approaches," are those concerned with the characteristics and influence of the individual consumer, such as memory, judgment and decision making, the role of physiological research, learning and classical conditioning, and effect and attitude change. Six chapters comprise part 2, "Macro Approaches"; they discuss the influence of social and environmental factors, including the role of mass media and of expectancies, organizational buying, the role of social expectations on buying behavior and consumption patterns, and public policy issues (e.g., deceptive and exploitative advertising). The final section, "Philosophy and Methods," focuses on research methods in the field. There are name and subject indexes.

COMPARATIVE PSYCHOLOGY AND ETHOLOGY

Indexes and Abstracts

640. **Animal Behaviour Abstracts**. Vol. 2- , No. 1- . New York, Cambridge University Press, 1972- . quarterly. $375.00/yr.(institutions). ISSN 0301-8695.

This unique index, easier to use than *Biological Abstracts* (see entry 387), is intended for advanced students and researchers in ethology. It was preceded by *Behavioural Biology Abstracts. Section A: Animal Behaviour*. Of particular interest is its coverage of biochemical and neurological aspects of innate behavior, issues in learning and memory, reproductive behavior, migration and evolution, behavioral ecology, and models and methodology. Citations are topically arranged, and there is an annual index.

Handbooks

641. Halliday, Tim R., and Peter J. B. Slater, eds. **Animal Behaviour**. New York, W. H. Freeman, 1983. 3v. index. price not reported. LC 83-5497.

Each volume in this set consists of contributed essays on specific aspects of animal behavior. Volume 1 focuses on areas of sensory stimuli, motor behavior, and motivation. Volume 2 concentrates on animal communication. Genetic determinants, the role of environment, and learning mechanisms and behavior comprise volume 3. Every essay covers general principles, a discussion of behaviors across species, and sources for further reading, and each volume contains its own reference list and index.

642. Lehner, Philip N. **Handbook of Ethological Methods**. New York, Garland STPM Press, 1979. 403p. index. (Garland Series in Ethology). price not reported. LC 77-90468. ISBN 0-8240-7024-0.

Lehner combines clear explanations of the scope and purpose of ethology with detailed descriptions of methodologies used to observe and study the behavior of nonhuman species. Issues in choosing appropriate populations, research design, data collection and manipulation, and discussions of results are presented in species-appropriate contexts and use examples from published research. A good bibliography, appendixes of statistical tables, and a subject index are appended.

643. Napier, John R., and P. H. Napier, eds. **Handbook of Living Primates: Morphology, Ecology and Behaviour of Nonhuman Primates**. London, Academic Press, 1967. 456p. index. price not reported. LC 66-30126.

Part 1 of this book, "Functional Morphology of Primates," details common anatomical and behavioral characteristics that distinguish primates from other mammals. In part 2, specific data on physiological characteristics and behavior are given for each genus, accompanied by an abundance of plates and citations to the literature. Finally, part 3 provides comparative physiological and behavioral data for each primate. There are an extensive reference list and an index to common and scientific names.

Dictionaries and Encyclopedias

644. Harre, Rom, and Roger Lamb, eds. **Dictionary of Ethology and Animal Learning.** Cambridge, Mass., MIT Press, 1986. 171p. index. $13.95pa. LC 87-10406. ISBN 0-262-58076-4.

Entries in this book were selected and updated from Harre and Lamb's *Encyclopedic Dictionary of Psychology* (see entry 170). Definitions differ in length from a few sentences to several pages. Cross-references are used liberally throughout, and brief bibliographies identify core works and items for further reading. Illustrations and tables are sparse and small but suitably placed. There is a detailed subject index. The number of updated references indicates that this book has seen more revision than other dictionaries derived from the parent work.

645. Immelmann, Klaus, and Colin Beer. **Dictionary of Ethology**. Cambridge, Mass., Harvard University Press, 1989. 336p. $35.00. LC 88-21360. ISBN 0-674-20506-5.

As noted in this work's preface, the language of animal behavior draws heavily from the fields of biology and psychology and from common parlance, yet it often has meanings unique to ethology. In about 200 words per entry, the authors define key terms and concepts, detail their historical significance in ethological research, and provide numerous examples from research on ecological occurrences with relevant species. Biographical entries are not included, although some terms are eponymous, and there are no illustrations. A brief bibliography lists references cited in the text, and cross-references compensate for the absence of a subject index.

646. McFarland, David, ed. **The Oxford Companion to Animal Behaviour**. New York, Oxford University Press, 1987. 685p. index. $19.95pa. LC 86-16173. ISBN 0-19-281990-9.

Claiming to be a handbook, this work is, in fact, a one-volume encyclopedia that introduces ethology and related areas in ecology, genetics, physiology, and psychology. It is a corrected reprint of the 1982 edition. Prior knowledge of biology and its nomenclature is not assumed, which is an advantage for beginning students or nonspecialists. Illustrations and charts are not numerous but are appropriately placed, and articles, generally 4 to 10 pages in length, are well written and comprehensible. There are few biographical entries. As appropriate, phenomena are discussed as they occur across a number of species, and cross-references are liberally used. There is a selective, cumulated reference list, although many more citations are appended to articles. Indexes to common and scientific names provide additional access points.

PARAPSYCHOLOGY

Guides

647. Ashby, Robert H. **The Ashby Guidebook for Study of the Paranormal.** rev. ed. Frank C. Tribbe, ed. York Beach, Maine, Samuel Weiser, 1987. 215p. $10.95pa. LC 86-34033. ISBN 0-87728-660-4.

Much of this guide is intended for those investigating phenomena such as extrasensory perception, poltergeists, psychokinesis, and dowsing. Essays deal with how to pursue and record first-hand experiences. However, Ashby also includes bibliographies of beginning and advanced material published though the mid-1980s, with lengthy, evaluative abstracts. There are annotated lists of relevant organizations, library collections and resource centers, and serial publications in the United States and United Kingdom. Brief biographies of over 100 persons influential in the development of psychic research are listed, and a glossary of terms is furnished.

648. White, Rhea A., and Laura A. Dale. **Parapsychology: Sources of Information**. Metuchen, N.J., Scarecrow, 1973. 303p. index. $22.50. LC 73-4854. ISBN 0-8108-0617-7.

649. White, Rhea A. **Parapsychology: New Sources of Information, 1973-1989**. Metuchen, N.J., Scarecrow, 1990. 699p. index. $67.50. LC 90-21327. ISBN 0-8108-2385-3.

These volumes comprise the most complete and authoritative guide to parapsychology and its literature. Together they contain citations to almost 500 English-language books, classified according to 24 broad categories. Also included are organizations, periodicals, academic institutions offering graduate work in parapsychology, lists of doctoral and masters' theses completed, and coverage of selected topics in general and specialized encyclopedias. The newer edition discusses current and emerging research topics and the interest of the U.S. government in parapsychology research. White excludes topics in the occult, astrology, and witchcraft; instead, her coverage concentrates on unexplained phenomena of human experience and the research base of parapsychology.

In addition to evaluative annotations, citations include information on the suggested audience, the types of library collections for which each is appropriate, and citations to reviews. Each of the subject sections delineates the scope and provides cross-references to other areas. The appendixes list books that have such features as glossaries, illustrations, and extensive bibliographies. Others rank books by reading levels and type of appropriate library collection. Additionally, there are a glossary of terms and chronologies of important events in the field. Indexes by name, title, and subject; a detailed table of contents; and brief essays preceding each chapter make both volumes easy to use, especially for students.

Bibliographies

650. **Catalogue of the Library of the Society for Psychical Research**. Boston, G. K. Hall; distr., New York, Macmillan, 1976. 341p. $80.00. LC 76-358758. ISBN 0-8161-0008-X.

This volume reproduces the catalog of the Society's Gurney Library in London, which was founded in 1883. The collection of over 5,000 items includes both rare and widely published volumes, pamphlets, collections of letters and biographies, bibliographies, and treatises from the early nineteenth century to the mid-1970s. Most works are English-language, with limited coverage of other European-language materials. Contents are divided between the author and title catalogs.

Coverage encompasses a wide range of paranormal phenomena, with emphasis on witchcraft and occultism, spiritualism and survival of bodily death, mediumship, hypnotic states, psi, and telepathy. Also included are selected volumes on the philosophy of mind, psychopathology, and other areas of study tangential to parapsychology.

651. Goss, Michael, comp. **Poltergeists: An Annotated Bibliography of Works in English, circa 1880-1975**. Metuchen, N.J., Scarecrow, 1979. 351p. index. $29.50. LC 78-11492. ISBN 0-8108-1181-2.

Poltergeists are defined as unexplained presences; auditory phenomena accompanied by physical disruption, such as flying objects; apparitions; or touches or shoves directed at people. In his introduction, Goss clearly defines the literature on poltergeists and related phenomena, including the structure and bibliographic problems of collating disparate literature of sometimes dubious origins and the history of publishing in this area of psychical research.

Goss cites 1,111 books, articles from academic journals and popular magazines, books, reviews, reference works, and published correspondence in English. Items are listed by author, or by title in the case of anonymous works, and have brief, descriptive annotations. Items considered by the compiler to require technical or working knowledge of psychical research methods are preceded by the phrase "research level," and these are usually afforded longer annotations.

Cross-references help consolidate items of commentary or reactions or tie together multiple reports of the same instance of poltergeist activity. There is a combined subject, author, and title index, as well as a geographic index by poltergeist sighting locales.

652. White, Rhea A. **Parapsychology: Sources on Applications and Implications**. Dix Hills, N.Y., Parapsychology Sources of Information Center, 1988. 131p. $20.00. ISBN 0-944446-08-6.

Over 900 unannotated citations to English-language research and popular literature in this work afford a comprehensive, if not exhaustive, overview of circumstances or settings in which paranormal phenomena (e.g., precognition, telepathy) have demonstrated or potential uses. A subject list arranges citations under 39 categories, such as business applications, techniques used in criminal investigations and locating lost people or objects, techniques used to predict events, healing and personal growth, creativity, use in military contexts, and behavior control. Both material supporting and disputing applications and results are cited, although the former are far more numerous, as a considerable number of the academic journal citations are drawn from the body of parapsychological literature. There is also a listing by first author, including the complete bibliographic citation and a code reflecting one or more of the 39 categories. Citations cover the early 1900s to 1987 in a variety of formats: magazine and academic journal articles, conference proceedings, books and chapters, and doctoral and master's theses. Occasionally a phrase will be included if a citation's title is not indicative of its content.

653. Zorab, George, comp. **Bibliography of Parapsychology**. New York, Parapsychology Foundation, 1957. 127p. index. price not reported. LC 57-8446.

Zorab lists approximately 1,000 unannotated references, most of them dated from the early 1800s to 1956. Although much of the material was published in books or journals, some represent obscure reports in a variety of languages. Works on magic and the occult are not included. The book's primary arrangement is under 10 broad categories, among them reference and historical works, extrasensory perception, physical phenomena, ghosts and poltergeists, research methods, and the relationship of parapsychology with other disciplines (e.g., biology, religion, medicine). Most are divided into several subcategories. Author and subject indexes are supplied.

654. Wolman, Benjamin B., ed. **Handbook of Parapsychology**. New York, Van Nostrand Reinhold, 1977; repr., Jefferson, N.C., McFarland, 1986. 967p. index. $55.00. LC 85-2863. ISBN 0-89950-186-9.

This volume provides a substantive alternative to frivolous and sensational guidebooks on paranormal phenomena. Its 36 chapters are divided under 11 broad subject areas, such as history, research methods, theories, healing, after-death experiences, Soviet research, and parapsychological phenomena related to various disciplines in the humanities and sciences. Topics are discussed in the context of historical, theoretical, and research trends. Reference lists accompanying each essay are extensive, with citations drawn from the international research literature. This is especially important in discussions of such popular topics as ESP, poltergeists, reincarnation, and telepathy. Part 11 contains an annotated list of over 60 books recommended for further reading and a glossary of parapsychology terms. Finally, there are name and subject indexes.

Indexes and Abstracts

655. **Parapsychology Abstracts International.** Vol. 1- . No. 1- . Dix Hills, N.Y., Parapsychology Sources of Information Center, 1983- . biannual. $50.00/yr.(institutions). ISSN 0740-7629.

At present, about 100 journals whose major thrust is parapsychology are regularly indexed and abstracted per year in this title. Other periodicals, such as popular ones or those representing other disciplines, are selectively included. Each issue contains about 250 citations and abstracts to journal articles, books, dissertations, chapters, and conference proceedings. The primary arrangement is by categories for parapsychology journals, nonparapsychology journals, articles from general interest periodicals, and nonperiodical formats.

A recent change is that beginning with volume 6 (1988), *PAI* has focused on current coverage. (Previously it attempted some retrospective coverage as well as current publication indexing.) Also, the first issue of each volume contains only English-language source publications, and the second issue focuses on non-English publications. In the latter case, all titles and abstracts are in English. Author and title indexes appear in each issue, whereas the subject indexes for both appear only in the second issue (December).

Dictionaries and Encyclopedias

656. Berger, Arthur S., and Joyce Berger. **The Encyclopedia of Parapsychology and Psychical Research**. New York, Paragon House, 1991. 554p. index. $ 45.00. LC 89-28857. ISBN 1-55778-043-9.

In this book, over 1,400 entries deal with paranormal phenomena, famous individuals (living and deceased) in its history and research, unusual individuals or phenomena, and research techniques. There is especially good coverage of non-Western traditions of paranormal phenomena and belief. Many paranormal experiences more often associated with religious belief and unorthodox healing are also included.

Essays are generally dispassionate, describing each item according to the available research and authoritative observation. Many essays contain a brief bibliography (or selected writings in the case of individuals), with numerous cross-references. Following the entries is a lengthy appendix in which, for each of 18 countries, a brief essay describes the history and current activity in parapsychological research, a list of research institutes and professional associations in that country, and university academic departments involved in relevant research. There are also an index to entries by country and a lengthy bibliography with many citations to current works. This is probably the best of the recent reference works in parapsychology, especially because it does not rely as heavily on older, previously published material.

657. Bletzer, June G. **The Donning International Encyclopedic Psychic Dictionary**. Norfolk, Va., Donning, 1986. 875p. $29.95; $19.95pa. LC 84-13808. ISBN 0-89865-372-X; 0-89865-371-1pa.

Bletzer provides definitions and discusses the uses of approximately 8,000 words and terms in psychic research, the occult, and the entire realm of paranormal experience. Abundant cross-references, synonyms, and word origins are provided. A broad view is taken of the concept of *paranormal* to include such concepts as biofeedback, relaxation, and altered states.

The value of this work lies in the definitions, generally from 10 to 150 words in length, of terms from all traditions, both East and West. There are seven appendixes, including guides to the independent development of one's psychic abilities, a categorization of terms under four broad categories that represent skills and various subcategories, and a lengthy bibliography of general works on parapsychology.

658. **Encyclopedia of Occultism & Parapsychology**. 3d ed. Leslie Shepard, ed. Detroit, Gale, 1991. 2v. index. $295.00/set. ISBN 0-8103-4907-8.

Shepard revises and updates two classic reference encyclopedias: Lewis Spence's 1920 *Encyclopedia of Occultism* and Nandor Fordor's 1934 *Encyclopaedia of Psychic Science*. The result is a comprehensive, cogent reference on paranormal phenomena. Concepts, organizations, major and influential publications, and biographical entries of both real and fictional persons are discussed in terms of their contemporaneous importance and lasting contributions (or notoriety) in the history of psychical investigation. *See also* references are provided in boldface type within articles. Reference lists tend to emphasize late nineteenth- and early twentieth-century publications, although lists have been updated substantially. Articles range in length from a paragraph to several pages. In addition to a general index, a series of topical indexes lists references to articles under nine broad categories: fauna, demons, gems, places associated with unusual occurrences, gods, paranormal phenomena (and subheadings under type of phenomena), periodicals, flora and plant life, and societies.

659. **Encyclopedia of the Unexplained: Magic, Occultism and Parapsychology**. Richard Cavendish, ed. New York, McGraw-Hill, 1974; repr., London, Arkana, 1989. 304p. index. $19.95pa. LC 90-160904. ISBN 0-14-019190-9.

In his introduction, Cavendish describes the three primary areas covered in this book: psychical research, such as telepathy and mediumship; magic and the occult, from Atlantis to witchcraft; and systems of divination, such as astrology, the zodiac, and Tarot. His emphasis is on the modern Western experience, although there is good coverage of ancient traditions and Eastern movements. There are many biographical entries of persons both obscure and famous in literature and the arts, as well as those from mainstream psychology; all were influential in the history of psychic research, or their works were used by others in support of paranormal claims. There are many illustrations, especially those purported to be of apparitions, monsters, UFOs, and other phenomena. There is a bibliography of over 500 unannotated references and indexes by personal name and cited book titles.

660. Riland, George. **The New Steinerbooks Dictionary of the Paranormal**. New York, Steinerbooks; distr., Blauvelt, N.Y., Garber, 1980. 358p. (Spiritual Science Library, v.5). $16.00; $8.00pa. LC 79-93353. ISBN 0-89345-028-6; 0-89345-225-4pa.

Approximately 2,800 entries in this work cover the Western and Eastern traditions of paranormal experiences, spiritualism, and the occult. Articles define terms, detail key concepts and belief systems, describe organizations, and give the historical importance and impact of individuals. Entries are generally a few sentences to a page in length, although key-concept articles tend to be longer. Numerous cross-references substitute for an index. This is a good supplemental dictionary to *The Donning International Encyclopedic Psychic Dictionary* (see entry 657).

PERSONNEL AND PROFESSIONAL ISSUES

Bibliographies

661. Feldman, Saul, Carole Goldstein, and Joan Offutt, eds. **Mental Health Administration: An Annotated Bibliography**. Rockville, Md., National Institute of Mental Health, U.S. Department of Health, Education, and Welfare, 1978. 449p. index. (DHEW Publication No. (ADM) 77-548). (SuDoc HE 20.8113: M52).

662. Feldman, Saul, ed. **Mental Health Administration: An Annotated Bibliography. Volume II**. Rockville, Md., National Institute of Mental Health, U.S. Department of Health and Human Services, 1981. 324p. index. (DHHS Publication No. ADM 81-1155). price not reported. (SuDoc HE 20.8113: M52/982).

These volumes contain over 1,800 citations to literature in medicine, social work, law and public policy, and psychology and psychiatry that pertain to the management of mental health programs and organizations in a variety of settings. The material cited includes not only journals and books but also reports generated by the federal government and professional associations, technical reports, dissertations, and conference papers. Literature concerning general business administration principles and practices is excluded. Both volumes arrange citations and their descriptive abstracts under 12 broad topics, including funding and accountability, program planning, organizational behavior, political and legal issues, the role of citizen participation and governing bodies, management information, personnel issues, and the role of the administrator. Only author indexes are provided.

Feldman and his collaborators have done an excellent job of differentiating the unique functions and demands of mental health service organizations (emphasizing American models). These volumes are a particularly good source for the areas of community psychiatry, the evaluation of services, and mental health delivery systems.

Handbooks

663. Cohen, Ronald J., and William E. Mariano. **Legal Guidebook in Mental Health.** New York, Free Press/Macmillan, 1982. 492p. index. price not reported. LC 81-71323. ISBN 0-02-905740-X.

Despite the changing nature of information dealing with the legal responsibilities and liabilities of mental health practice, this handbook is a detailed guide to legislative, regulatory, and judicial aspects of mental health law. It is a compendium of original source materials and discussion. Broad subject areas covered include regulation; malpractice; and various causes associated with patient suits, including medication, liability for negligence and referral, lack of informed consent, assault, sexual impropriety, and breach of confidentially. Chapter 4 discusses other issues in professional legal aspects, such as defamation, self-incrimination, and right to treatment. Countersuits and malpractice and the psychotherapist round out the volume. Also provided are an extensive bibliography of further information (in addition to reference lists in the chapters) classified by type of suit or legal issue (e.g., suicide, privacy, malpractice insurance); an index to statutes, regulations, and other legal citations; and a general index by subject.

664. **Ethical Principles in the Conduct of Research with Human Participants.** By the American Psychological Association. Washington, D.C., American Psychological Association, 1982. 76p. index. $10.00. LC 85-208810. ISBN 0-912704-82-9.

Formulated by the Committee for the Protection of Human Participants in Research and endorsed by the American Psychological Association in 1982, this work is designed to insure the safety and confidentiality of subjects who participate in psychological research. The principles are capsulated in 10 brief statements that cover such elements as the integrity of the research process, informed consent of participants and respect for their safety and welfare, the right of subjects to decline participation, and confidentiality. The remainder of the guide discusses the practical use of each principle, including issues arising in the course of research and discussion of potential problem situations. There is a subject index.

665. **A Hospital Practice Primer for Psychologists.** By the American Psychological Association. Washington, D.C., American Psychological Association, 1985. 51p. index. $25.00. ISBN 0-912704-41-1.

Recognizing that an increasing number of clinical psychologists hold hospital privileges, APA's Committee on Professional Practice of the Board of Professional Affairs has responded by addressing concerns relevant to hospital practice. Among the issues included in this work are formal education and training requirements, the professional privileges afforded psychologists performing inpatient care, and how these professional activities can be integrated into a hospital's structure and mission. Less formal coverage is given to the restrictions on psychologists' practices, on-call and billing practices, treatment teams, and other elements of hospital "culture." A glossary, a list of further readings, a typical hospital organization chart, and sample forms are included. The *Primer* does not reflect APA policy, and the contents should serve as guidelines only.

666. Keith-Spiegel, Patricia, and Gerald P. Koocher. **Ethics in Psychology: Professional Standards and Cases.** New York, Random House; distr., Hillsdale, N.J., Lawrence Erlbaum, 1985. 494p. $27.00. LC 84-27542. ISBN 0-89859-713-7.

This title covers a number of issues of continuing concern to psychologists that are not discussed frequently in the literature, such as peer review, fees and insurance reimbursement, the advertisement of professional services, and the popularization of psychological theories and research in the mass media. Contemporary and historical perspectives are viewed in light of current legislation, accepted professional standards, and areas of public concern and accountability.

In each chapter, hypothetical or public domain cases illustrate related ethical dilemmas. Issues and illustrations are drawn from mental health practice, the teaching of psychology as a discipline, the integrity of research methods, obligations of those giving expert testimony, animal rights in research, testing, and social responsibilities of all members of the profession. The 1981 *Ethical Principles of Psychologists,* revised edition (it has since been revised again in 1992), written, published, and endorsed by APA, serves as the reference document. It and other codes addressing professional conduct are appended.

667. Sales, Bruce Dennis, ed. **The Professional Psychologist's Handbook**. New York, Plenum, 1983. 779p. index. $75.00. LC 83-4038. ISBN 0-306-40934-8.

In this handbook, seven areas of professional practice are discussed in considerable detail: standards of practice, the role of a professional organization (specifically the American Psychological Association), the education and training of psychologists, legal responsibilities and liability, private practice as a business, the ethics of practice, and the political and regulatory environments. Predictably, most chapters address clinical and counseling psychology, with fewer references to psychologists employed in other specialties and settings. Four appendixes reprint professional standards most widely applicable to the profession.

Legislation and adjudication will affect the currency of the text and accompanying tables. However, the material on such controversial issues as licensing, legal liability and accountability, and insurance reimbursement status will remain usable for many years.

Author/Title Index

The numbers in this index refer to entries. Numbers followed by "n" refer to entry annotations.

Subject Index

The numbers in this index refer to entries. Numbers followed by "n" refer to entry annotations.